SEYCHELLES

COUNTRY STUDY GUIDE

STRATEGIC INFORMATION AND DEVELOPMENTS

International Business Publications, USA
Washington DC, USA

SEYCHELLES
COUNTRY STUDY GUIDE
STRATEGIC INFORMATION AND DEVELOPMENTS

UPDATED ANNUALLY

Cover Design: **International Business Publications, USA**

We express our sincere appreciation to all government agencies and international organizations which provided information and other materials for this guide

2018 Edition Updated Reprint International Business Publications, USA
ISBN 1-4330-4428-5

This guide provides basic information for starting or/and conducting business in the country. The extraordinary volume of materials covering the topic, prevents us from placing all these materials in this guide. For more detailed information on issues related to any specific investment and business activity in the country, please contact Global Investment Center, USA
Please acquire the list of our business intelligence and marketing reports and other business publications. We constantly update and expand our business intelligence and marketing materials. Please contact the center for the updated list of reports on over 200 countries.

For additional analytical, business and investment opportunities information,
please contact Global Investment & Business Center, USA
at (703) 370-8082. Fax: (703) 370-8083. E-mail: ibpusa3@gmail.com
Global Business and Investment Info Databank - www.ibpus.com

Printed in the USA

For additional analytical, business and investment opportunities information,
please contact Global Investment & Business Center, USA
at (703) 370-8082. Fax: (703) 370-8083. E-mail: ibpusa3@gmail.com
Global Business and Investment Info Databank - www.ibpus.com

SEYCHELLES

COUNTRY STUDY GUIDE

STRATEGIC INFORMATION AND DEVELOPMENTS

TABLE OF CONTENTS

STRATEGIC AND DEVLOPMENT PROFILES

STRATEGIC PROFILES

Capital and largest city	Victoria 4°37′S 55°27′E4.617°S 55.450°E
Official languages	• English • French • Seychellois Creole
Ethnic groups	• 93.2% Creoles • 3.0% British • 1.8% French • 0.5% Chinese • 0.3% Indian • 1.2% others
Demonym	• Seychellois • Seychelloise • Seselwa (Creole)
Government	Presidential republic
• President	Danny Faure
• Vice President	Vincent Mériton
Legislature	National Assembly
Independence	
• from the United Kingdom	29 June 1976
Area	
• Total	459 km^2 (198th) 177 sq mi
• Water (%)	negligible
Population	
• estimate	92,000 (195th)
• Density	186.2/km^2 (60th) 482.7/sq mi
GDP (PPP)	2016 estimate
• Total	$2.608 billion
• Per capita	$28,148
GDP (nominal)	2016 estimate
• Total	$1.419 billion
• Per capita	$15,319
Gini	65.8 very high
HDI	0.772 high · 64th
Currency	Seychellois rupee (SCR)
Time zone	SCT (UTC+4)
• Summer (DST)	not observed (UTC+4)
Drives on the	left
Calling code	+248

ISO 3166 code	SC
Internet TLD	.sc

Seychelles officially the **Republic of Seychelles** is an archipelago country in the Indian Ocean. The capital of the 115-island country, Victoria, lies 1,500 kilometres (932 mi) east of mainland East Africa. Other nearby island countries and territories include Comoros, Mayotte (region of France), Madagascar, Réunion (region of France) and Mauritius to the south. With a population of roughly 94,228, it has the smallest population of any sovereign African country.[5]

Seychelles is a member of the African Union, the Southern African Development Community, the Commonwealth of Nations, and the United Nations. After proclamation of independence from the United Kingdom in 1976, Seychelles has developed from a largely agricultural society to a market-based diversified economy, with agriculture being supplanted by rapidly rising service and public sectors as well as tourism. From 1976 until 2015, nominal GDP output has increased nearly sevenfold and the purchasing power parity nearly sixteenfold. In late 2010s, the President Danny Faure and the National Assembly presented plans to encourage foreign investment[*disambiguation needed*] in order to further upgrade these sectors.

Today, Seychelles boasts the highest nominal per capita GDP in Africa, excluding the French regions. It is one of only a handful of countries in Africa with a high Human Development Index. Despite the country's newfound economic prosperity, poverty remains widespread due to a high level of economic inequality, one of the highest in the world, and unequal wealth distribution among the populace which vastly favors the upper and ruling class.[6]

Background:	A lengthy struggle between France and Great Britain for the islands ended in 1814, when they were ceded to the latter. Independence came in 1976. Socialist rule was brought to a close with a new constitution and free elections in 1993.

GEOGRAPHY

Location:	Eastern Africa, group of islands in the Indian Ocean, northeast of Madagascar
Geographic coordinates:	4 35 S, 55 40 E
Map references:	Africa
Area:	total: 455 sq km land: 455 sq km water: 0 sq km
Area - comparative:	2.5 times the size of Washington, DC
Land boundaries:	0 km
Coastline:	491 km
Maritime claims:	contiguous zone: 24 NM continental shelf: 200 NM or to the edge of the continental margin exclusive economic zone: 200 NM territorial sea: 12 NM
Climate:	tropical marine; humid; cooler season during southeast monsoon (late May to September); warmer season during northwest monsoon (March to May)
Terrain:	Mahe Group is granitic, narrow coastal strip, rocky, hilly; others

	are coral, flat, elevated reefs
Elevation extremes:	lowest point: Indian Ocean 0 m highest point: Morne Seychellois 905 m
Natural resources:	fish, copra, cinnamon trees

An island nation, Seychelles is located to the northeast of Madagascar and about 1,600 km (994 mi) east of Kenya. The number of islands in the archipelago is often given as 115 but the Constitution of the Republic of Seychelles lists 155. The islands as per the Constitution are divided into various groups as follows.

There are 42 granitic islands, in descending order of size: Mahé, Praslin, Silhouette Island, La Digue, Curieuse, Felicite, Frégate, Ste-Anne, North, Cerf, Marianne, Grand Sœur, Thérèse, Aride, Conception, Petite Sœur, Cousin, Cousine, Long, Récif, Round (Praslin), Anonyme, Mamelles, Moyenne, Ile aux Vaches Marines, L'Islette, Beacon (Ile Sèche), Cachée, Cocos, Round (Mahé), L'Ilot Frégate, Booby, Chauve Souris (Mahé), Chauve Souris (Praslin), Ile La Fouche, Hodoul, L'Ilot, Rat, Souris, St. Pierre (Praslin), Zavé, Harrison Rocks (Grand Rocher).

There are two coral sand cays north of the granitics: Denis and Bird. There are two coral islands south of the granitics: Coëtivy and Platte.

There are 29 coral islands in the Amirantes group, west of the granitics: Desroches, Poivre Atoll (comprising three islands — Poivre, Florentin and South Island), Alphonse, D'Arros, St. Joseph Atoll (comprising 14 islands — St. Joseph Ile aux Fouquets, Ressource, Petit Carcassaye, Grand Carcassaye, Benjamin, Bancs Ferrari, Chiens, Pélicans, Vars, Ile Paul, Banc de Sable, Banc aux Cocos and Ile aux Poules), Marie Louise, Desnoeufs, African Banks (comprising two islands — African Banks and South Island), Rémire, St. François, Boudeuse, Etoile, Bijoutier.

There are 13 coral islands in the Farquhar Group, south-southwest of the Amirantes: Farquhar Atoll (comprising 10 islands — Bancs de Sable Déposés Ile aux Goëlettes Lapins Ile du Milieu North Manaha South Manaha Middle Manaha North Island and South Island), Providence Atoll (comprising two islands — Providence and Bancs Providence) and St Pierre.

There are 67 raised coral islands in the Aldabra Group, west of the Farquhar Group: Aldabra Atoll (comprising 46 islands — Grande Terre, Picard, Polymnie, Malabar, Ile Michel, Ile Esprit, Ile aux Moustiques, Ilot Parc, Ilot Emile, Ilot Yangue, Ilot Magnan, Ile Lanier, Champignon des Os, Euphrate, Grand Mentor, Grand Ilot, Gros Ilot Gionnet, Gros Ilot Sésame, Heron Rock, Hide Island, Ile aux Aigrettes, Ile aux Cèdres, Iles Chalands, Ile Fangame, Ile Héron, Ile Michel, Ile Squacco, Ile Sylvestre, Ile Verte, Ilot Déder, Ilot du Sud, Ilot du Milieu, Ilot du Nord, Ilot Dubois, Ilot Macoa, Ilot Marquoix, Ilots Niçois, Ilot Salade, Middle Row Island, Noddy Rock, North Row Island, Petit Mentor, Petit Mentor Endans, Petits Ilots, Pink Rock and Table Ronde), Assumption, Astove and Cosmoledo Atoll (comprising 19 islands — Menai, Ile du Nord (West North), Ile Nord-Est (East North), Ile du Trou, Goëlettes, Grand Polyte, Petit Polyte, Grand Ile (Wizard), Pagode, Ile du Sud-Ouest (South), Ile aux Moustiques, Ile Baleine, Ile aux Chauve-Souris, Ile aux Macaques, Ile aux Rats, Ile du Nord-Ouest, Ile Observation, Ile Sud-Est and Ilot la Croix).

Seychelles is divided into twenty-five administrative regions that comprise all of the inner islands. Eight of the districts make up the capital of Seychelles and are referred to as Greater Victoria. Another 14 districts are considered the rural part of the main island of Mahé with two districts on Praslin and one on La Digue which also includes respective satellite islands. The rest of the Outer Islands are not considered part of any district.

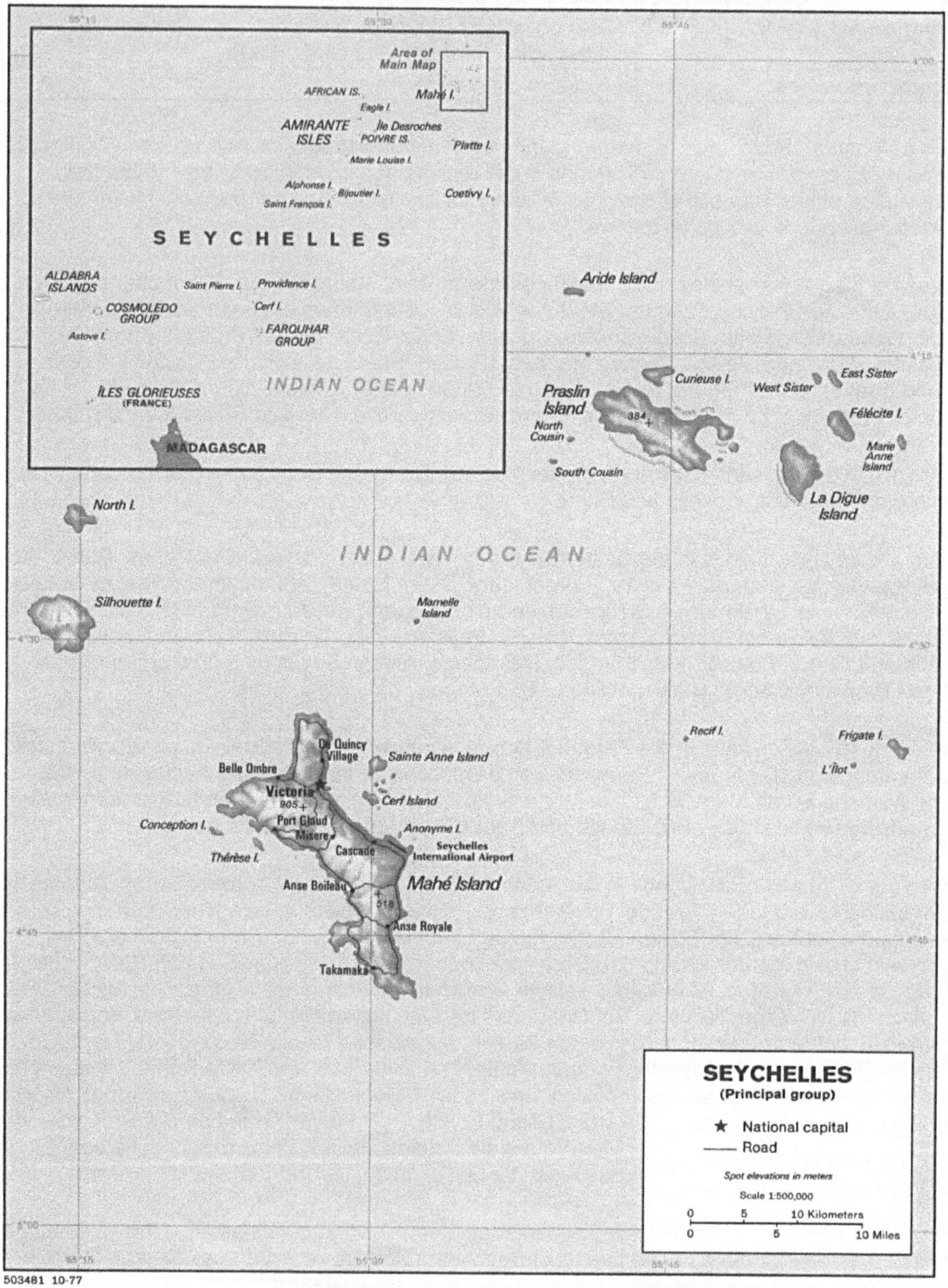

503481 10-77

Greater Victoria Rural Mahé Praslin

- Bel Air
- La Rivière Anglaise (*English River*)
- Les Mamelles
- Mont Buxton
- Mont Fleuri
- Plaisance
- Roche Caiman
- Saint Louis

- Anse aux Pins
- Anse Boileau
- Anse Etoile
- Au Cap
- Anse Royale
- Baie Lazare
- Beau Vallon
- Bel Ombre
- Cascade
- Glacis
- Grand'Anse Mahé
- Pointe La Rue
- Port Glaud
- Takamaka

- Baie Sainte Anne (Anse Volbert)
- Grand'Anse Praslin (Grande Anse)

La Digue and remaining Inner Islands

- La Digue (Anse Réunion)

Land use:	arable land: 2% permanent crops: 13% permanent pastures: 0% forests and woodland: 11% other: 74%
Irrigated land:	NA sq km
Natural hazards:	lies outside the cyclone belt, so severe storms are rare; short droughts possible
Environment - current issues:	water supply depends on catchments to collect rainwater
Environment - international agreements:	party to: Biodiversity, Climate Change, Desertification, Endangered Species, Hazardous Wastes, Law of the Sea, Marine Dumping, Nuclear Test Ban, Ozone Layer Protection, Ship Pollution signed, but not ratified: Climate Change-Kyoto Protocol
Geography - note:	40 granitic and about 50 coralline islands

PEOPLE

Population:	79,715
Age structure:	0-14 years: 28.27% (male 11,367; female 11,167) 15-64 years: 65.47% (male 25,453; female 26,737) 65 years and over: 6.26% (male 1,673; female 3,318)
Population growth rate:	0.49%
Birth rate:	17.66 births/1,000 population
Death rate:	6.65 deaths/1,000 population

Net migration rate:	-6.15 migrant(s)/1,000 population
Sex ratio:	at birth: 1.03 male(s)/female under 15 years: 1.02 male(s)/female 15-64 years: 0.95 male(s)/female 65 years and over: 0.5 male(s)/female total population: 0.93 male(s)/female
Infant mortality rate:	17.3 deaths/1,000 live births
Life expectancy at birth:	total population: 70.69 years male: 65.17 years female: 76.37 years
Total fertility rate:	1.83 children born/woman
Nationality:	noun: Seychellois (singular and plural) adjective: Seychelles
Ethnic groups:	Seychellois (mixture of Asians, Africans, Europeans)
Religions:	Roman Catholic 90%, Anglican 8%, other 2%
Languages:	English (official), French (official), Creole
Literacy:	definition: age 15 and over can read and write total population: 58% male: 56% female: 60%

GOVERNMENT

Country name:
conventional long form: Republic of Seychelles
conventional short form: Seychelles
local long form: Republic of Seychelles
local short form: Seychelles
etymology: named by French Captain Corneille Nicholas MORPHEY after Jean Moreau de SECHELLES, the finance minister of France, in 1756

Government type:
presidential republic

Capital:
name: Victoria
geographic coordinates: 4 37 S, 55 27 E
time difference: UTC+4 (9 hours ahead of Washington, DC, during Standard Time)

Administrative divisions:
25 administrative districts; Anse aux Pins, Anse Boileau, Anse Etoile, Anse Royale, Au Cap, Baie Lazare, Baie Sainte Anne, Beau Vallon, Bel Air, Bel Ombre, Cascade, Glacis, Grand Anse Mahe, Grand Anse Praslin, Inner Islands, La Riviere Anglaise, Les Mamalles, Mont Buxton, Mont Fleuri, Plaisance, Pointe Larue, Port Glaud, Roche Caiman, Saint Louis, Takamaka

Independence:

29 June 1976 (from the UK)

National holiday:
Constitution Day, 18 June (1993); Independence Day (National Day), 29 June (1976)

Constitution:
previous 1970, 1979; latest drafted May 1993, approved by referendum 18 June 1993, effective 23 June 1993; amended several times, last in 2011 (2016)

Legal system:
mixed legal system of English common law, French civil law, and customary law
International law organization participation:
has not submitted an ICJ jurisdiction declaration; accepts ICCt jurisdiction

Citizenship:
citizenship by birth: no
citizenship by descent only: at least one parent must be a citizen of the Seychelles
dual citizenship recognized: no
residency requirement for naturalization: 5 years

Suffrage:
18 years of age; universal

Executive branch:

chief of state: President Danny FAURE (PL) (since 16 October 2016); Vice President Vincent MERITON (since 28 October 2016); note - James Alix MICHEL resigned the presidency effective 16 October 2016; the president is both chief of state and head of government

head of government:

President Danny FAURE (PL) (since 16 October 2016); Vice President Vincent MERITON (since 28 October 2016); note - James Alix MICHEL resigned the presidency effective 16 October 2016; the president is both chief of state and head of government

cabinet: Council of Ministers appointed by the president

elections/appointments: president directly elected by absolute majority popular vote in two rounds if needed for a 5-year term (eligible for 2 more terms); election last held on 3-5 December 2015 with runoff on 16-18 December 2015 (next expected in December 2020)

election results: President James Alix MICHEL reelected president; percent of vote in second round - James Alix MICHEL (PP) 50.2%, Wavel RAMKALAWAN (SNP) 49.8%

Legislative branch:

description: unicameral National Assembly or Assemblee Nationale (up to 35 seats - the Assembly elected in September 2016 has 33 members; 25 members directly elected in single-seat constituencies by simple majority vote and up to 10 members elected by proportional representation vote; members serve 5-year terms)

elections: last held on 8-10 September 2016 (next to be held in 2021); note - the National Assembly was dissolved in July 2011 resulting in early elections

election results: percent of vote by party - LDS 49.6%, PL 49.2%, other 1.2%; seats by party - LDS 19, PL 14

Judicial branch:

highest court(s): Seychelles Court of Appeal (consists of the court president and 4 justices); Supreme Court of Seychelles (consists of the chief justice and 9 puisine judges); Constitutional Court (consists of 3 Supreme Court judges)

judge selection and term of office: all judges appointed by the president of the republic upon the recommendation of the Constitutional Appointments Committee, a 3-member body, with 1 member appointed by the president of the republic, 1 by the opposition leader in the National Assembly, and 1 by the other 2 appointees; judges appointed until retirement at age 70

subordinate courts: Magistrates' Courts of Seychelles; Family Tribunal for issues such as domestic violence, and child custody and maintenance; Employment Tribunal for labor-related disputes

Political parties and leaders:

People's Party (Parti Lepep) or PL [James Alix MICHEL] (formerly SPPF)

Popular Democratic Movement or PDM [Francesca MONNAIE]

Seychelles National Party or SNP [Wavel RAMKALAWAN] (formerly the United Opposition or UO)

Seychelles Party for Social Justice and Democracy or SPSD

Seychellois Democratic Alliance (Linyon Demokratik Seselwa) or LDS [Roger MANCIENNE] (alliance consisting of SNP, Seychelloise Alliance, SPSD, and SUP)

Seychelloise Alliance (Lalyans Seselwa) [Patrick PILLAY]

Seselwa (Seychelles) United Party or SUP [Robert ERNESTA] (formerly the New Democratic Party or NDP)

International organization participation:

ACP, AfDB, AOSIS, AU, C, CD, COMESA, EITI (candidate country), FAO, G-77, IAEA, IBRD, ICAO, ICC (NGOs), ICCt, ICRM, IDA, IFAD, IFC, IFRCS, ILO, IMF, IMO, InOC, Interpol, IOC, IOM, IPU, ISO (correspondent), ITU, MIGA, NAM, OIF, OPCW, SADC, UN, UNCTAD, UNESCO, UNIDO, UNWTO, UPU, WCO, WHO, WIPO, WMO, WTO (observer)

Diplomatic representation in the US:

chief of mission: Ambassador Ronald Jean JUMEAU (since 8 September 2017)
chancery: 800 Second Avenue, Suite 400C, New York, NY 10017
telephone: [1] (212) 972-1785
FAX: [1] (212) 972-1786
consulate(s) general: New York

Diplomatic representation from the US:
the US does not have an embassy in Seychelles; the US Ambassador to Mauritius is accredited to Seychelles

Flag description:
five oblique bands of blue (hoist side), yellow, red, white, and green (bottom) radiating from the bottom of the hoist side; the oblique bands are meant to symbolize a dynamic new country moving into the future; blue represents sky and sea, yellow the sun giving light and life, red the peoples' determination to work for the future in unity and love, white social justice and harmony, green the land and natural environment

National symbol(s):
coco de mer (sea coconut); national colors: blue, yellow, red, white, green

National anthem:
name: "Koste Seselwa" (Seychellois Unite)
lyrics/music: David Francois Marc ANDRE and George Charles Robert PAYET

ECONOMY

Economy - overview:

Since independence in 1976, per capita output in this Indian Ocean archipelago has expanded to roughly seven times the pre-independence, near-subsistence level, moving the island into the upper-middle-income group of countries. Growth has been led by the tourist sector, which employs about 30% of the labor force and provides more than 70% of hard currency earnings, and by tuna fishing.

In recent years, the government has encouraged foreign investment to upgrade hotels and other services. At the same time, the government has moved to reduce the dependence on tourism by promoting the development of farming, fishing, and small-scale manufacturing.

In 2008, having depleted its foreign exchange reserves, Seychelles defaulted on interest payments due on a $230 million Eurobond, requested assistance from the IMF, and immediately enacted a number of significant structural reforms, including liberalization of the exchange rate, reform of the public sector to include layoffs, and the sale of some state assets. In December 2013, the IMF declared that Seychelles had successfully transitioned to a market-based economy with full employment and a fiscal surplus. Seychelles grew at 4.3% in 2015 because of a strong tourist sector and expanding private sector credits; its fiscal surplus reached 4% of GDP.

GDP (purchasing power parity):
$2.417 billion (2015 est.)
$2.316 billion (2014 est.)
$2.181 billion (2013 est.)
note: data are in 2015 US dollars
country comparison to the world: 192

GDP (official exchange rate):
$1.375 billion (2015 est.)

GDP - real growth rate:
4.4% (2015 est.)
6.2% (2014 est.)
5% (2013 est.)
country comparison to the world: 35

GDP - per capita (PPP):
$26,300 (2015 est.)
$25,400 (2014 est.)
$24,200 (2013 est.)
note: data are in 2015 US dollars
country comparison to the world: 67

Gross national saving:
21.3% of GDP (2015 est.)
15.5% of GDP (2014 est.)
26.7% of GDP (2013 est.)
country comparison to the world: 119

GDP - composition, by end use:
household consumption: 52.9%
government consumption: 25.2%
investment in fixed capital: 38.3%
investment in inventories: -0.1%
exports of goods and services: 72%
imports of goods and services: -88.3% (2015 est.)

GDP - composition, by sector of origin:
agriculture: 2.6%
industry: 14%
services: 83.4% (2015 est.)

Agriculture - products:
coconuts, cinnamon, vanilla, sweet potatoes, cassava (manioc, tapioca), copra, bananas; tuna

Industries:
fishing, tourism, beverages

Industrial production growth rate:
2.2% (2015 est.)
country comparison to the world: 100

Labor force:
39,560 (2006 est.)
country comparison to the world: 195

Labor force - by occupation:
agriculture: 3%

industry: 23%
services: 74% (2006)

Unemployment rate:
3% (2014 est.)
3.3% (2013 est.)
country comparison to the world: 21

Population below poverty line:
NA%

Household income or consumption by percentage share:
lowest 10%: 4.7%
highest 10%: 15.4%

Budget:
revenues: $477.3 million
expenditures: $444.3 million (2015 est.)

Taxes and other revenues:
34.7% of GDP (2015 est.)
country comparison to the world: 62

Budget surplus (+) or deficit (-):
2.4% of GDP (2015 est.)
country comparison to the world: 13

Public debt:
63.2% of GDP (2015 est.)
64.5% of GDP (2014 est.)
country comparison to the world: 60

Fiscal year:
calendar year
Inflation rate (consumer prices):
4% (2015 est.)
1.4% (2014 est.)
country comparison to the world: 159

Central bank discount rate:
11.17% (31 December 2010)
country comparison to the world: 19

Commercial bank prime lending rate:
12.36% (31 December 2015 est.)
11.65% (31 December 2014 est.)

country comparison to the world: 65

Stock of narrow money:
$492.7 million (31 December 2015 est.)
$407.2 million (31 December 2014 est.)
country comparison to the world: 164

Stock of broad money:
$567.8 million (31 December 2014 est.)
$529.3 million (31 December 2013 est.)
country comparison to the world: 177

Stock of domestic credit:
$491.6 million (31 December 2015 est.)
$427.3 million (31 December 2014 est.)

country comparison to the world: 173

Market value of publicly traded shares:
$NA

Current account balance:
-$195 million (2015 est.)
-$300 million (2014 est.)
country comparison to the world: 87

Exports:
$449.4 million (2015 est.)
$538.9 million (2014 est.)
country comparison to the world: 175

Exports - commodities:
canned tuna, frozen fish, petroleum products (reexports)

Exports - partners:
France 18.2%, UK 17.9%, Mauritius 10%, Japan 9.2%, Italy 7.8%, Spain 4.5% (2015)

Imports:
$922.4 million (2015 est.)
$1.081 billion (2014 est.)
country comparison to the world: 183

Imports - commodities:
machinery and equipment, foodstuffs, petroleum products, chemicals, other manufactured goods

Imports - partners:
Saudi Arabia 22.5%, Spain 11.1%, Singapore 7.4%, China 4.5%, South Africa 4.1%, France 4% (2015)
Reserves of foreign exchange and gold:
$536.2 million (31 December 2015 est.)
$465 million (31 December 2014 est.)
country comparison to the world: 147

Debt - external:
$2.758 billion (31 December 2015 est.)
$2.837 billion (31 December 2014 est.)
country comparison to the world: 142

Exchange rates:
Seychelles rupees (SCR) per US dollar -
13.314 (2015 est.)
12.747 (2014 est.)
12.747 (2013 est.)
13.7 (2012 est.)
12.381 (2011 est.)

ENERGY

Electricity access:
population without electricity: 2,795
electrification - total population: 97%
electrification - urban areas: 97%
electrification - rural areas: 97%

Electricity - production:
400 million kWh (2014 est.)
country comparison to the world: 172

Electricity - consumption:
300 million kWh (2014 est.)
country comparison to the world: 176

Electricity - exports:
0 kWh (2013 est.)
country comparison to the world: 192

Electricity - imports:
0 kWh (2013 est.)
country comparison to the world: 198

Electricity - installed generating capacity:
100,000 kW (2014 est.)
country comparison to the world: 177

Electricity - from fossil fuels:
100% of total installed capacity (2012 est.)

country comparison to the world: 25

Electricity - from nuclear fuels:
0% of total installed capacity (2012 est.)
country comparison to the world: 177

Electricity - from hydroelectric plants:
0% of total installed capacity (2012 est.)
country comparison to the world: 199

Electricity - from other renewable sources:
0% of total installed capacity (2012 est.)
country comparison to the world: 125

Crude oil - production:

0 bbl/day (2015 est.)
country comparison to the world: 187

Crude oil - exports:
0 bbl/day (2013 est.)
country comparison to the world: 184

Crude oil - imports:
0 bbl/day (2013 est.)
country comparison to the world: 122

Crude oil - proved reserves:
0 bbl (1 January 2016 es)
country comparison to the world: 186

Refined petroleum products - production:
0 bbl/day (2013 est.)
country comparison to the world: 128

Refined petroleum products - consumption:
6,500 bbl/day (2014 est.)
country comparison to the world: 162

Refined petroleum products - exports:
0 bbl/day (2013 est
country comparison to the world: 130

Refined petroleum products - imports:
5,956 bbl/day (2013 est.)
country comparison to the world: 148

Natural gas - production:
0 cu m (2013 est.)
country comparison to the world: 125

Natural gas - consumption:
0 cu m (2013 est.)
country comparison to the world: 191

Natural gas - exports:
0 cu m (2013 est.)
country comparison to the world: 175

Natural gas - imports:
0 cu m (2013 est.)
country comparison to the world: 130

Natural gas - proved reserves:
0 cu m (1 January 2014 es)
country comparison to the world: 190

Carbon dioxide emissions from consumption of energy:
1.4 million Mt (2013 est.)

country comparison to the world: 165

COMMUNICATIONS

Telephones - fixed lines:
total subscriptions: 21,341

subscriptions per 100 inhabitants: 23 (July 2015 est.)
country comparison to the world: 184

Telephones - mobile cellular:
total: 148,000
subscriptions per 100 inhabitants: 160 (July 2015 est.)
country comparison to the world: 184

Telephone system:
general assessment: effective system
domestic: combined fixed-line and mobile-cellular teledensity exceeds 180 telephones per 100 persons; radiotelephone communications between islands in the archipelago
international: country code - 248; direct radiotelephone communications with adjacent island countries and African coastal countries; satellite earth station - 1 Intelsat (Indian Ocean) (2015)

Broadcast media:
the government operates the only terrestrial TV station, which provides local programming and airs broadcasts from international services; multi-channel cable and satellite TV are available through 2 providers; the government operates 1 AM and 1 FM radio station; there is 1 privately operated radio station; transmissions of 2 international broadcasters are accessible in Victoria (2016)

Internet country code:
.sc

Internet users:
total: 54,000
percent of population: 58.1% (July 2015 est.)
country comparison to the world: 184

TRANSPORTATION

National air transport system:
number of registered air carriers: 1
inventory of registered aircraft operated by air carriers: 3
annual passenger traffic on registered air carriers: 497,496
annual freight traffic on registered air carriers: 19,234,992 mt-km (2015)

Civil aircraft registration country code prefix:
S7 (2016)

Airports:
14 (2013)
country comparison to the world: 150

Airports - with paved runways:

total: 7
2,438 to 3,047 m: 1
914 to 1,523 m: 5
under 914 m: 1 (2013)
Airports - with unpaved runways:
total: 7
914 to 1,523 m: 2
under 914 m: 5

Heliports: 1

Roadways:
total: 526 km
paved: 514 km
unpaved: 12 km (2015)
country comparison to the world: 195

Merchant marine:
total: 9
by type: cargo 1, carrier 1, chemical tanker 6, petroleum tanker 1
foreign-owned: 3 (Hong Kong 1, Nigeria 1, South Africa 1) (2010)
country comparison to the world: 117

Ports and terminals:
major seaport(s): Victoria

MILITARY

Military branches:
Seychelles People's Defense Forces (SPDF): Army (includes infantry, Special Forces (Tazar)), Coast Guard (includes Naval Wing, Air Wing) (2015)

Military service age and obligation:
18 years of age for voluntary military service (younger with parental consent); no conscription

Military expenditures:
0.89% of GDP
0.82% of GDP (2011)
0.89% of GDP (2010)
country comparison to the world: 109

TRANSNATIONAL ISSUES

Disputes - international:
Mauritius and Seychelles claim the Chagos Islands (UK-administered British Indian Ocean Territory)

IMPORTANT INFORMATION FOR UNDERSTANDING SYSHELLS

GEOGRAPHY

- Seychelles lies 4° south of the Equator, 1800km east of Kenya
- Seychelles archipelago consists of 115 islands
- Seychelles boasts the only mid-ocean granitic islands in the world
- 40 granitic islands and 75 coralline islands form the archipelago
- Seychelles enjoys an average temperature of 29ºC daily
- Seychelles lies beyond the cyclone belt

Seychelles is an archipelago occupying the western part of the Indian Ocean and spread out over an Exclusive Economic Zone (EEZ) of no less than 1.3 million square kilometres. The main part of this island group is situated between 4 and 5 degrees south of the equator at a longitude between 55 and 56 degrees east. The main island of Mahé lies some 1800 kilometres east of the east African coast of Kenya and to the north-east of Madagascar. There are over 100 named islands forming the Seychelles group. Most are coralline and are spread over a large area towards the south and south east. Some 40 of these islands, however, are granitic and are found within a radius of 50 kilometres from the main granitic island of Mahé.

Mahé is 27 kilometres long and 12 kilometres wide with a total land area of 154 square kilometres. This compares with a land area of 291 square kilometres for all the outer islands. Mahé is mountainous with a highest peak of 905 metres.

The vegetation remains green all year round, but suffers a little during the dry season. The most common Seychelles soil has a greyish brown colour and contains only 1% organic matter; the red coloured soil has even less organic matter. Fertilisers must be added to the soil to assist in the growing of high yield crops. The soil has a low retention capacity for water and is constantly washed down to the sea leaving sand granules or exposing bare granite rocks.

Seychelles has a mean maximum temperature of 29ºC and 12 hours of daylight. Rainfall recorded during the two monsoons, the south east from May to October (the dry season) and the north west from November to April, has averaged 2013 mm annually over the last 6 years. The heaviest rainfall is usually during mid-December to mid-January. Seychelles archipelago lies outside the cyclone belt and enjoys stable weather year round.

In Seychelles, there are many species of birds, fish and other marine life together with a rich flora, some of which are unique. Two of the outstanding species of birds found only in Seychelles are the black parrot and the paradise fly-catcher.

The archipelago consists of 115 islands and thirty prominent rock formations scattered throughout a self-proclaimed exclusive economic zone (EEZ--see Glossary) of more than 1.35 million square kilometers of ocean (see fig. 7). Some forty islands are granitic and lie in a ninety-kilometer radius from Mahé, the main island. The remaining islands are coralline, stretching over a 1,200-kilometer radius from Île aux Vaches in the northeast to the Aldabra Atoll in the southwest. The islands are all small-- the aggregate land area is only 444 square kilometers, about twoand -a-half times the size of Washington, D.C.

Mahé is twenty-five kilometers long and no more than eight kilometers wide. It contains the capital and only city, Victoria, an excellent port. Victoria lies approximately 1,600 kilometers east of Mombasa, Kenya; 2,800 kilometers southwest of Bombay; 1,700 kilometers north of Mauritius; and 920 kilometers northeast of Madagascar. The only other important islands by virtue of their size and population are Praslin and La Digue, situated about thirty kilometers to the northeast of Mahé.

The granitic islands are the peaks of the submarine Mascarene Plateau, a continental formation theorized to be either a part of Africa separated when Asia began to drift away from the original single continent of Gondwanaland, or the remnants of a microcontinent that existed up to the beginning of the Tertiary Period, approximately 50 million years ago. The granitic islands are characterized by boulder-covered hills and mountains as high as 940 meters rising abruptly from the sea. Elsewhere, narrow coastal plains extend to the base of the foothills. Extensively developed coral reefs are found mainly on the east coasts because of the southwest trade winds and equatorial current. Ninety-nine percent of the population is located on the granitic islands, and most are on Mahé.

The coralline islands differ sharply from the granitic in that they are very flat, often rising only a few feet above sea level. They have no fresh water, and very few have a resident population. Many, like Île aux Vaches, Île Denis, the Amirante Isles, Platte Island, and Coetivy Island are sand cays upon which extensive coconut plantations have been established. Some of the coralline islands consist of uplifted reefs and atolls covered with stunted vegetation. Several of these islands have been important breeding grounds for turtles and birds, as well as the sites of extensive guano deposits, which formerly constituted an important element of the Seychellois economy but now for the most part are depleted. Aldabra Islands, the largest coralline atoll with an area greater than Mahé, is a sanctuary for rare animals and birds.

The uniqueness of the Seychelles' ecology is reflected in the US$1.8 million project of the Global Environment Trust Fund of the World Bank (see Glossary) entitled Biodiversity Conservation and Marine Pollution Abatement, that began in 1993. The World Bank study for this project states that the islands contain, out of a total of 1,170 flowering plants, "at least seventy-five species of flowering plants, fifteen of birds, three of mammals, thirty of reptiles and amphibians, and several hundred species of snails, insects, spiders and other invertebrates" found nowhere else. In addition, the waters contain more than 900 kinds of fish, of which more than one-third are associated with coral reefs. Specific examples of unique birds are the black paradise flycatcher, the black parrot, the brush warbler, and a flightless rail.

As a result of extensive shipping to Seychelles that brings needed imports and the discharge of commercial tuna fishing, the waters are becoming polluted. Furthermore, goats brought to Aldabra Islands are destroying much of the vegetation on which giant turtles, including two species unique to Seychelles--the green and the hawksbill--feed or seek shade.

Seychelles began addressing the conservation problem in the late 1960s by creating the Nature Conservancy Commission, later renamed the Seychelles National Environment Commission. A system of national parks and animal preserves covering 42 percent of the land area and about 26,000 hectares of the surrounding water areas has been set aside. Legislation protects wildlife and bans various destructive practices. In Seychelles' 1990-94 National Development Plan, an effort was made to include in the appropriate economic sectors of the development plan environment and natural resources management aspects.

Also connected with ecology is a World Bank project dealing with the environment and transportation. Launched in 1993 with a loan of US$4.5 million, it is designed to improve the infrastructure of Seychelles with regard to roads and airports or airstrips so as to encourage tourism as a source of income, while simultaneously supporting environmental programs in resource management, conservation, and the elimination of pollution.

The climate of Seychelles is tropical, having little seasonal variation. Temperatures on Mahé rarely rise above 29 C. or drop below 24 C. Humidity is high, but its enervating effect is usually ameliorated by prevailing winds. The southeast monsoon from late May to September brings cooler weather, and the northwest monsoon from March to May, warmer weather. High winds are rare inasmuch as most islands lie outside the Indian Ocean cyclone belt; Mahé suffered the only such storm in its recorded history in 1862. Mean annual rainfall in Mahé averages 2,880 millimeters at sea level and as high as 3,550 millimeters on the mountain slopes. Precipitation is somewhat less on the other islands, averaging as low as 500 millimeters per year on the southernmost coral islands. Because catchment provides most sources of water in Seychelles, yearly variations in rainfall or even brief periods of drought can produce water shortages. Small dams have been built on Mahé since 1969 in an effort to guarantee a reliable water supply, but drought can still be a problem on Mahé and particularly on La Digue.

CLIMATE

- The drier South East monsoon blows from May-September
- The North West monsoon blows from November-March
- Average temperature is 29 degrees centigrade daily
- Average humidity is 75%
- The islands are beyond the cyclone belt

The weather in Seychelles is generally warm and humid. The tropical climate is influenced primarily by trade winds.

May to September when the south east trade winds blow is a relatively dry period. The season's temperature averages between 24-30C, with cooling breezes, lower humidity (80%), and light rainfall.

The climate and the pattern of rainfall explain the lush vegetation and profusion of plants not found elsewhere in the region.

The northwest trade winds bring in their path tropical rainfall, particularly in December and January. The season, which extends from November to January, has irregular wind patterns which results in high humidity and higher temperatures (up to a maximum of 32C). The transition periods of April and October are fairly hot, with little breeze and calm seas. Unlike its Indian Ocean neighbours the Seychelles lies beyond the cyclone belt.

NATURE

- 46% of the land area is set aside for National Parks, Nature Reserves and Protected areas
- Ten endemic species and seventeen endemic sub-species of bird can be found on the granitic islands of Seychelles
- Three endemic species of birds can be found on the coraline islands
- Seychelles has large breeding colonies of sea-birds
- The flora of Seychelles is as unique as the islands themselves
- There are 75 plants which are endemic to Seychelles
- The Tropicbird Orchid is the national flower of Seychelles

- Coco-de -Mer is the worlds largest nut
- 150,000 Giant Tortoise live on Aldabra, that's five times more than on Galapagos
- The largest tortoise in the world is Esmeralda who weighs 320kg and lives on Bird
- The Tiger Chameleon is endemic to Seychelles
- Four of the seven species of Turtle are found in Seychelles
- There are three species of snake in Seychelles and they are all harmless
- There are two types of lizards in Seychelles the Geckos and the Skinks
- The Black Bellied Terrapin is so rare it may have become extinct
- There are no dangerous spiders
- Seychelles has seven species of Caecilians and five species of Frogs
- There is no Malaria in Seychelles
- The Tenebrionid Beetle can only be found on Fregate
- There are five species of stick insect endemic to Seychelles
- Seychelles Fruit Bats are a common sight in the sky at dusk
- Tenerecs have the world record for the largest number of nipples.....24!
- Whaleshark numbers around Seychelles are increasing
- The best months for spotting Whalesharks are August and November
- Whaleshark tagging programmes are available from selected diving centres

The forty-one granitic islands of Seychelles were cast adrift in mid-ocean when the supercontinent of Pangaea broke up. The huge landmass split in two, Laurasia to the north, Gondwanaland to the south, separated by the sea of Tethys. As the process continued, Gondwanaland itself fragmented. South America, Africa, Madagascar, India, Australia and Antarctica drifted apart on giant plates. India moved most rapidly, crossing the Equator to merge with Asia, forcing the shores of Tethys to rise up and become the highest mountain peaks on the globe. Somewhere amidst this tectonic turbulence, the Seychelles Islands were being born. There were no land mammals on earth then and the ocean barrier excluded them from Seychelles for millennia, with the exception of bats. A"lost world" had been created where a unique flora and fauna evolved in isolation.

Similarly the outer coralline islands of Seychelles became home to distinctive forms of wildlife, particularly on the inhospitable limestone crags of Aldabra Atoll. Far from the main shipping routes, this dry, unforgiving place is the most unspoilt island in the Indian Ocean and is now a World HeritageSite.

This is Seychelles magic. Not only does it have different origins from other island groups on earth, but whereas so many countries have destroyed their natural heritage in the name of progress, the Seychelles environment has largely been preserved. Forty-six percent of the land area is set aside as National Parks, Nature Reserves and Protected Areas.

HISTORY OF ISLANDS

- **1502** Portuguese explorer Vasco de Gama discovers the Amirantes islands.
- **1609** John Jourdain first Britain to set foot on Seychelles soil.
- **1742** Frenchman Lazare Picault leads an expedition to Mahe (ile d' Abondance)
- **1756** Stone of Possession laid by Irishman Corneille Morphey on behalf of King Louis XV of France.
- **1794** de Quinssy capitulates for the first of seven times to British Warships.
- **1814** Treaty of Paris confirms British Sovereignty.
- **1835** Abolition of slavery.
- **1903** Seychelles becomes a crown colony.

- **1971** Airport opened.
- **1976 29th June** Seychelles becomes independent from Britain.
- **1977 5th June** Prime Minister Albert René seizes power with a coup d'etat.

Although there is much speculation of early Persian and Arab seafarers visiting the islands hundreds of years before Christ was born no documentary evidence exists. However in the ninth century the Seychelles appear for the first time on Arab charts and are referred to as the "Tall Islands" following an expedition to the Maldives. A few hundred years later the Seychelles appear on more Arabic maps and are referred to as "Zarin" ("the Sisters").

Several historical books record that Vasco da Gama discovered the Seychelles. However that is not strictly true as he only discovered part of them, the group of islands known as the Amirantes islands in 1502. A fellow countryman, Joao de Nova, discovered the Farquhar group the year before but rarely makes it into the history books.

The first British landing has been credited to John Jourdain who landed on the islands of North and Silhouette in 1609. His men went ashore and stocked the ship with local produce, he wrote in his journal that his men "*brought so many tortells as they could carrie. The tortells were good meate, as good as fresh beefe, but after twoe or three meals our men would not eate them, because they did looke so uglie before they were boyled*".

In 1742 Lazare Picault became the first Frenchman to visit Seychelles from an expedition from Ile de France (Mauritius), So impressed was he with Mahé that he christened it the Ile d'Abondance ("Isle of Abundance") . After only four days he left the island having taken 300 giant tortoises and 600 coconuts on board.

Two years later in 1744 Picault returned and named the island Mahe after the governor of Mauritius, Le Vicomte Mahé. He sent him back to make a more complete survey. The French believed that the European war between Britain and France in 1740 could spread to the Indian Ocean and that Seychelles would be of strategic importance.

On the 9th November 1756 an Irish sea captain, Corneille Morphey, laid official claim to Mahé and the seven islands to the east on behalf of Louis XV of France by laying a stone of Possession. The group was then named after Jean Moreau de Sechelles who was the minister of finance for King Louis XV from 1754 to 1756.

In 1789 the French Revolution began. The inhabitants in Seychelles at the time comprised 69 French, 32 free coloureds and 487 slaves. In 1790 they decided to form an Assembly and declared independence from Ile de France thus laying claim to the whole of the Seychelles group.

This newly found independence was not to last long. In 1794 the French send in Captain Queau de Quinssy (later spelled Quincy) who became Governor. Later that year he was attacked by the British Navy by four ships which had on board 166 cannons and 1200 soldiers. With such heavy odds against him he was forced to sign an Act of Capitulation, mainly drawn up by himself which in effect guaranteed that the island would be run by him and he would oversee law and order. As soon as the British left de Quinssy took down the British flag and hoisted the French, from then until 1811 he capitulated to the British a further seven times.

In 1814 the treaty of Paris is signed which confirms British sovereignty over the Seychelles. De Quinssy was by now held in high regard by the British and was invited to stay on in service of the King. This he did until his death at the age of 79 in 1827.

In 1835 slavery was abolished by the British Government and a little over 6500 slaves were set free. Reluctance to work for their former masters turns the agriculture industry into a disaster. Over the next five years the population shrank to 4360 and the emphasis on the islands economy shifted from cotton to coconut plantations which produced copra and coconut oil.

In 1903 Seychelles became a crown colony in its own right. The new British Governor, Mr Sweet-Escott, commemorated the event by erecting a clock tower in the centre of Victoria, which was modelled on the clock standing outside Victoria railway station in London.

By 1914 the population had risen to 24,000, With the First World War now having a great effect on trade around the world, exports plumitted and the Seychelles economy suffered with the result of serious poverty amongst many of the inhabitants. At one stage 2,500 people are being held in custody by the authorities in crime related incidences.

In 1923 electricity was available for the first time in Victoria . Eleven years later the official currency became the Seychelles Rupee but the country still struggled due to heavy import demands against weaker exports. In 1940 a taxpayers association was formed to help raise taxes to run the island. These four members were subsequently re-elected in each of the elections until 1964.

During the year 1964, two political parties were formed by two opposing lawyers. The Seychelles Democratic party was led by James Mancham and the Seychelles People United Party was formed and lead by Albert René. Who would have guessed that over thirty years on, these two figure heads would still be at the centre of the Seychelles political stage.

The International airport was opened in 1971 and when the first plane landed, a British Overseas Airways Corporation (BOAC) VC10, the landing was witnessed by practically the whole island. This was an important step in strengthening the tourism industry which had previously relied on ships arriving via Africa.

In 1975 the Seychelles Democratic Party (SDP) and the Seychelles People United Front (SPUF) formed a coalition government. In 1976 on June 29th the Seychelles became an independent republic. James Mancham became the first President whilst Albert René was elected as Prime Minister.

On the 5th June 1977 whilst James Mancham was at a Commonwealth Conference in London, Prime Minister Albert René overthrew the government with a bloodless political coup and was installed as the new President. The SPUP was later renamed the Seychelles People's Progressive Front (SPPF). Many of James Mancham's supporters went into exile where they remained for many years.

Under a stable government the tourism industry flourished and the economy boomed whilst the crime rate became negligible. The new government also declared 46% of total land area as Nature Reserve or Parks in an effort to conserve the very reason for people visiting the islands...... its natural beauty.

Although known and visited by traders from the Persian Gulf area and East Africa in earlier times, the Seychelles Archipelago first appeared on European maps at the beginning of the sixteenth century after Portuguese explorers sighted the islands during voyages to India. Recorded landings did not occur until 1609, however, when members of the British East India Company spent several days on Mahé and other nearby islands. A French expedition from Mauritius reached the islands in 1742, and during a second expedition in 1756 the French made a formal claim to them. The name "Seychelles" honors the French minister of finance under King Louis XV. Settlement began in 1778 under a French military administration but barely survived its first decade. Although the settlers were supposed to plant crops only to provision the garrison and passing French ships, they also found it lucrative to exploit the islands' natural resources. Between 1784 and 1789, an estimated 13,000 giant tortoises were shipped from Mahé. The settlers also quickly devastated the hardwood forests--selling them to passing ships for repairs or to shipyards on Mauritius. In spite of reforms to control the rapid elimination of trees, exploitation of the forest continued for shipbuilding and house building and later for firing cinnamon kilns, ultimately destroying much of the original ecology.

Possession of the islands alternated between France and Britain several times during the French Revolution and the Napoleonic wars. France ceded Seychelles--which at that time included the granitic group and three coral islands--to Britain in 1814 in the Treaty of Paris after rejecting a British offer to take French holdings in India in place of Seychelles. Because Britain's interest in the islands had centered mainly on halting their use as a base for French privateering, its main concern was to keep the islands from becoming burdens. Britain administered Seychelles as a dependency of Mauritius, from which they received little attention and few services.

The first European settlers were French who had been living on Mauritius, Reunion, or in French settlements in India. Many lived in conditions of poverty quite similar to those of their African slaves, who from early on greatly outnumbered the remainder of the population. After the abolition of slavery in the islands in 1834, many settlers left, taking their slaves with them. Later, large numbers of Africans liberated by the British navy from slaving ships on the East African coast were released on Seychelles. Small numbers of Chinese, Malaysians, and Indians moved to the islands, usually becoming small traders and shopkeepers. Intermarriage among all groups except the Indians was common, however, and left so few families of pure descent that by 1911 the practice of categorizing residents according to race was abandoned.

Before 1838 most Seychellois worked on white-owned estates as slaves, producing cotton, coconut oil, spices, coffee, and sugarcane, as well as sufficient food crops to support the population. After the abolition of slavery, they became agricultural wage laborers, sharecroppers, fishers, or artisans, settling as squatters where they liked. Labor-intensive field crops rapidly gave way to crops that required relatively little labor, including copra, cinnamon, and vanilla. Only those industries related to processing the cash crops or exploiting natural resources developed. As a result, the increasing population quickly came to depend on imports for most basic necessities, including food and manufactured goods.

CROWN COLONY STATUS, 1903

Political development proceeded very slowly. From 1814 until 1903, when the islands became a crown colony, they were granted increasing administrative autonomy from Mauritius. In 1888 separate nominated administrative and executive councils were established for Mauritius and Seychelles. Thus, for the first time, some landed white Seychellois were allowed to serve in official advisory positions. In 1897 the administrator of Seychelles was given the powers of a colonial governor, although it was not until 1903 that the islands were separated from Mauritius. When Seychelles became a separate colony, the other islands of the archipelago, except for Coetivy and the Farquhar Islands, were added to the original group acquired by Britain in 1814. Coetivy was transferred from Mauritius in 1908 and the Farquhars in 1922 after World War I.

Widespread involvement of Seychellois in their own political affairs began in 1948 after World War II, when Britain granted suffrage to approximately 2,000 adult male property owners, who then elected four members to the Legislative Council that advised the governor. The winning candidates were drawn from a group known as the Seychelles Taxpayers' and Producers' Association (STPA), which represented the landed strata of society--known colloquially as the *grands blancs* (great whites). The STPA defended its members' interest in matters of crop marketing and other issues and was the principal political force in the nation until the early 1960s, when representatives of the small new urban professional and middle class began to win seats.

Two parties emerged to represent this new constituency: the DP, led by James Mancham, and the SPUP, led by France Albert René. Both men were London-educated lawyers who had returned to Seychelles determined to improve local conditions and to develop popularly based local politics.

Although community rivalries and the differing styles of the two leaders were important in attracting followers, the two parties also differed in substantive ways. The SPUP called itself socialist, favored worker-oriented policies, and pressed for complete independence from Britain and a nonaligned foreign policy. The pressure for independence was intensified after Britain in 1965 removed Île Desroches, the Aldabra Islands, and the Farquhar Islands from Seychelles and made them part of the British Indian Ocean Territory. The DP took a more laissez-faire capitalist approach and wanted to continue the association with Britain and to allow British and United States bases on the islands.

STEPS TOWARD INDEPENDENCE, 1967-76

Continuous and mounting demands for an increased share in running the colony's affairs prompted Britain to enact a series of constitutions for Seychelles, each of which granted important new concessions. In 1967 Britain extended universal suffrage to the colony and established a governing council to run it, the majority of whose members for the first time were elected. That year almost 18,000 Seychellois voted, and the DP emerged in control of the council. In 1970 Britain set up a ministerial form of government and gave Seychellois the responsibility to administer all but external affairs, internal security, the civil service, and the government's broadcasting service and newspaper. The DP won ten seats, and the SPUP won five in the Legislative Assembly. Mancham became the islands' chief minister and René, the leader of the opposition.

The opening of an international airport on the east coast of Mahé in 1971 improved contact with the outside world. Before this most journeys to and from Seychelles had involved long voyages on bimonthly steamers running between East Africa and India and often required inconvenient transits in Mombasa and Bombay. Air service had been available only on a restricted basis at an airstrip used by the United States in building a satellite station on Mahé. The end of the islands' relative isolation triggered tourism and concomitant booms in foreign capital investment and the domestic construction industry. The construction of the international airport changed the economy from a traditional agricultural and fishing one within a few years into one where services accounted for the major portion of employment and gross domestic product (GDP--see Glossary). The two parties differed on the ways to manage the new tourist industry and to apportion its benefits. The SPUP favored controlling the growth of tourism and at the same time developing the entire economy, whereas the SDP wanted to stimulate the rapid growth of tourism and to establish the islands as an international financial center.

Independence from Britain was the dominant issue between the two parties in the early 1970s, however. The SPUP insisted on cutting the colony's ties with Britain, whereas Mancham argued for even closer association. But when it became plain that the independence issue was popular and Britain showed no interest in retaining close relations, the SDP also shifted to a proindependence policy. Moreover, the disfavor with which African and Asian nations viewed colonialism had put the SDP into disrepute in the region. The SDP won the election campaign in 1974 but the election provoked angry controversy. The SPUP charged that the results had been rigged; because of the way constituencies had been demarcated, the SDP won thirteen of the fifteen seats with only 52.4 percent of the vote, lending credibility to the charges. Thereafter, relations between the two parties, already personalized and bitter, worsened steadily.

Despite their differences, the two parties formed a coalition under Mancham to lead Seychelles to independence. Five members from each party were added to the Legislative Assembly in an attempt to equalize political representation. One year later, Britain granted the colony complete independence, and on June 29, 1976, the Republic of Seychelles became a sovereign nation, with Mancham as president and René as vice president. As a gesture of goodwill, Britain returned Île Desroches, the Aldabra Islands, and the Farquhar Islands. In addition, Britain made a series of grants to the new nation to smooth the transition to an independent economy. Both parties agreed to support the coalition government until elections were held in 1979.

Coup by René Supporters, 1977

On June 4-5, 1977, sixty supporters of the SPUP who had been training in Tanzania staged a coup and overthrew Mancham while he was in London. René, who denied knowing of the plan, was then sworn in as president and formed a new government.

A year later, the SPUP combined with several smaller parties and redesignated itself the Seychelles People's Progressive Front (SPPF), or simply the Front. A new constitution adopted in 1979 stipulated that the SPPF be the sole recognized party. The constitution provided for a strong executive headed by the president and a legislature of twenty-three elected and two appointed members.

In the first election, held in June 1979, René was the single candidate for president. He won with 98 percent of the vote. The results were viewed as a popular endorsement of the socialist policies pursued by the government in the two years following the coup. The SPPF proceeded with its program to set minimum wage levels, raise government salaries, improve housing and health facilities, broaden educational opportunities, increase social security coverage, and generate employment in agriculture and fisheries. The lives of most Seychellois were enhanced, and most citizens appeared to favor the government's policies.

The decision to turn the nation into a one-party state based on socialist ideology, as well as certain initiatives of the government, caused some bitterness, especially among the upper and middle classes. Censorship of the media and control over public expression were unpopular. A number of groups attempted to oust the René government between 1978 and 1987. The most notable was a group of mercenaries who tried to enter the country in 1981 disguised as tourists from South Africa. The mercenaries were exposed as they came through customs at the international airport but most of them, including their leader, Colonel Michael "Mad Mike" Hoare, escaped after commandeering an Air India passenger plane to South Africa. Although the South African government prosecuted and jailed some of the mercenaries for air hijacking, Hoare testified that South African military and intelligence officials were involved in the coup attempt. During this period, the Seychelles government received support from Tanzania, which deployed troops to the islands to strengthen the government's hand.

Mancham and other exiled opposition figures based principally in London formed several groups that sought to turn international opinion against the René government, stigmatizing it as antidemocratic, procommunist, and pro-Soviet. As part of its efforts to stifle opposition, the government embarked on a campaign in 1987 to acquire parcels of land owned by dissident Seychellois living abroad. The takeovers were not subject to legal challenge, but the amount of compensation--in the form of bonds payable over twenty years--could be appealed in court. The government's authoritarianism finally brought it under growing pressure from its chief patrons--Britain and France. Finally, in 1991 René and the SPPF consented to liberalize the political system, inviting opposition leaders to return to Seychelles and help rewrite the constitution to permit multiparty politics.

POPULATION

The population of Seychelles is 75,000

- Official languages are English , Creol and French

During the earlier years of the history of Seychelles, there were two events which were to have important consequences: the abolition of slavery in 1835 and the establishment of the Roman Catholic Church in 1853. The first had a profound effect in, creating the Seychellois people who are of mixed race primarily of African, Malagasy and French origin, totally integrated and with a common Creole language which is French-based. The official languages spoken in Seychelles are Creole, French and English. The second event resulted in considerable cultural change, especially in the field of education.

In 1901, the Seychelles population was 19,237, with a growth rate of 1.2% per annum. By the end of 1962 the population was 43,748 with growth of 2.5% per annum. Twenty years later it reached 64,413. By then, the rate of growth had fallen to 1.4% per annum. The population at mid-1994 was estimated to be 73,850 and the actual growth rate dropped to 1.1% per annum.

According to a July 1994 estimate, the nation's population was 72,113--double what it had been in 1951. The growth rate of 0.8 percent annually had slackened from the 2.1 percent rate recorded in the late 1970s. The infant mortality rate in 1994 was estimated at 11.7 per 1,000 live births. There were twenty-two births per 1,000 of population annually and only seven deaths per 1,000; the outward migration rate of seven per 1,000 helped stem population growth.

About 90 percent of all Seychellois live on Mahé; most of the remainder live on Praslin (6,000) and La Digue (1,800). The population of the outer coralline group is only about 400, mostly plantation workers gathering coconuts for copra. To restrict population growth on Mahé, the government has encouraged people to move to Praslin and other islands where water is available.

The birth rate has declined by one-third from thirty-two per 1,000 in 1974 and is relatively lower than most African and Asian countries. By 1980 about one-third of all Seychellois women of reproductive age were reported to be using some form of contraception, which is considered unusually high compared with other African and Asian countries. Death rates are exceptionally low, in part because of the young age structure, but also because of the availability of free medical services to all segments of society, and the healthy climate and living conditions. The average life expectancy at birth in 1994 was 66.1 years for males and 73.4 for females.

ETHNIC GROUPS

The population is a relatively homogeneous one of mixed European and African descent, and most citizens consider themselves as Seychellois, possessors of a unique culture and society. Contrary to other Indian Ocean island nations, the Asian population is relatively small; it consists almost entirely of Indians and Chinese. However, the intermixing of the Indian and Chinese communities with the larger society is greater than was common elsewhere. Some twenty *grand blanc* planter families, descendants of the original French settlers, represent a separate group but under the socialist government no longer command the power and social prestige they once had. About 2,000 foreign workers and their families lived in Seychelles in the early 1990s.

Languages

Creole, the mother tongue of 94 percent of the nation in 1990, was adopted as the first official language of the nation in 1981. English is the second language and French the third, all of them officially recognized. The increased emphasis on Creole is designed to facilitate the teaching of reading to primary-level students and to help establish a distinct culture and heritage. Opponents of the René government thought it a mistake to formalize Creole, which had no standardized spelling system. They regarded it as a great advantage for Seychellois to be bilingual in French and English; treating Creole as a language of learning would, they feared, be at the expense of French and English.

Creole in Seychelles developed from dialects of southwest France spoken by the original settlers. It consists basically of a French vocabulary with a few Malagasy, Bantu, English, and Hindi words, and has a mixture of Bantu and French syntax. Very little Seychelles Creole literature exists; development of an orthography of the language was completed only in 1981. The government-backed Kreol Institute promotes the use of Creole by developing a dictionary, sponsoring literary competitions, giving instruction in translation, and preparing course material to teach Creole to foreigners.

More than one-third of Seychellois can use English, and the great majority of younger Seychellois can read English, which is the language of government and commerce. It is the language of the People's Assembly, although speakers may also use Creole or French. The principal journals carry articles in all three languages.

Although discouraged by the René regime as a colonialist language, French continues to carry prestige. It is the language of the Roman Catholic Church and is used by older people in correspondence and in formal situations. Some 40 percent of television transmissions are in French--beamed by satellite to an earth station provided by the French government--and most Seychellois can speak and understand the language.

the program is said to reflect favoritism on behalf of SPPF supporters.

GOVERNMENT AND POLITICAL SYSTEM - STRATEGIC INFORMATION AND DEVELOPMENTS

GOVERNMENT ORGANIZATION

PRESIDENT

	4th President of Seychelles
	Incumbent
	Assumed office 16 October 2016
Vice President	Vincent Meriton
Preceded by	James Michel
	Vice President of Seychelles
	In office 1 July 2010 – 16 October 2016
President	James Michel
Preceded by	Joseph Belmont
Succeeded by	Vincent Meriton
	Personal details
Born	8 May 1962 (age 56) Kilembe, Uganda
Political party	People's Party
Spouse(s)	Jeanine Faure (div. 2016)[1]

Danny Faure (born 8 May 1962) is a Seychellois politician who has been President of Seychelles since 16 October 2016. Previously, he served as Vice President of Seychelles from 2010 to 2016. Faure is a member of the People's Party (PP)

Faure was born to Seychellois parents in the western Ugandan town of Kilembe. He completed his primary and secondary education in Seychelles. He studied at a university in Cuba, graduating with a degree in political science.[2][3]

In 1985, at the age of 23, Faure started working as an assistant curriculum officer at the Seychelles education ministry. He also worked as a lecturer at both the National Youth Service and the Seychelles Polytechnic.[3]

In 1993, following the return of multiparty democracy to the island nation, Faure became the leader of government business in the National Assembly, serving in that capacity until 1998. That year, he was appointed as Minister of Education. Over the years, he has served in various ministerial capacities including youth, finance, trade and industries, public administration and information and communication technology.[3]

In 2006, he was appointed as Minister of Finance by President James Michel. During his tenure at finance, Seychelles embarked on a series of economic reforms, recommended by the International Monetary Fund. Faure oversaw the first generation reforms, which ran from October 2008 to October 2013. Faure served as designated minister between 2004 and 2010. He became Vice President on 1 July 2010, while retaining the finance portfolio.[2][3]

President James Michel announced on 27 September 2016 that he would resign, effective on 16 October, and transfer power to Vice President Faure. The announcement coincided with the election of an opposition majority in the National Assembly. As there were four years of Michel's term remaining, it was to count as a full term for Faure.[4] Faure was accordingly sworn in on 16 October 2016

CABINET OF SEYCHELLES

October 2016–Present

Portfolio	Incumbent
President Foreign Affairs Public Administration Legal Affairs Defense	H.E. Danny Faure
Vice President of Seychelles Information, Blue Economy Investment and Industry, Information, Communications and Technology (ICT) Risk and Disaster Management	H.E.Vincent Mériton
Minister of Health and Social Affairs	Jean-Paul Adam
Minister of Finance, Trade and Economic Planning	Peter Larose
Minister of Internal Affairs	Mitcy Larue
Minister of Habitat, Infrastructure and Land Transport	Charles Bastienne
Minister of Youth, Sports and Culture	Idith Alexander
Minister of Employment, Entrepreneurship Development and Business Innovation	Wallace Cosgrow
Minister of Agriculture and Fisheries	Michael Benstrong
Minister of Tourism, Civil Aviation, Ports and Marine	Alain St Ange
Minister of Environment, Energy & Climate Change	Didier Dogley
Minister of Education and Human Resources Development	Joël Morgan
Designated Minister and Minister of Local Government	Macsuzy Mondon

GOVERNMENT

Seychelles is a republic within the Commonwealth. The 1993 constitution provides for a president, who is directly elected to serve a five-year term and is limited to a maximum of three successive terms. The president is head of both state and government and commander in chief of the armed forces. There is a single-chamber, 33-member national assembly, 22 of its members elected by direct universal suffrage and 11 by proportional representation. It serves a four-year term.

Seychelles is a **unitary state.** A **unitary state** is a state governed as a single power in which the central government is ultimately supreme and any administrative divisions (sub-national units) exercise only the powers that the central government chooses to delegate. The majority of states in the world have a unitary system of government. Of the 193 UN member states, 165 are governed as unitary states.

In a unitary state, sub-national units are created and abolished (an example being the 22 mainland regions of France being merged into 13), and their powers may be broadened and narrowed, by the central government. Although political power may be delegated through devolution to local governments by statute, the central government remains supreme; it may abrogate the acts of devolved governments or curtail their powers.

The United Kingdom of Great Britain and Northern Ireland is an example of a unitary state. Scotland, Wales and Northern Ireland have a degree of autonomous devolved power, but such power is delegated by the Parliament of the United Kingdom, which may enact laws unilaterally altering or abolishing devolution (England does not have any devolved power).[1] Many unitary states have no areas possessing a degree of autonomy.[2] In such countries, sub-national regions cannot decide their own laws. Examples are the Republic of Ireland and the Kingdom of Norway.[3]

Unitary states are contrasted with federations, or federal states. In such states, the sub-national governments share powers with the central government as equal actors through a written constitution, to which the consent of both is required to make amendments. This means that the sub-national units have a right of existence and powers that cannot be unilaterally changed by the central government.

EXECUTIVE

- Ministry of Defence
- Ministry of Internal Affairs
- Ministry of Environment and Transport
- Ministry of Economic Planning
- Ministry of Finance
- Ministry of Information Technology and Communication
- Ministry of Industries and International Business
- Ministry of Local Government and Sports
- Ministry of Tourism and Civil Aviation
- Ministry of Social Affairs and Manpower Development
- Ministry of Foreign Affairs
- Ministry of Youth and Culture
- Ministry of Land Use and Habitat
- Ministry of Health

- Ministry of Administration
- Ministry of Education
- Ministry of Agriculture and Marine Resources

Politics of Seychelles takes place in a framework of a presidential republic, whereby the President of Seychelles is both head of state and head of government, and of a multi-party system. Executive power is exercised by the government. Legislative power is vested in both the government and the National Assembly.

THE 21ST CENTURY

Early elections originally set for 2003 were called in August/September 2001. The Government Party SPPF once again prevailed, although the main Opposition Party, Seychelles National Party (previously known as the United Opposition Party) headed by Rev. Wavel Ramkalawan, made a surprisingly strong showing and collected 46% of the total votes. The DP, headed by Mr. Mancham, did not take part in the elections.

In April 2004, Rene retired as President passing the office to his Vice President, James Michel. At the next Presidential election in July 2006, James Michel polled 53.7% of valid votes, Wavel Ramkalawan 45.7% and Phillip Boulle 0.6%. In the May 2007 National Assembly elections, Seychelles People's Progressive Front took 56.2% of votes and Seychelles National Party in coalition with Seychelles Democratic Party took 43.8%. This gave SPPF 18 directly elected seats plus 5 nominated, total 23 seats with the SNP/DP coalition taking 7 directly elected plus 4 nominated, total 11 seats.

EXECUTIVE BRANCH

The Seychelles president, who is both head of state and head of government, is elected by popular vote for a five-year term of office. The previous president, France Albert René, was democratically elected after the constitutional reforms of 1992, though he had been in power since a coup d'état in 1977. He stood down in 2004 in favour of his vice-president, James Michel. The cabinet is presided over and appointed by the president, subject to the approval of a majority of the legislature.

LEGISLATIVE BRANCH

The National Assembly/Assemblée Nationale has 34 members, elected for a term of five years, 25 members elected in single-seat constituencies and 9 members elected by proportional representation.

ADMINISTRATIVE DIVISIONS

Seychelles is divided in 25 administrative districts; Anse aux Pins, Anse Boileau, Anse Etoile, Anse Royale, Au Cap, Baie Lazare, Baie Sainte Anne, Beau Vallon, Bel Air, Bel Ombre, Cascade, English River, Glacis, Grand' Anse (on Mahe), Grand' Anse (on Praslin), Inner Islands, Les mamelles, Mont Buxton, Mont Fleuri, Plaisance, Pointe Larue, Port Glaud, Roche Caiman, Saint Louis, Takamaka

LEGISLATIVE

The National Assembly has 33 seats, 22 of which are elected by direct popular vote and 11 selected proportionately from parties which have won 9% or more of the vote. Five year term. The SPPF (82% of the popular vote) holds twenty-seven seats, Democratic Party (15%) five seats and United Opposition Party (3%) one seat.

JUDICIAL

The legal system is based on English common law, French civil law (Napoleonic Code) and Seychelles common law. It comprises five magistrates' courts, a Supreme Court and a Court of Appeal. As of 1996, all of the judges were citizens of other countries, working on contract.

POLITICAL PARTIES

- Seychelles People's Progressive Front or SPPF (led by France Albert Rene)
- Democratic Party or DP (Sir James Mancham)
- New Democratic Party (Christopher Gill)
- United Opposition or UO (Wavel Ramakalawan), a coalition of the following: Seychelles Party or PS (Wavel Ramakalawan), Seychelles Democratic Movement or MSPD (Jacques Hondoul) and Seychelles Liberal Party or SLP Ogilvie Berlouis

Budget
Revenues: US$216 million (1995)
Expenditures: US$235 million, including capital expenditures of $41 million

Foreign Relations
Member of the United Nations, Commonwealth of Nations, Organization of African Unity, Indian Ocean Commission and the Nonaligned Movement. Seychelles' basic foreign policy is that of "positive nonalignment."

United Nations

Ambassador Harold Walter GEISEL
Suite 900F, 820 Second Avenue,
New York, NY 10017, U.S.A
1-212-972-1785
Fax: 1-212-972-1786
Telex: 220032 SMUN UR

EMBASSIES

United States of America
Ambassador Harold Walter GEISEL
Suite 900F, 820 Second Avenue,
New York, NY 10017, U.S.A
1-212-972-1785
Fax: 1-212-972-1786
Telex: 220032 SMUN UR

France
51 Avenue Mozart
75016 Paris, France
(33 1) 42 30 57 47
Fax: (33 1) 42 30 57 40
e-mail: ambsey@aol.com
Telex: 649 140 SEYPA

INTERNATIONAL ORGANIZATIONS

Seychelles is a member of ACCT, ACP, AfDB, C, ECA, FAO, G-77, IBRD, ICAO, ICFTU, ICRM, IFAD, IFC, IFRCS, ILO, IMF, IMO, InOC, Intelsat (nonsignatory user), Interpol, IOC, ISO (correspondent), NAM, OAU, OPCW, SADC, UN, UNCTAD, UNESCO, UNIDO, UPU, WCL, WHO, WMO, WToO, WTrO (applicant)

MILITARY

Branches: Army (500 personnel; 1 infantry, 2 artillery and 1 support unit), Presidential Protection Unit (300), National Guard (1,000), Coast Guard (120), Air Wing (100), Marines (80), Police Force (560).

Military manpower: available males age 15-49, 22,677; fit for military service, 11,345 (2000 est.).
Military expenditures: $13.7 million

Maritime Claims
Continental shelf: 200 nm or to the edge of the continental margin
Exclusive economic zone: 200 nm
Territorial sea: 12 nm

ENVIRONMENTAL

Current issues: water supply depends on catchments to collect rain water

INTERNATIONAL AGREEMENTS:

party to: Biodiversity, Climate Change, Desertification, Endangered Species, Hazardous Wastes, Law of the Sea, Marine Dumping, Nuclear Test Ban, Ozone Layer Protection, Ship Pollution, Whaling *signed, but not ratified:* Climate Change-Kyoto Protocol

Between 1979 and 1993, Seychelles was governed under a single-party socialist system. President René, who had assumed power in a military coup d'état in 1977, had been the sole candidate in the presidential elections of 1979, 1984, and 1989, each time winning an affirmative vote of more than 90 percent.

The SPPF agreed to relinquish its monopoly of power in December 1991 when a party congress approved René's proposal to allow other political groups to be registered (see Return to a Multiparty System , this ch.). Groups receiving sufficient popular support were permitted to take part in revising the constitution. A first effort to produce a new constitution failed in a referendum in November 1992, but after further negotiations constitutional changes were approved the following June. Multiparty elections followed in July 1993 in which René and the SPPF were again victorious.

IMPORTANT OFFICIAL MATERIALS

INAUGURAL ADDRESS OF PRESIDENT DANNY FAURE, 16TH OCTOBER, 2016

Dear Seychellois Brothers and Sisters

It is with much humility that I address you today. Today is the start of a new chapter. A new chapter because a new generation is taking the helm from the generation that fought for our Independence, built the Seychellois nation, and created a modern society.

I appreciate that for us to reach where we are today, many people have worked hard and made many sacrifices. We have come from quite far. Indeed from very far. Today I say to you a huge Thank You. On behalf of the Seychellois Nation, I pay my respects to President Mancham, President Rene and President Michel for their leadership roles. I also take this opportunity to salute the people of Seychelles for their contribution in making Seychelles what it is today.

President Michel, this month it will be exactly 31 years since, as Minister of Education at the time, you gave me the opportunity to share my knowledge with the children and the youth of Seychelles. Thank you, President, for that opportunity, which allowed many other opportunities, not just for me, but for thousands of young people today.

During the course of our journey filled with many challenges for our small country, I have learnt from you to always keep our sights focused on the issues greater than ourselves: that is, the welfare of the people of our country.

Under your Presidency, Seychelles has witnessed an unprecedented economic transformation. You worked very hard to give Seychelles its rightful place in the world. Much has been said about what you have done for Seychelles and Seychellois. In time, much will also be written. What is clear to me is that your work and legacy will speak for itself with the passage of time.

Today, after you have completed 39 years in the Cabinet of Ministers, including 12 years as President, I salute you for your personal sacrifice, your hard work and your dedication in the service of the people of Seychelles. I join the entire Seychellois nation in wishing you all the very best in your retirement, and to accord you the respect that you deserve.

Dear Seychellois Brothers and Sisters, I believe in our Nation. I believe in Seychelles. I believe in a Seychelles that will remain forever united, and in a free and proud Seychelles.

Today, the Seychelles that we all love, offers us an extraordinary opportunity to view the future with confidence and optimism. Our Seychelles that we all believe in, calls each one of us to join together to overcome the differences and obstacles that still divide us. Often, without realising it, we become victims of our past, and we feel trapped in the politics of the past. I understand this.

During these 39 years, Seychelles has developed. Seychelles has progressed. For many of our citizens, Government has done much to make their lives happier and better. Nevertheless, there remain other brothers and sisters who believe that Government is the reason for their pain and suffering, and to them, I present a sincere apology.

As your President, I believe that for Seychelles to really achieve national unity in every sense, we must undergo a process of true reconciliation.

We stand to achieve much more as a nation and as a people if we overcome that which divides us. Let the differences in our political opinions be a source of strength that dynamises our democracy, and not one that chokes it. We must see the diversity within our unity as a new force that strengthens this National Unity that we truly want for our Seychelles.

Dear Seychellois Brothers and Sisters, Seychelles is greater than us. Seychelles is our true homeland. We all have a place within it.

Each one of us can interpret election results in different ways. What is absolutely clear is that through the will of the people, Seychellois have asked us to engage in dialogue and to work together. So today, more than ever, we must work together for the benefit of our people and Seychelles.

I am ready to work with our National Assembly. I have informed Hon Patrick Pillay, Speaker of the National Assembly, that in accordance with Article 92 (1) of our Constitution, on Tuesday 18th October 2016, I shall address the National Assembly, that institution where I started my political career 23 years ago. I shall use that occasion to speak about the work of our Government.

Dear Seychellois Brothers and Sisters, I am a child of SPUP, the party of the poor, the party of workers, the party that struggled to bring Independence. We have not yet achieved all of the vision that SPUP had for Seychelles. The development of Seychelles must remain focused on its people, it is the only way to eliminate poverty.

The principles that will bring greater vigour to the implementation of our development are: fairness, equal opportunities, social justice and a fair redistribution of wealth. I shall do everything to ensure that our policies reflect these principles.

Dear Brothers and Sisters, People of Seychelles, I believe in the principle of doing good for our brothers and sisters. When each one of us also does good, collectively our society becomes a happier one. On this journey, we must all remove ill-will, remove malice, remove injustice, and remove insults that lower us in the eyes of our Creator.

I believe in a Seychelles where none of our citizens is left behind, in a society which is compassionate. In a nation where true human dignity is respected. That no one is above the law, and the law applies equally for all.

I believe firmly in a system of universal social protection which is the basis for the maintenance of social cohesion and harmony, and which is also a condition for lasting peace.

I believe in a Seychelles where there is room for different ideas to co-exist, and as a nation, we are ready to create more space where diverging views and ideas can be heard and respected. And as our Constitution requires, we shall provide our citizens access to information.

I believe in honesty, integrity, and frankness. If any of our citizens have any complaint, or any evidence of wrong-doing where laws are not being respected, or where someone's human rights are being violated, or abused, he or she should, without fear, approach the relevant authorities for redress. In this regard, all citizens must take responsibility for their actions.

I believe in the strength of our Seychellois workforce, and in its capacity to move Seychelles forward. I believe in discipline, hard work, and a society where all work is valued and recognised. Irrespective of our political opinion, religious beliefs, whether we are in the public or private sectors, the important thing is that you do the work that you have been assigned, and you discharge it with all the necessary responsibilities. As employers, we pay workers their due salaries in accordance with the law. And we treat all our workers well, without exception. Along this line, the partnership between public and private sectors and civil society must show greater engagement. It is only through a more solid partnership that we can have greater shared prosperity among our people.

Dear Seychellois Brothers and Sisters, I have reached where I am today because there have been many alongside me. You know who you are. I know what you feel. I am the product of the opportunities that, 52 years ago, SPUP had set off to provide for the youth of Seychelles. Today I say to them Thank You. I thank my parents: my mother Violet Samson, my father Jean Faure. Both Seychellois. They cradled me, brought me up to appreciate obedience, respect, discipline and hard work. I thank my two brothers and my three sisters who have always been by my side. A very special thank you to my family who have given me unwavering support throughout.

I say thank you to Father Lafortune for the guidance that he gave me as the altar boy in the Anse Royale Church.

I salute the generation of the children of 1962, especially my school friends and teachers.

Each one of us has been inspired by different people, by different personalities. Me, I draw my inspiration from President René. Today I would like to say a Big Thank You to him. His principles, such as liberty and social justice which fuelled our struggle for Independence and the creation of a more fair society.

As President of the Republic, I am more determined than ever to create that society, evermore fair, ever more fraternal, ever more united, ever more prosperous and ever more humane. Today I call on you, my Seychellois brothers and sisters, to hold hands and scale our next phase. Where, together, we do not abandon peace and freedom, and where we remain forever united and together.

I stand as your servant, ready to serve the people of Seychelles and Seychelles.

Long live the people of Seychelles!

ADDRESS BY PRESIDENT DANNY FAURE ON THE OCCASION OF TWO YEARS IN OFFICE

Dear Seychellois brothers and sisters,

On the 16th of October, 2016, I took the Oath of Office.

I declared and affirmed that I would always be faithful and bear true allegiance to the Constitution of Seychelles, and that I would preserve, protect and defend the Constitution of Seychelles.

I promised that I would faithfully and diligently perform my duties and discharge my responsibilities as the President of Seychelles, that I would always be loyal to the Republic of Seychelles, that I would uphold the Constitution and the laws of Seychelles, and that I would dedicate myself to the service and betterment of the people of Seychelles, without fear or favour, affection or ill will.

I took the Oath of Office at a time where Seychelles was divided. It was a time where politics had divided families, divided friends, and divided workplaces.

Faced with this situation, as the fourth President of the Republic of Seychelles, I took a decision.

I refused to choose the path of confrontation; the path of partisan politics, the path of division. My decision was to choose a path of dialogue; to communicate directly with the opposition, to consult all actors and partners in society. I chose a path of working together, a path of national unity, and a path of true reconciliation. A path where I place Seychelles above everything else.

On the 16th of October 2016, when I addressed you for the first time as the President of the Republic, I presented you with the principles and values that I believe in. I also shared my vision for our people – a Seychelles where each one of us has a place. An inclusive society where everyone – irrespective of our political opinions or religious beliefs, irrespective of whether we come from the private sector, the public sector or from civil society – we all work together with integrity, responsibility, compassion, peace, and respect for one another, to continue to create and share the wealth of our country.

For us to be able to achieve this Vision, I asked all citizens to come together and join me to overcome our differences. In the last two years, I have remained faithful to my declarations of the 16th October 2016. I have followed an approach of consultation on all that concerns the wellbeing of Seychelles and Seychellois. I did not hesitate to review decisions when it was necessary to do so. We have worked hard to bring Seychellois together; to have a common vision for Seychelles.

Today, I feel reassured by the way our citizens have responded to the call for us to work together for our country. Today, there is a more stable situation in our country. A situation where families that were divided because of politics have made peace, where there is unity and harmony in workplaces and in communities. I see a people, despite our differences, coming together for a single purpose: Seychelles, our country.

To me, this is the result of working together and the shared conviction that the path of reconciliation, the path of national unity, the path of dialogue is the best path for our small country. Every Seychellois has played a role to maintain this stability, this tranquillity and harmony that our country enjoys. This stability has ensured that we continue to welcome visitors to Seychelles, our economy continues to grow, and that we continue to make progress; succeeding both locally and internationally.

Sometimes in life there is the temptation to go back to the path of confrontation; but we need the maturity to put Seychelles, which is bigger than us all, before everything. My experience is that the politics of confrontation, partisan politics, may bring short term gains but not long term gains for our Nation.

Brothers and sisters,

In the last two years, much has been done to open spaces for increased participation in the governance and steering of our country. I continue to increase the participation of the private sector on the governing boards of institutions. We can now see at the head of many Boards, individuals from the private sector or civil society. This has led us to a place where the private sector and the civil society have a better understanding and appreciation of the challenges that Government faces. This new way of composing the Boards has also created an opportunity for individuals to share their expertise and to reinforce the performance and governance of institutions.

When I spoke about development in 2016, I talked about the fundamental principles that would ensure successful growth such as equal opportunities, social justice, and fair redistribution of the country's wealth. Since then, many policies have been reviewed in order to espouse the principles of good governance, transparency and accountability as we continue to accelerate our development.

We are in a new stage where the execution of work has to be done in line with the new framework. We must continue.

Seychellois sisters and brothers, our vibrant democracy continues to evolve. In the last two years, we have worked together to put in place frameworks that will guarantee the existence of strong institutions, because I believe that strong institutions practise good governance and defend and protect the rights of citizens and ensure the country's progress.

We continue to implement policies and procedures to ensure that there is transparency and accountability in the functioning of Government. I have practised a leadership of non-interference in institutions so that all institutions have the space to do their work in line with the law that governs them. Such a practice has allowed institutions to comfortably take decisions as they should and to be held accountable for those decisions. This new way of working has necessitated a change in the way we think.

It is important that all Seychellois recognise the direction that our country is taking and that we all know how to participate in the development of the country without fear. To facilitate this, Government introduced a law on Access to Information. We also created the space for the media to play a more active role in informing citizens. We have reinforced our communication with citizens, so that members of the public may participate in the decision making process on issues that affect their lives.

We are witnessing a situation in our country where our citizens are living with all of their freedoms. With a sense of responsibility, respect and tolerance for the opinions of others, we can continue to make positive contributions to improve the quality of life in our country and become an example for the world.

Seychellois sisters and brothers, we all know the expression, "*No one is a prophet in his own land*". It happens often that focussed on our problems, we forget to acknowledge and celebrate our accomplishments. Seychelles has accomplished a lot and much has been recognised on the international scene. In September 2018, the United Nations Human Development Index, placed Seychelles in the 62nd position out of 189 countries. We are the first country in Africa. The Human Development Index measures the achievements of a country in three dimensions, that of health, education and the standard of living.

At the end of its mission in Seychelles on the 2nd of October this year, the International Monetary Fund (IMF) reported very positive results for Seychelles. IMF described our macroeconomic performance as strong, and our economy, despite a difficult world economic environment, on the right path with a positive prediction for 2019.

Another recognition of our achievements occurred recently on the 12th of October when the World Bank placed Seychelles as 43rd out of 157 countries on the Human Capital Index. Again, we are first in Africa and first in the region. The Human Capital Index looks at whether a country is making available the conditions that will allow its families to flourish. By looking at health, education and adult survival rates, the Index assesses the likelihood of a child born in that country will live to realise all its potential. The World Bank has informed us that our country is the one that has made the most significant progress in the last five years in Human Capital Development.

Seychellois Brothers and Sisters, our achievements have not happened by chance. The accomplishments of our country are thanks to the dedication, hard work and participation of every Seychellois – from the young person who takes their education and their future seriously, to the conscientious and committed employee who works tirelessly, to the parent that raises their child with care and good habits, to the senior citizen who gives guidance and prays for the country. Each one of us have played an important role to create this environment of peace, stability, compassion and tranquillity where progress has been able to flourish. Together, let us resist any efforts to disturb our tranquillity, our national unity, our peace. Let us come together, always together, to move Seychelles forward.

Seychellois Brothers and Sisters, the country is in good hands, the country is on the right path. Let us continue to work together with love, peace and in unity, with the conviction that our country is more important than our differences.

Tonight I wish to renew my commitment to work for all Seychellois and to work even harder, for our Seychelles that is greater than us all.

Thank you and good evening.

GOVERNMENT SYSTEM DEVELOPMENTS

Under the constitution that took effect in 1979, all political activity, in particular that regarding the formulation and debate of policy, was conducted under the auspices of the Front. The party constitution was attached as a supplement to the national constitution. The president, as head of state and commander in chief of the armed forces, was nominated by the national congress of the SPPF and stood for election on a yes-no basis. All Seychellois aged seventeen or older could vote. The president served a five-year term and could be elected no more than three times in succession.

The constitution provided few checks on executive powers. The president appointed a cabinet without review by the People's Assembly. The latter consisted of twenty-three members elected for four-year terms from twenty-three constituencies, plus two members named by the president to represent the inner and outer islands. The president appointed the chair of the assembly. The SPPF selected candidates for assembly seats. In some constituencies, only one candidate was nominated, but in others the voters could choose from as many as three SPPF nominees. The legislature exercised no independent role, simply enacting into law bills proposed by the executive branch. Debates on issues occurred and were reported in the media, but criticism of the president or the government was not tolerated.

RETURN TO A MULTIPARTY SYSTEM

Several factors contributed to the shift away from singleparty rule. Political changes in the former Soviet Union and Eastern Europe, and a movement toward multiparty systems in Africa, left Seychelles conspicuously out of step with trends in the rest of the world. Britain and France trimmed their foreign aid programs, tying future aid to progress on the political front. Exiled Seychelles political figures were active in drawing attention to the autocratic features of the Seychelles system In addition, domestic opposition to domination by the SPPF had become increasingly open by 1991. The Roman Catholic Church, the business community, and even a few figures in the SPPF had begun to express dissatisfaction. Embryonic local government had been introduced by combining the role of local party branch leaders and district councillors, but this step failed to satisfy sentiment for a more open and democratic system.

On December 3, 1991, at a special congress of the SPPF, President René announced that, beginning in January 1992, political groupings of at least 100 members would be permitted to register and that multiparty elections for a commission to participate in drafting a new constitution would be held six months later. In April 1992, former president James Mancham returned from Britain to lead the New Democratic Party (NDP), which tended to represent the commercial and wealthy in the election campaign. Six additional parties were also registered. In the voting for the constitutional commission, the SPPF gained 58.4 percent of the votes and the NDP, 33.7 percent. None of the other parties gained enough to be represented, although the most successful of these, the Seychellois Party (Parti Seselwa) led by Wavel Ramkalanan and calling for restoring free enterprise, was granted one seat on the commission. As a prelude to the constitutional conference, in September 1992 the government ended the eleven-year state of emergency declared after the 1981 attempted mercenary coup.

During the subsequent constitutional conference, the NDP delegation withdrew, objecting to closed sessions and claiming that the SPPF was forcing through an undemocratic document that reinforced the wide powers of the current president. The SPPF members, who constituted a quorum, continued the commission's work, and the draft constitution was submitted for popular referendum in November 1992.

The vote in favor of the new constitution was 53.7 percent, well short of the 60 percent needed for acceptance. The NDP campaigned for rejection of the draft, claiming that it would perpetuate domination by the president. The draft stipulated that half of the assembly seats would be allocated by proportional representation based on the presidential election results, thus guaranteeing the president a majority. The Roman Catholic Church also objected to the legalization of abortion called for in the document.

In January 1993, the constitutional commission reconvened to resume negotiations on a new draft constitution. The proceedings were conducted more openly, live television coverage was permitted, and interest groups could submit proposals. The new constitution, which had the support of both the SPPF and the NDP, was approved by 73.9 percent of the voters in a second referendum held on June 18, 1993. The text emphasized human rights and the separation of executive, legislative, and judicial powers. The presidency was again limited to three terms of five years each. The constitution provided for a leader of the opposition to be elected by the National Assembly. The assembly consisted of thirty-three members, twenty-two of them elected, and eleven designated by proportional representation.

In the first election under the new constitution, held on July 23, 1993, René was again elected president with 60 percent of the vote. Mancham of the NDP received 37 percent, and Philippe Boullé of the United Opposition Party, a coalition of the smaller parties, received 3 percent. Of the elective seats for the National Assembly, SPPF candidates won twenty-one and the NDP, one. Of the total thirty-three seats in the assembly, twentyseven went to the SPPF, five to the NDP, and one to the United Opposition Party.

Although Seychelles security forces intimidated some antiSPPF candidates in 1992, no coercion was reported during the 1993 voting. Fears of loss of jobs and benefits are believed to have played a part in the SPPF victory, however.

OPPOSITION MOVEMENTS AND INTEREST GROUPS

Most domestic critics of the government had been silenced by harassment or had been forced into exile during the period of one-party rule from 1977 to 1991. Opposition groups, about which little information is available, included the Movement for Resistance (Mouvement pour la Résistance), the Seychelles Liberation Committee, and the Seychelles Popular Anti-Marxist Front. Government control over the press and radio and television broadcasts also made it difficult for any opposition views to be heard, although newspapers printed by exiles were smuggled in from abroad or received by fax. The Roman Catholic and Anglican churches were allowed to comment on social and political issues during broadcasts of religious services, which each was allowed on alternate Sundays. The Roman Catholic bishop exercised a degree of influence and was regarded as one of the few checks against abuse by the René regime.

Until 1992 the Seychelles government tolerated no manifestation of domestic opposition, and opposition figures were forced to carry on their anti-SPPF campaigns from abroad, mainly in London. One exile leader, Gérard Hoarau, head of the Seychelles National Movement, was assassinated in 1985 in a crime that the British police were unable to solve.

The leading member of the exile community, however, was Mancham, former head of the Seychelles Democratic Party who was overthrown as president in 1977. In April 1992, Mancham returned to Seychelles to revive his political movement. Since 1989 Mancham had mounted what he called a "fax revolution" from London by sending facsimile messages designed to stir up opposition to the 200 fax machines in Seychelles. His program, entitled the Crusade for Democracy, was intended to restore democracy to Seychelles peacefully. Data transmitted by fax included accounts of human rights violations in Seychelles and charges of corruption of the René regime. René's government made it illegal to circulate a seditious fax in Seychelles, but fax owners eluded this regulation by photocopying the original before turning it in to the police. René then sought to counter the criticism through a government media campaign, but in so doing he admitted the existence of an opposition in Seychelles. The end result was that he was obliged to give way and allow multiparty democracy to exist. René recognized Mancham as official Leader of the Opposition, and Mancham received a salary as a government employee with various perquisites.

A third opposition leader was Anglican clergyman Wavel Ramkalanan. In a 1990 radio sermon, Ramkalanan denounced violations of human rights by the René government. Although forced off the air, he continued to distribute copies of his sermons charging government corruption. Ramkalanan formed the Parti Seselwa when the government lifted its political ban but obtained only a 4.4 percent return in the 1992 election for delegates. The Parti Seselwa and five other newly registered parties allied themselves with Mancham's NDP but later broke away to form the United Opposition Party, charging Mancham with being too willing to compromise with René and the SPPF.

The Roman Catholic Church continued to wage opposition to the René regime. In early 1993, the Roman Catholic bishop appeared before the constitutional commission several times to complain about past human rights violations by the René government. He also demanded that the new constitution adopt a ban on abortion and provide for religious education in the schools.

INFORMATION MEDIA

During the rule of René and the SPPF through 1991, political expression was tightly controlled. The only daily newspaper was the government-owned *Seychelles Nation*, which had an estimated circulation of 4,000. Published by the Department of Information and Telecommunications, it has a government bias and does not present independent views. *L'Écho des Îles*, a Roman Catholic weekly that touches on current events, is not subject to censorship and often carries views critical of the government. Its circulation is about 2,000. After the political liberalization of 1992, several opposition journals appeared and were allowed to publish without government harassment. Foreign publications are imported and sold without interference.

The state-owned Seychelles Broadcasting Corporation (SBC), previously closely controlled, was granted autonomous status in 1992. Television and radio continued to show a pro-SPPF bias but began to broadcast material critical of the government in their news. Party political broadcasts were permitted, and SBC coverage of the campaigns and constitutional deliberations was followed closely.

LEGAL SYSTEM

The three-tiered judicial system consists of magistrates' or small claims courts, the Supreme (or trial) Court, and the Court of Appeal. The Court of Appeal hears appeals from the Supreme Court in both civil and criminal cases. The Supreme Court has jurisdiction of first instance as well as acting as an appeals court from the magistrates' courts. The system is based on English common law, with influences of the Napoleonic Code (e.g., in tort and contract matters), and customary law. Criminal cases are heard in magistrates' courts or the Supreme Court depending on the seriousness of the charge. Juries are called only in cases of murder or treason. Normal legal protections are extended to defendants. They include public trials, the right of the accused to be present, and the accused's right to confront witnesses, to appeal, to qualify for bail in most cases, and to be represented by counsel, on a *pro bono* basis if indigent. Judges from other Commonwealth countries--mostly African or Asian--are employed on a contract basis. Judges remain independent from influence by the executive in spite of occasional government pressure.

Under the penal code, a detained person must be brought before a magistrate within forty-eight hours. Before repeal of the Public Security Act in 1992, persons could be detained indefinitely on security charges. The president still has broad personal powers to detain persons regarded as security threats. Since 1989 only a few brief detentions have been reported, all under the Public Security Act.

Much progress in human rights has occurred since political freedoms were restored in 1992. Both military and police engaged in physical harassment of members of opposition parties before the 1992 election of constitutional delegates, but later elections were free of intimidation. The government's control of jobs, housing, and land enables it to reward supporters and discourage dissent. Legislation still on the books brings the risk of prosecution and imprisonment for publishing defamatory material against the president or for publishing or possessing publications banned by the government for security reasons. The close association of the armed forces with the SPPF represents a further threat to the full exercise of political rights. In an attempt to mollify domestic and foreign critics, René removed the deputy secretary general of the SPPF as chief of staff of the defense forces in 1992.

The number of crimes and other offenses reported in 1990 was 4,564, of which 35 percent involved violations of traffic ordinances. Thefts, burglaries, housebreaking, and other forms of stealing made up most of the remaining 1,559 offenses. There were five cases of homicide; thirteen cases of rape and indecent assault; 634 aggravated or common assaults; 287 offenses against property such as trespass and arson; and 403 incidents of disorderly conduct. The general trend appears to be downward, although the sharpest decline is in vehicular offenses. Theft in tourist hotels is said to be on the rise. Juvenile delinquency-- linked to boredom and isolation--is a growing problem.

Official statistics are not available on sentencing or the prison population. The United States Department of State described living conditions at the Police Bay prison as spartan but said that in 1993 both SPPF and opposition members drafting the constitution had been allowed, to visit and found conditions satisfactory. Weekly family visits are allowed, and inmates have access to printed materials.

FOREIGN RELATIONS

Officials characterize the nation's foreign policy as one of "positive nonalignment," under which the country pursues an active and independent course in the conduct of its international relations. Seychelles is a member of the United Nations (UN) and a number of related agencies, including the IMF. It is also a member of the Commonwealth, which has assisted it in transition to multiparty democracy; the Organization of African Unity (OAU); and the Nonaligned Movement. In 1984 Seychelles became linked with Mauritius and Madagascar in the Indian Ocean Commission (IOC); later joined by Comoros and France on behalf of Reunion, the IOC seeks to promote economic cooperation in the region and expand interisland trade.

Although the René government often has sided with the more radical members and causes of the Nonaligned Movement, neither the positions taken nor the radical rhetoric in which they were expressed have been allowed to interfere with essentially pragmatic decisions directly affecting the nation's interests. Seychelles is particularly active in promoting the concept of the Indian Ocean as a zone of peace, campaigning for the removal of all foreign powers and bases in the region. It is committed to seeking the end of the United States naval presence on Diego Garcia, an island territory of Britain situated about 1,900 kilometers east of Mahé. In a spirit of solidarity with the more radical states of the nonaligned spectrum, Seychelles has pursued political ties with the German Democratic Republic (East Germany), Libya, Cuba, Iraq, and the Democratic People's Republic of Korea (North Korea). It has supported the former Soviet Union on such controversial issues as its invasion of Afghanistan.

Seychelles also seeks to strengthen its relations with the littoral nations of the Indian Ocean. Such states include other island governments such as those of French-administered Reunion, and independent Maldives and Mauritius as well as more distant nations such as India, Bangladesh, Tanzania, and Kenya. India has been a source of funding for Seychelles projects and in October 1990 René paid his third visit to the country following the first meeting of the Indo-Seychelles Joint Commission. The body has continued to meet biennially to discuss common trade, investment, and communications matters. In addition, the navies of the two countries cooperate. In February 1992, the Seychelles minister of education visited Bangladesh to expand bilateral cooperation in education, literacy programs, and rural development. Relations with the Tanzanian government were especially close during the early years of the René regime. Tanzanians had helped train and equip the initiators of the coup that brought René to power, and Tanzanian advisers had helped establish and train the Seychelles People's Liberation Army. With both Tanzania and Kenya, Seychelles has discussed sharing labor resources and with Tanzania, the sharing of its EEZ, tourism promotion, and air flights.

In a practical sense, Seychelles' links with the countries of the West have been much more significant than its political kinship with more radical developing countries. Seychelles has succeeded in attracting relatively large amounts of aid; foreign assistance per capita was US$223 annually in 1975-79, US$295 in 1980-85, and US$331 in 1985-90. France has been the leading donor, providing US$53.9 million in bilateral assistance between 1982 and 1990, in addition to contributions through the World Bank and the EC. Loans placed through the Seychelles Development Bank and direct investments are also important. Examples of projects France has funded for Seychelles included in 1990 assistance to the television station to promote broadcasting in French and provision of devices to improve airport security. Britain has been second in total aid, supplying US$26.1 million in the 1982-90 period. Australia has extended modest amounts of aid, primarily in the form of education and training programs, as part of its efforts to become more fully engaged in the Indian Ocean region. Before the Soviet Union broke up in 1990, it was a significant contributor, granting such aid as fuel oil to assist in patrolling the EEZ. The relative prosperity of the islands has brought a decline in aid from most sources. The British aid level had fallen to about US$1.5 million annually in 1991.

In addition to Peace Corps volunteers working in Seychelles, United States assistance, which earlier amounted to US$3.3 million annually, was US$1.3 million in fiscal year (FY--see Glossary) 1993. The preeminent feature of United States-Seychelles relations over the preceding thirty years was the United States Air Force satellite tracking station situated on Mahé on land leased from Seychelles at US$4.5 million annually as of 1993. The Seychelles economy benefits by a further US$5 to US$6 million annually in local spending linked to the station. The facility's complement consists of four uniformed air force personnel, about seventy-five civilian contract personnel who operate the equipment, and some 175 Seychellois employees. United States naval vessels periodically pay calls at Victoria. Restrictions on British and United States ships carrying nuclear weapons had not been enforced since 1983.

Furthermore, Seychelles has sought to promote economic relations particularly with countries from which it might receive loan assistance. For example, it obtained a US$1 million loan for elementary education in December 1988 from the OPEC Fund for International Development. In August 1990 Seychelles signed an agreement on economic and technological cooperation with China.

The Seychelles government condemned apartheid policies in South Africa and joined in the voting in the OAU for trade sanctions. Although René declared that his government would take steps to reduce Seychelles' reliance on South African products, South Africa's relatively low prices and short delivery times have in fact brought South Africa a growing share of Seychelles' trade. In 1991 South Africa accounted for 13.5 percent of total imports. Numerous factors combined to curtail tourism from South Africa in the early 1980s--the René government's hostility, the apparent South African involvement in the 1981 coup attempt, a reduction in air links, and the recession in South Africa. Beginning in 1988, however, tourist arrivals began to increase dramatically, climbing to 13,570 in 1993.

As negotiations proceeded to convert to a multiracial political system in Pretoria, Seychelles modified its hostile political stance, agreeing to enter into commercial and consular relations in April 1992. South Africa also agreed in August 1992 to pay compensation of US$3 million for the abortive 1981 coup. In November 1993 the two countries agreed to establish relations at the ambassadorial level.

EU SEYCHELLES RELATIONS

STRATEGIC OBJECTIVES OF THE EU'S RELATIONSHIP WITH SEYCHELLES

The overarching objective of European Union's (EU) relationship with the Seychelles under the 11 th European Development Fund (EDF) is to promote the development of a common strategic approach for the sustainable development and the gradual integration of Seychelles into the world economy. Following the support of the 10th

macroeconomic reform programme under the EDF, the Government of Seychelles in collaboration with other development partners and other areas of EU intervention is pushing the cooperation agenda for the coming years further under the theme 'From Stabilisation to Sustained Growth' based on the challenges ahead in order to solidify sustained and inclusive growth. Gender equality being an important objective under the Seychelles development goals is supported in the implementation ofthis National Indicative Programme where feasible.

In this perspective, Seychelles has consistently been showing high political commitment at various international fora in seeking donor support for implementing a sustainable development strategy. The government adopted the "Seychelles Sustainable Development Strategy (SSDS) 2011-20" which mainstreams sustainability in a wide range of thematic sectors, policies and other institutional frameworks of the Seychelles that provides strategic direction and guidance on the country development vision. As a framework document the SSDS is wide-ranging but comprehensive blueprint for Seychelles medium term sustainable development and is one that reflects Seychelles endeavour to mainstream sustainable development in its national development strategy which is currently under preparation. The SSDS is also coherent in mainstreaming the regional integration agenda ofthe island.

In this context, the EU will be primarily focusing on the need to respond to capacity constraints and increased pressure on the existing local human resources in order to meet developmental needs. The intervention of the EU will be aligned with the emerging areas of intervention within the framework of the SSDS and regional integration agenda. It will also promote better donor complementarity to ensure the best allocation of resources in order to do more with less and to unlock the potential under the principle of additionality. EU cooperation with Seychelles under the 10th EDF (2009 -2014) is characterized by support to environment related fields, social sector, in particular education, and infrastructure such as water and sanitation, improvement in bandwidth connectivity and more recently climate change, which are the largest sectors in the SSDS, as key to secure inclusive and sustainable growth, which is a focus in EU's recent agenda for change.

Given that the future financial allocation for Seychelles under the National Indicative Programme (NIP) is EUR 2.2 million, the EU would concentrate on the provision of well-targeted, and small-scale interventions through technical assistance under a TCF (feasibility studies, etc); for instance to assist in the provision of grants for project preparation to facilitate access to innovative financing such as blending operations to leverage infrastructure investments, Public-Private Partnerships (PPP) operations, or to facilitate other funding possibilities including the EDF regional funds.

In addition, the European Union will maintain the dynamic approach of mobilising a number of additional financial instruments, as done in the last few years, including environment and climate change and fisheries related budget lines; support to Non State Actors under the civil society organisations -local authorities (CSO-LA) thematic pro gramme to address human rights and governance issues, further enhance synergies and coherence with the sizeable grants made available under the fisheries agreement and provision of mechanism to address high vulnerability to external shocks.

1.2 Choice of sectors

Within the overall policy context of the SSDS, a general provision for a Technical Cooperation Facility is envisaged.

Seychelles has come a long way since the 2008 economic crisis, but a number of weaknesses and challenges remain to be addressed. Seychelles faces a number of constraints similar to Small Island Developing States (SIDS) and is highly vulnerable to external shocks. With a population of around 90,000 inhabitants, the country faces heavy pressure on its limited manpower. As a result, there is a mismatch between the demand and supply of human resources which creates constraints and bottlenecks in ensuring sustainable growth. In this context, the African Development Bank (AIDB) is assisting Seychelles in the formulation of a National Human Resource Development Strategy (NHRDS) in order to evaluate the human resource needs of Seychelles which is also one of the core areas of focus of the National Development Strategy (NDS) currently under preparation. Seychelles needs to enhance its human resource capabilities in order to respond effectively to the emerging challenges inherent to its small size.

The SSDS identifies issues relating to the environment and sustainability which are integrated into all the main sectors. This is being further developed under the concepts of Green and Blue Economies.

In view of the sensitive nature of the physical and natural environment of the Seychelles, there is enormous pressure placed on ecosystems due to increasing demands for natural resources (such as food, fish, construction materials, etc.), water and energy, growth in solid waste, and intense competition for land use. Water and energy consumption has significantly increased and will continue to do so over the next ten years. The fact that tourism is one of the main pillars of the economy, the demand for consumption of resources will place increasing strains on the environment. The challenge of preserving the environment and making prudent use of the natural resource base is therefore critical to Seychelles' sustainable development and future growth.

Seychelles is also confronted with limited regional and international connectivity in the field of digital communication and maritime links, which hampers generating welfare benefits for the population.

Emphasis on the implementation of the Interim Economic Partnership Agreement (I EPA) should also be taken into account, these are aimed at promoting trade between the EU and the ACP - and through trade development, sustainable growth and poverty reduction. The i-EPAs set out to help ACP countries integrate into the world economy and share in the opportunities offered by globalisation.

In accordance with the objective of the EU cooperation under the 11th EDF, the cooperation is identified on the basis of the following criteria:

Consistency with the Seychelles Sustainable Development Strategy

Consistency with the Barbados Programme of Action and the Mauritius Strategy for the Sustainable Development of SIDS

The need to respond to capacity constraints and increased pressure on the existing local resources in order to meet developmental needs

The need to take timely measures to reduce the economic and environmental vulnerability ofthe country

Ensuring alignment between country needs and EU interventions and complementarities with other development partners.

Moreover, the issue of division of labour makes it advisable to take a back seat in sectors such as macroeconomic reform and public finance management already covered by the International Monetary Fund (IMF) and the World Bank (WB) in order to concentrate expertise and financial resources, which renders further flexibility a necessity. Based on the above criteria, and given the fact that the SSDS covers a wide range of sectors, the TCF would focus on a few key strategic areas of intervention that would add value and give a comparative advantage to EU cooperation.

A number of programmes and policy changes require a multi-sectoral approach as well as institutional mechanisms that need to be geared for developing such coherence and coordination. A number of relevant sectors and stakeholders (such as policy makers, private sector and civil society in the country) would need to be involved and consulted in the process of implementing appropriate policy measures designed to move forward in a "pro-active" manner rather than a "reactive" mode of operation. Well-organised and policy coordination mechanisms are required at institutional level as there is a strong need to set up a proper donor coordination framework as well as intra-institutional coordination mechanisms for implementation of national and regional programmes.

The TCF will undertake capacity building to develop appropriate coordination and monitoring mechanisms to ensure that the country's policy makers have sufficient information, technical resources and capacities to effectively take decisions and achieve the set objectives of achieving sustainable develo~ment. As a concrete example, small-scale technical support provided under the lOt EDF to the Office of the Auditor General and to the Finance and Public Accounts Committee of the National Assembly has had a significant impact in the discharge of duties for external audit and legislative scrutiny and was widely recognised by the Government and development partners.

Given more pressing government budgetary priorities, the country is very often constrained in providing only limited resources for capacity building so as to provide more resources to other areas of governmental operations. Such budgetary prioritisation choices or constraints often result in a diminished technical capacity at the technical and institutional level. Moreover, there is relatively poor inter-agency coordination in policymaking. The existence of adequate technical support to relevant institutions, experienced and knowledgeable experts is essential to overcome those shortcomings and add to the preparedness of Seychelles to engage in the implementation of sustainable development priorities and policies. Technical assistance in the area of competition may also be included in that support.

Any intervention would need a strong support capacity building component in view of the limitations noted in Seychelles. In addition, in order to enable Seychelles access innovative financing schemes and develop public-private partnerships to unleash the emerging developmental potential, relevant studies would need to be undertaken and provision made for technical support back-up to implement sectoral reforms that would lead to a quantum leap in its development agenda.

Finally, taking into account the importance of the Information and Communication Technologies (ICT) and their applications as proven drivers of inclusive and sustainable growth, innovation and entrepreneurship, in meeting the challenges facing Seychelles the Technical Cooperation Facility (TCF) will pay particular attention to the deployment of ICTs and the full exploitation of their potential in providing or facilitating sustainable solutions, considering especially the island's shortages or shortcomings in the field of digital communications, as indicated earlier

SECURITY AND ARMY

Seychelles confronts no external security threat. However, during the Cold War, Seychelles faced several threats from foreign powers interested in the country's strategic position astride the Indian Ocean's oil-tanker lanes. In particular, President France Albert René feared South African aggression. On at least two occasions, he accused South Africa of trying to overthrow his regime. Both incidents involved Colonel "Mad Mike" Hoare, a mercenary who allegedly had been acting on behalf of the South African government. The first coup attempt occurred in November 1979, when René announced that he had foiled a plot "sponsored from abroad with the cooperation of mercenaries standing ready in Durban." The authorities arrested but later released eighty coup plotters. Although a South African connection could not be ruled out, some Western observers believed the affair was French-inspired.

The second, more serious coup attempt occurred on November 25, 1981, when a group of forty-five European mercenaries, led by Colonel Hoare, arrived at Mahé International Airport on a commercial flight from Swaziland to overthrow the René regime. The Seychellois authorities quickly thwarted the coup attempt, known as Operation Anvil, and the mercenaries hijacked an Air India plane and forced the captain to fly them to Durban, South Africa. As soon as the aircraft arrived, the South African police arrested all the mercenaries. Several of the mercenaries, including Colonel Hoare, served time in jail for their involvement in Operation Anvil. On May 7, 1985, Colonel Hoare gained his freedom as a result of a general presidential pardon.

In the aftermath of Operation Anvil, there were indications that Pretoria and Victoria, the capital of Seychelles, had concluded a secret agreement. In exchange for the release of South African prisoners in Seychelles, the South African government promised to refrain from future actions against the René regime, help guarantee Seychellois security, and provide an indemnity payment to Seychelles. In July 1992, Pretoria announced that it would pay Victoria about 8 million rand in compensation for Operation Anvil. Since then, Seychellois-South African relations have improved to the point that, on November 8, 1993, the two countries established diplomatic relations at the ambassadorial level.

In 1986 another coup attempt against the René regime occurred, supposedly involving the United States, France, and Britain. In addition to this foreign connection, the plot, known as Operation Distant Lash, included thirty mercenaries and some 350 partisans in Seychelles. The figurehead of this coup attempt was Minister of Defense Ogilvy Berlouis who reportedly was groomed to be the country's new pro-Western president. The security forces uncovered the conspiracy before the plotters could act and subsequently arrested Berlouis. Also, the government forced several Seychelles People's Liberation Army (SPLA) officers to resign.

In July 1987, British police uncovered yet another plot to overthrow the René regime and to abduct leading members of the South African opposition movement, the African National Congress (ANC), who were based in London. The authorities eventually arrested four men and charged them with conspiracy to kidnap the ANC members; the charges were later withdrawn because of insufficient evidence.

Since independence numerous internal threats against the Seychellois government have arisen. After overthrowing James Mancham's regime on June 5, 1977, René quickly established a socialist one-party state, censored the rival newspaper, and abolished religious fee-paying schools. Additionally, René created an army and a large security apparatus for the first time in the country's history. Such controversial policies caused considerable popular resentment against the René regime.

Resentment caused thousands of Seychellois to go into exile and to organize an array of opposition groups seeking to overthrow René. In April 1978, some of James Mancham's followers unsuccessfully tried to overthrow the government when René was on a state visit to North Korea and the PRC. The Movement for Resistance (Mouvement pour la Résistance), which sought to restore democracy in Seychelles, indicated that about 100 of its members had financed the November 1981 coup attempt. The Seychelles Liberation Committee, established in 1979 by exiles in Paris, also wanted to remove René and abolish his one-party state. The Seychelles National Movement maintained that it was a broad-based opposition group with followers in Seychelles, Britain, and Australia. The Seychelles Popular Anti-Marxist Front (SPAMF) declared that it had unsuccessfully tried to persuade the South African government to support a SPAMF coup attempt against René. Most Western observers believed that, notwithstanding the November 1981 coup attempt, these exile organizations had little chance of effecting a change of government in Seychelles, largely because they had few supporters in the country and minimal resources. With the end of the Cold War and the emergence of multiparty politics in Seychelles, the external and internal threats against the René regime have dissipated.

ARMED FORCES IN NATIONAL LIFE

Prior to 1977, Seychelles had no armed forces. Instead, there was a small police force modeled along British lines. René believed that the military would help preserve the country's revolution and advance socialism. Although the armed forces have been largely loyal to René, on at least one occasion, the SPLA staged a mutiny against the René regime. On August 17-18, 1982, some eighty-eight noncommissioned officers and enlisted personnel seized the Victoria radio station and port, police stations, telegraph facilities, and the Union Vale army camp. The mutineers demanded redress of numerous grievances such as a change in the composition and ideological orientation of the René regime, the expulsion of all Tanzanian military advisers, and an improvement in the living conditions of the ordinary soldier. Within thirtysix hours, loyalist forces, supported by approximately 400 Tanzania People's Defence Force personnel, crushed the mutiny and recaptured all key installations. In April 1983, the government concluded a secret court martial of the mutineers. Since then, the armed forces have acquiesced in the goals and policies of the René regime.

SEYCHELLES PEOPLE'S DEFENSE FORCES

The Seychelles People's Defense Force (SPDF) consist of the SPLA, a people's navy, and a people's air force. In December 1992, the government amalgamated the Seychelles People's Navy and the Seychelles People's Air Force to form the Seychelles Coast Guard. Each service commander reports to the armed forces chief of staff, who is responsible to the commander in chief, René. The president also retains the minister of defense portfolio. The Defence Forces Council, which is chaired by the armed forces chief of staff, manages the SPDF.

The 1,000-man SPLA comprises one infantry battalion, two artillery troops, and one support company. The army possesses six BDRN and eight Shorland reconnaissance vehicles, four BTR-152 armored personnel carriers, three D-130 122-mm towed artillery pieces, two BM-21 122-mm multiple rocket launchers, six M-43 82- mm mortars, ten SA-7 surface-to-air missiles, and an unknown number of RPG-7 rocket launchers. The SPLA's mission includes defending the nation's territorial integrity and, when necessary, assisting the People's Militia in preserving domestic law and order. Because much of its equipment requires maintenance work, the army has minimal capabilities. Western observers believe that the army would be ineffective against a professional military force.

The 100-member air wing of the coast guard operates one Britten-Norman BN-2A Maritime Defender and a Cessna A-150 Aerobat trainer. The former aircraft, which the British government donated in 1980, patrols the EEZ, which extends over an area of almost 1 million square kilometers. The Britten-Norman, which normally operates in conjunction with patrol boats from the navy wing of the coast guard, searches for vessels conducting illegal fishing and smuggling activities. The aircraft also conducts light transport, search and rescue, and medical evacuation missions. The air wing is the most effective service with equipment in good operating condition.

The navy wing of the coast guard, based in Port Victoria, owns one Topaz coastal patrol boat, one Andromache, one Zoroaster, and two Zhuk inland patrol boats, and one amphibious landing craft. The navy wing patrols the country's EEZ and conducts antidrug and search and rescue missions. The navy wing's effectiveness is extremely limited, largely because it rarely has more than two of its vessels operational at one time.

STATE SECURITY SERVICES

The People's Militia has existed since the beginning of the René regime. On June 10, 1977, the president called for volunteers to register for training in the People's Militia, which was to guard against a countercoup by James Mancham. By the early 1990s, the 800-member People's Militia consisted largely of untrained and unfit volunteers. Its mission is to defend the country from external aggression and preserve the revolution. In June 1989, René assumed overall control of the People's Militia while the chief of staff is responsible for running it on a dayto -day basis. The People's Militia is divided into five military regions (north, central, west, south Mahé, and Praslin). Most Western observers consider the People's Militia a totally ineffective force.

The national police, which is organized along British lines and commanded by a police commissioner, includes a regular 500- member unit and a sixty-member paramilitary mobile unit. Members of the force normally are unarmed but mobile unit personnel are equipped with modern weapons, including 7-62 SLR rifles. For operational and administrative purposes, Seychelles is divided into the Central Police Division, which comprises the capital; North Police Division; South Police Division; and the Praslin/La Digue Police Division. A senior police officer commands each of these formations. Seychelles maintains a total of seventeen police stations in all divisions. The police organization includes headquarters, Criminal Investigation Department (CID), Special Force (Police Mobile Unit), general duties, and special branch. A commandant manages the police training school at Praslin. This school provides fifteen-week and refresher training courses for recruits, two-week supervisory officers' courses, two-week promotion courses, and four-week basic courses. Each district also has field training. Most Western observers agree that the national police are under strength and poorly paid. As a result, the police have limited military value.

René maintains a 300-man Presidential Guard for his own protection. This unit, which includes an unknown number of European mercenaries, possesses high-quality personnel and weapons.

Information about Seychelles defense spending is limited. The 1991 defense expenditures, which were decided by René, amounted to approximately US$16 million.

TRAINING AND MORALE

Historically, with the exception of the air wing, the armed forces have been poorly trained and suffered from low morale. Beginning in the late 1980s, the government began to establish a military training infrastructure. On May 16, 1987, the first noncommissioned officers (NCOs) passed through a three-month refresher course at the SPDF NCO Training School. At the graduation ceremony, Chief of Staff James Michel told the NCOs that a new career development program would give each of them "an equal opportunity to develop his career and rise up the promotion scale to the highest ranks." On May 7, 1988, the SPDF, supported by the People's Militia, conducted a simulated offensive at the Grand Police Military Training Center. The troops covered offensive and defensive military tactics, weapons training, field communications and engineering, first aid, map reading, and other military subjects. On June 2, 1990, officials opened the Seychelles Defence Academy, which provided training courses for the SPDF, the People's Militia, and the police. Despite these efforts, the SPLA and the navy wing have failed to improve their capabilities. Personnel suffer from low morale, poor qualifications, and ineffective combat skills.

The air wing, however, shows a relatively high degree of professionalism. All pilots receive training in the Cessna A-150 before moving on to the Britten-Norman. After building up the requisite number of flying hours and obtaining the necessary commercial licenses, most pilots are seconded to the national airline, Air Seychelles. Some pilots are assigned to the Seychelles government, which operates one Cessna Citation and one Cessna Caravan II as passenger and light transport aircraft.

FOREIGN MILITARY ASSISTANCE

Seychelles traditionally received foreign military assistance from numerous nations, including Tanzania, India, the former Soviet Union, North Korea, and the United States. Of these, Tanzania has been Seychelles' most important military ally. The two countries initiated military relations shortly after René established the People's Militia; twelve Tanzanian military advisers arrived in Seychelles to help train the militia. By 1980 the TPDF maintained an estimated 140-member contingent on Seychelles, including a 30-member training team. After the expulsion of French technicians in 1979, Tanzania reinforced its presence in Seychelles. In June 1979, Seychellois military units participated in a joint exercise with TPDF and Malagasy units. On November 26, 1981, the day after Colonel Hoare's coup attempt failed, 400 TPDF personnel started patrolling Mahé International Airport and the coast to prevent a return of Hoare's mercenaries. According to some Western observers, the intervention of Tanzanian military personnel during the August 1982 SPDF mutiny probably saved the René regime.

India has been one of René's oldest military allies. On June 5, 1982, India gave Seychelles two Chetak helicopters as a Liberation Day gift for the people's air force; after one crashed, Bombay provided another. By the early 1990s, the Indian presence in Seychelles included a colonel who managed the Seychelles Defense Academy, and two police advisers.

Between 1979 and 1990, the former Soviet Union provided an array of military aid to Seychelles, including small arms, ammunition, SA-7 surface-to-air missiles, artillery, patrol boats, and petroleum. Additionally, the former Soviet Union deployed an unknown number of Soviet military and technical advisers to Seychelles. By December 1990, changing political conditions in Moscow forced the former Soviet Union to terminate its military aid program and withdraw all its advisers from Seychelles. In exchange for aid provided, the former Soviet Union hoped to gain access to Seychelles naval ports. However, although he allowed Soviet warships to make port calls, René never signed a formal access agreement with Moscow.

By 1983 North Korea had deployed a fifty to sixty-member military advisory team to Seychelles. These personnel assumed responsibility for training the SPLA. Unconfirmed reports also indicated that the North Koreans instructed the Presidential Guard. By 1988, according to Michel, the North Koreans had departed Seychelles.

The United States provided security assistance to Seychelles to retain access to the United States Air Force Tracking Station at La Misére. Aid activities focused on the IMET program, civic action, and coastal security. Since FY 1984, a small number of Seychellois military personnel have attended IMET courses in technical and professional areas such as communications and studied at infantry and command and staff level military schools. Other training include basic infantry, naval, and coast guard operations courses. During the early 1990s, the United States hoped to expand its security assistance to the Seychelles to include biodiversity, air-sea rescue, explosives ordinance disposal, and military working dog training.

Since the end of the Cold War, Seychelles increasingly has relied on India and the United States for foreign military assistance. France also has provided some maintenance aid to the Seychellois coast guard. Some Western observers maintain that, with the establishment of diplomatic relations, South Africa could initiate a military aid program in Seychelles within a few years.

PENAL SYSTEM

The Seychellois penal system is based on English common law and Napoleonic civil law. The judiciary system includes the Supreme Court and an Appeals Court. The president also exercises quasi-judicial powers, especially in national security cases. Seychellois law requires that military personnel be tried by court martial unless the president decrees otherwise.

The courts often sentence criminals to the Grand Police Camp, a high security prison run by the army on Mahé Island. Amnesty International reports that prison authorities often require prisoners to perform excessively strenuous labor.

ECONOMY AND ECONOMIC DEVELOPMENT - STRATEGIC INFORMATION

The **economy of Seychelles** is based on fishing, tourism, the processing of coconuts and vanilla, coir (coconut fiber) rope, boat building, printing, furniture and beverages. Agricultural products include cinnamon, sweet potatoes, cassava (tapioca), bananas, poultry and tuna.

The public sector, comprising the government and state-owned enterprises, dominates the economy in terms of employment and gross revenue, employing two-thirds of the labor force. Government consumption absorbs over one-third of the GDP.

Since independence in 1976, per capita output has expanded to roughly seven times the old near-subsistence level. Growth has been led by the tourist sector, which employs about 30% of the labour force and provides more than 70% of hard currency earnings, and by tuna fishing.

In recent years the government has encouraged foreign investment in order to upgrade hotels and other services. These incentives have given rise to an enormous amount of investment in real estate projects and new (mostly five star) resort properties. Hilton, Four Seasons and Banyan Tree are all new entrants to Seychelles. Development projects projected in the hundreds of millions of dollars each are in the beginning stages for Emirates Airlines, Qatar Airways, Raffles, Shangri-La. Other private developments such as Ile Aurore, Per Aquam and Eden Island are projected at over $2 billion.

At the same time, the government has moved to reduce the dependence on tourism by promoting the development of farming, fishing, small-scale manufacturing and most recently the offshore sector. The vulnerability of the tourist sector was illustrated by the sharp drop in 1991–1992 due largely to the country's significantly overvalued exchange rate and the Gulf War, and once again following the September 11, 2001, attacks on the United States.

Other issues facing the government are the curbing of the budget deficit, including the containment of social welfare costs, and further privatisation of public enterprises. The government has a pervasive presence in economic activity, with public enterprises active in petroleum product distribution, insurance (has now been privatized), banking (is being privatized very soon), imports of basic products (now being privatized), telecommunications (four private ISP/telecom companies), and a wide range of other businesses. Beginning at the turn of the millennium the Seychelles Petroleum Company (SEPEC) started to develop the first fleet of modern petroleum double-hull tankers (five vessels), which was completed by late 2007/early 2008 with the possibility to build more in the near future. The Seychelles President claims that this has opened the door to a new industry for his country and encouraged economic growth by further removing over-reliance on traditional trades like fisheries and tourism, which is now falling rapidly as the country's main income but nevertheless, has experienced significant growth in recent years.

Growth slowed in 1998–2001, due to sluggish tourist and tuna sectors. Also, tight controls on exchange rates and the scarcity of foreign exchange have impaired short-term economic prospects. The black market value of the Seychellois rupee is anywhere from two thirds to one half the official exchange rate. The next few years were also a bit slow due to the worldwide economic downturn and the fear of flying brought on by September 11, 2001. More recently though, tourism has roared back at a record pace setting successive records in 2006 and again in

2007 for number of visitors. The increased availability of flights to and from the archipelago due in part to new entrants Emirates and Qatar airlines is also beginning to show. New five star properties and the devaluation of the currency by nearly 33% by the Seychelles Government is having a positive influence on the tourism sector as well. Both at official exchange rates and at purchasing power parity (PPP), Seychelles remains the richest territory in Africa in terms of GDP per capita (US$9,440.095 at real exchange rates and US$17,560.062 at PPP 2008 estimate),

Because of economic contraction (the economy declined by about 2% in 2004 and 2005 and lost another 1.4% in 2006 according to the International Monetary Fund) the country was moving downwards in terms of per capita income. However, the economy came roaring back in 2007, growing by 5.3% due in part to the record tourism numbers but also the booming building and offshore industries which also continue to set records. The IMF has forecast further growth in 2008 with continuing increase in the GDP per capita. (See footnote and 5. Report for Selected Countries and Subjects [Seychelles]).

Seychelles is, per capita, the most highly indebted country in the world according to the World Bank, with total public debt around 122.8% of GDP. Approximately two thirds of this debt is owed domestically, with the balance due to multilaterals, bilaterals, and commercial banks. Current external debt is estimated at 35.5% according to the IMF (2007) The country is in arrears to most of its international creditors and has had to resort to pledged commercial debt to continue to be able to borrow. This high debt burden is a direct consequence of the overvalued exchange rate. In essence, the country is living beyond its means, and financing its lifestyle by borrowing domestically and internationally.

Seychelles is also the smallest country in the world that has a completely independent currency - one that is neither pegged, nor an adopted foreign currency, nor a common currency used within a larger monetary union. When the Seychellois rupee became freely floated on November 3, 2008, its value quickly fell drastically.

> The rupee traded at an average 19.97 per euro by noon in the capital Victoria, compared with 11.3421 last week, according to Caroline Abel, head of monetary analysis and statistics at the Central Bank of Seychelles. It traded at 15.58 per dollar, from 8.9090, she said. Against the pound, it dropped to 25.02, from 14.3227.

The decision to let the currency trade freely is part of a package of measures approved by the International Monetary Fund, which on October 31 agreed to give the Seychelles an emergency loan to help it meet spiraling debt-servicing costs. The country's $800 million external foreign debt is equivalent to almost 175 percent of gross domestic product

The **economy of Seychelles** rests on tourism and fishing.

Since Seychelles' independence in 1976, per capita output in this Indian Ocean archipelago has expanded to roughly seven times the old near-subsistence level. Growth has been led by the tourist sector, which employs about 30% of the labor force and provides more than 70% of hard currency earnings, and by tuna fishing. In recent years the government has encouraged foreign investment in order to upgrade hotels and other services. At the same time, the government has moved to reduce the dependence on tourism by promoting the development of farming, fishing, and small-scale manufacturing. The vulnerability of the tourist sector was illustrated by the sharp drop in 1991-92 due largely to the Gulf War. Although the industry has rebounded, the government recognizes the continuing need for upgrading the sector in the face of stiff international competition. Other issues facing the government are the curbing of the budget deficit and further privatization of public enterprises. Growth slowed in 1998-99, due to sluggish tourist and tuna sectors

TOURISM AND FISHING

Presently, tourism accounts for about 12.7% of the GDP and the manufacturing and construction sectors (including industrial fishing) account for about 28.8%. In 2000, industrial fishing surpassed tourism as the most important foreign exchange earner.

Tourism is one of the most important sectors of the economy, accounting for approximately 16.6% (2000) of GDP. Employment, foreign earnings, construction, banking, and commerce are all dominated by tourism-related industries. Tourism earned $631 million in 1999-2000. About 130,046 tourists visited Seychelles in 2000, 80.1% of them from Europe (United Kingdom, Italy, France, Germany, and Switzerland).

Industrial fishing in Seychelles, notably tuna fishing, is rapidly becoming a significant factor in the economy. Earnings are growing annually from licensing fees paid by foreign trawlers fishing in Seychelles' territorial waters. In 1995, Seychelles saw the privatization of the Seychelles Tuna Canning Factory, 60% of which was purchased by the American food company Heinz. Similarly, some port operations have been privatized, a trend that has been accompanied by a fall in transshipment fees and an increase in efficiency. Overall, this has sparked a recovery in port services following a drastic fall in 1994.

THE TRADITIONAL PLANTATION ECONOMY

While the tourism and industrial fishing industries were on a roll in the late 1990s, the traditional plantation economy atrophied. Cinnamon barks and copra -- traditional export crops—dwindled to negligible amounts by 1991. There were no exports of copra in 1996; 318 tons of cinnamon bark was exported in 1996, reflecting a decrease of 35% in cinnamon bark exports from 1995.

Despite attempts to improve its agricultural base and emphasize locally manufactured products and indigenous materials, Seychelles continues to import 90% of what it consumes. The exceptions are some fruits and vegetables, fish, poultry, pork, beer, cigarettes, paint, and a few locally made plastic items. Imports of all kind are controlled by the Seychelles Marketing Board (SMB), a government parastatal which operates all the major supermarkets and is the distributor and licensor of most other imports.

In an effort to increase agricultural self-sufficiency, Seychelles has undertaken steps to make the sector more productive and to provide incentives to farmers. Much of the state holdings in the agricultural sector have been privatized, while the role of the government has been reduced to conducting research and providing infrastructure.

INDUSTRY

Many of the other industrial activities are limited to small scale manufacturing, particularly agro-processing and import substitution. Agriculture (including artisanal and forestry), once the backbone of the economy, now accounts for only around 3% of the GDP. The public sector, comprising the government and state-owned enterprises, dominates the economy in terms of employment and gross revenue. It employs two-thirds of the labor force. Public consumption absorbs over one-third of the GDP.

VULNERABILITY

The country's economy is extremely vulnerable to external shocks. Not only does it depend on tourism, but it imports over 90% of its total primary and secondary production inputs. Any decline in tourism quickly translates into a fall in GDP, a decline in foreign exchange receipts, and budgetary difficulties. Furthermore, recent changes in the climate have greatly affected the tuna industry.

ECONOMIC GROWTH

Growth slowed in 1998–2001, due to sluggish tourist and tuna sectors. Also, tight controls on exchange rates and the scarcity of foreign exchange have impaired short-term economic prospects. The black market value of the Seychellois rupee is anywhere from two thirds to one half the official exchange rate.[citation needed] The next few years were also a bit slow due to the worldwide economic downturn and the fear of flying brought on by September 11, 2001.

More recently though, tourism has roared back at a record pace setting successive records in 2006 and again in 2007 for number of visitors. The increased availability of flights to and from the archipelago due in part to new entrants Emirates and Qatar airlines is also beginning to show. New five star properties and the devaluation of the currency by nearly 33% by the Seychelles Government is having a positive influence on the tourism sector as well.[citation needed] Both at official exchange rates and at purchasing power parity (PPP), Seychelles remains the richest territory in Africa in terms of GDP per capita (US$9,440.095 at real exchange rates and US$17,560.062 at PPP 2008 estimate),[4]

Because of economic contraction (the economy declined by about 2% in 2004 and 2005 and lost another 1.4% in 2006 according to the International Monetary Fund) the country was moving downwards in terms of per capita income. However, the economy bounced back in 2007, growing by 5.3% due in part to record tourism numbers and the booming building and offshore industries. The IMF forecast further growth in 2008 with continuing increase in the GDP per capita.[5]

In October 2008, as tourism and fishing revenue began slowing, the Seychelles defaulted on a $230 million debt. The International Monetary Fund stepped with a two-year, $26 million rescue package. The rescue package came with a few stipulations; The country laid off 1,800 government workers, floated its currency, lifted foreign exchange controls and sold off state assets.[6] At the time, the country's $800 million external foreign debt was equivalent to almost 175 percent of its gross domestic product.[7]

The decision to let the currency trade freely as part of the IMF rescue package means that Seychelles is the smallest country in the world that has a completely independent currency - one that is neither pegged, nor an adopted foreign currency, nor a common currency used within a larger monetary union. When the Seychellois rupee became freely floated on November 3, 2008, its value quickly fell drastically, decreasing from eight per U.S. dollar to 16, effectively doubled the prices of imports.[8]

The rupee traded at an average 19.97 per euro by noon in the capital Victoria, compared with 11.3421 last week, according to Caroline Abel, head of monetary analysis and statistics at the Central Bank of Seychelles. It traded at 15.58 per dollar, from 8.9090, she said. Against the pound, it dropped to 25.02, from 14.3227.

The global recession and piracy in the Indian Ocean hit Seychelles hard in 2009, with the GDP projected to contract by 7.5 percent. However the government exceeded its fiscal targets, with a primary surplus of 13.4% of GDP in the first nine months of 2009 according to the IMF. They report expenditure has been tightly controlled and revenue has held up well despite the difficult economic environment.[9]

In May 2010 an International Monetary Fund mission visited Seychelles and concluded the country is making progress. The head of the mission, Mr. Jean Le Dem, said at the conclusion of the visit:[10]

The economy is recovering from a recession that put real gross domestic product (GDP) to almost a stand in 2009. Real GDP is projected to grow at 4 percent in 2010, reflecting primarily a rebound in tourism earnings. Twelve-month inflation, which was negative during the past few months, is expected to return to about 1 percent by year-end

MINISTRY OF FINANCE

The Ministry of Finance is responsible for economic decisions and budgetary policy. A separate Monetary Authority supervises the banking system and manages the money supply. Although foreign banks operate branches in Seychelles, the government owns the two local banks—the Development Bank of Seychelles, which mobilizes resources to fund development programs, and the Seychelles Saving Bank, a bank for savings and current accounts. The commercial banking sector is presently made up of the following:

- Barclays;
- Banque Francaise Commercial Ocean Indien;
- Bank of Baroda;
- Habib Bank; and
- Seychelles International Mercantile Credit Banking Corporation (SIMBC) trading under the name "Nouvobanq".

The first four are branches of foreign banks and the latter is a joint venture between the Seychelles government and the Standard Chartered Bank Africa. Commercial banks offer the full range of services.

OFFSHORE OIL AND GAS

New detailed studies and exploration shows that the Seychelles potentially have large off-shore petroleum reservoirs which are yet to be discovered. Drills have proven the presence of:

1. Oil-prone source rocks containing Type II kerogen in coaly deltaic shales of the Middle Jurassic and in marine shales of the Upper Jurassic;
2. Mixed source rocks bearing Type II/III kerogen in deltaic marine shales of the Lower Cretaceous that are II correlative of oil-generating shales in Somalia;
3. Gas-prone sources containing Type I kerogen in Upper Triassic fluvial shales and Paleocene marine shales, the latter being correlative of oil and gas generating source rocks of the Deep Continental Shelf trend of the Bombay High Oil Province offshore west India;
4. Evidence of hydrocarbon generation and migration with well shows, such as 0.7 ml benzene in DST-1 of Reith Bank-1, 10,010 ppm of 99.8% n-C4 headspace gas coincident with as small fault in the same well and 20% petrol vapours at an immature level of volcanics in Owen Bank A-1;
5. Clastic reservoirs with measured porosities up to 22% in the Early-Middle Jurassic; and
6. Sealing lithologies both locally in syn-rift, and regionally in post-rift sequences. An extensive seismic dataset, plus a variety of remote sensing data have been collected which bolster the well data by confirming the presence of:
7. A variety of trapping styles, dominated by tilted fault blocks, stratigraphic pinchouts and reefs;
8. Multiple heating events, with the principal event post-dating trap formation; and
9. Hydrocarbon generation and migration with the presence of: a) numerous DHIs on seismic, including gas chimneys, flat spots, bright spots, phase changes and chemosynthetic reefs; b) gas sniffer anomalies, involving ethane/iso-butane in the southeast and propane/normal butane/total hydrocarbon in the north and northeast; c)

UV fluorescence anomalies, especially over the wells and in the southeast; and d) 4 types of beach-stranded tar that correlate to the local source rock stratigraphy.

However, to date all exploratory and stratigraphic test wells (a total of 9 since the 1970s) in the Seychelles have failed to find commercial hydrocarbons. The most recent wildcat by Enterprise Oil in 1995 detected gas but failed to find hydrocarbons.
Several oil and gas exploration companies are active in the Seychelles offshore. These include East African Exploration (EAX), Avana Petroleum and Petroquest.

FINANCIAL SERVICES

In addition to the now booming tourism and building/real estate markets, Seychelles has renewed its commitment to developing its financial services sector. Government officials and industry participants believe this could overtake the tourism industry as the chief pillar of the economy by 2017. The recent passage of a revised Mutual Fund Act 2007, Securities Act 2007 and Insurance Act 2007 are meant to be the catalysts to move Seychelles from just another offshore jurisdiction to a full-fledged Offshore Financial Center (OFC).

The Ministry of Finance is responsible for economic decisions and budgetary policy. A separate Monetary Authority supervises the banking system and manages the money supply. Although foreign banks operate branches in Seychelles, the government owns the two local banks—the Development Bank of Seychelles, which mobilizes resources to fund development programs, and the Seychelles Saving Bank, a bank for savings and current accounts.

The Seychelles International Business Authority (SIBA) is charged with overseeing the quickly growing offshore industry.

OFFSHORE OIL AND GAS

New detailed studies and exploration shows that the Seychelles potentially have large off-shore petroleum reservoirs which are yet to be discovered. Drills have proven the presence of:

1. Oil-prone source rocks containing Type II kerogen in coaly deltaic shales of the Middle Jurassic and in marine shales of the Upper Jurassic;
2. Mixed source rocks bearing Type II/III kerogen in deltaic marine shales of the Lower Cretaceous that are II correlative of oil-generating shales in Somalia;
3. Gas-prone sources containing Type I kerogen in Upper Triassic fluvial shales and Paleocene marine shales, the latter being correlative of oil and gas generating source rocks of the Deep Continental Shelf trend of the Bombay High Oil Province offshore west India;
4. Evidence of hydrocarbon generation and migration with well shows, such as 0.7 ml benzene in DST-1 of Reith Bank-1, 10,010 ppm of 99.8% n-C4 headspace gas coincident with as small fault in the same well and 20% petrol vapours at an immature level of volcanics in Owen Bank A-1;
5. Clastic reservoirs with measured porosities up to 22% in the Early-Middle Jurassic;
6. Sealing lithologies occur both locally in syn-rift, and regionally in post-rift sequences;[11]
7. An extensive seismic dataset, plus a variety of remote sensing data have been collected which bolster the well data by confirming the presence of:
8. A variety of trapping styles, dominated by tilted fault blocks, stratigraphic pinchouts and reefs;
9. Multiple heating events, with the principal event post-dating trap formation; and

10. Hydrocarbon generation and migration with the presence of: a) numerous DHIs on seismic, including gas chimneys, flat spots, bright spots, phase changes and chemosynthetic reefs; b) gas sniffer anomalies, involving ethane/iso-butane in the southeast and propane/normal butane/total hydrocarbon in the north and northeast; c) UV fluorescence anomalies, especially over the wells and in the southeast; and d) 4 types of beach-stranded tar that correlate to the local source rock stratigraphy.

However, to date all exploratory and stratigraphic test wells (a total of 9 since the 1970s) in the Seychelles have failed to find commercial hydrocarbons. The most recent wildcat by Enterprise Oil in 1995 detected gas but failed to find hydrocarbons.

Several oil and gas exploration companies are active in the Seychelles offshore. These include East African Exploration (EAX) (a subsidiary of Afren), Avana Petroleum (a subsidiary of Vanoil Energy) and WHL Energy.

Beginning at the turn of the millennium the Seychelles Petroleum Company (SEPEC) started to develop the first fleet of modern petroleum double-hull tankers (five vessels), which was completed by late 2007/early 2008 with the possibility to build more in the near future. The Seychelles President claims that this has opened the door to a new industry for his country and encouraged economic growth by further removing over-reliance on traditional trades like fisheries and tourism, which is now falling rapidly as the country's main income but nevertheless, has experienced significant growth in recent years

TRADE STATISTICS

The National Statistics Information and Library Service (NSILS) is a public library providing access to the statistical outputs of the Government Statistical Service (GSS). Tel: 020 7533 5888

Public reference libraries normally hold United Kingdom trade statistics; more detailed figures on United Kingdom overseas trade can be obtained from data retailers, for more information please contact:

HM Customs and Excise
Tariff and Statistical Office
Tel: 01702 367485

Imports by Principal Countries of Origin (1999 figures - Management & Information Systems Division)				
The following 7 countries accounted for 69% of Seychelles' imports in 1999				
Countries	R'000	Apr £'000	%of total	Major Categories
Italy:	308,497	34,277.44	13%	Machinery, Manufactures
South Africa:	247,307	27,478.55	11	Manufactures, Machinery, Chemicals, Food
Finland:	236,014	26,223.77	10	Machinery (one-off electricity project)
France:	229,247	25471.88	10	Manufactures, Machinery, Food
Saudi Arabia:	212,780	23642.00	9	Mineral Fuels

UK:	184,360	20,484	8	Machinery, Manufactures, Chemicals, Food
Singapore:	177,983	19,775.8	8	Machinery, Manufactures, Chemicals, Food

STANDARD OF LIVING

GNP per capita: US7,500 in 1999
Statistics and Database Administration Section (MISD): 1999 figures

PUBLIC EXPENDITURE

The 2001 budget outlay is R1225,565m. (approx. £136 m.), which is 3% higher than the previous year's budget.

Expenditure on healthcare and education have increased over 2000 figures, while capital project expenditure has halved.

Rs40m. of Government-owned property (mainly flats and houses) will be sold to occupier.

ECONOMY

Since independence in 1976, per capita output in this Indian Ocean archipelago has expanded to roughly seven times the old near-subsistence level. Growth has been led by the tourist sector, which employs about 30% of the labor force and provides more than 70% of hard currency earnings, and by tuna fishing. In recent years the government has encouraged foreign investment in order to upgrade hotels and other services. At the same time, the government has moved to reduce the dependence on tourism by promoting the development of farming, fishing, and small-scale manufacturing. The vulnerability of the tourist sector was illustrated by the sharp drop in 1991-92 due largely to the Gulf war. Although the industry has rebounded, the government recognizes the continuing need for upgrading the sector in the face of stiff international competition. Other issues facing the government are the curbing of the budget deficit and further privatization of public enterprises. Growth slowed in 1998-99, due to sluggish tourist and tuna sectors.

Industry
Tourism; fishing; processing of coconuts and vanilla, coir (coconut fiber) rope, boat building, printing, furniture; beverages

Agriculture
Products: coconuts, cinnamon, vanilla, sweet potatoes, cassava (tapioca), bananas, chickens, tropical fruit.

Agriculture in Seychelles faces an uphill battle because of the lack of arable land with decent soil (only 400 hectares - about 1000 acres or 1.5 sq miles) and extreme rainfall patterns throughout the year. The government provides great assistance to the industry by having reduced import taxes and duties on agricultural equipment and fertilizers and by eliminating income taxes for registered farmers. Currently, tea and products to support the tourism industry (fruits, vegetables, poultry and pork) are doing well. Other foodstuffs, including rice, are imported. Cinnamon, vanilla, copra and tobacco are not doing as well due to world market conditions. Together, agriculture and fishing contribute about 3.5% of the GNP.

Fishing
Because of its exceptionally large Exclusive Economic Zone, Seychelles is a world leader in transshipment of tuna fish and products. Considerable income is produced by the foreign fishing vessel licensing and by supplies and services for those ships. Indian Ocean Tuna (a majority of which is owned by Heinz International) processes over 110 tons each day resulting in over $20 million, the largest single export. Almost all commercial fishing activity goes through Victoria harbour.

Manufacturing
Manufacturing is the largest industrial sector, contributing 19% of the GNP. Products are mostly foodstuffs and soft goods including tea, coffee, UHT milk, fruit juices, coconut cream, animal feed, tobacco and beer. Soap, detergents, plastics and handicrafts for tourists are also produced. A lack of market and raw material is the chief impediment.

Tourism
The largest foreign cash inflow to Seychelles results from tourism. Over 125,000 visitors arrived in 1999, contributing well over $100 million (70% of foreign exchange revenue). Most tourists are from Europe (France, Great Britain, Germany, Italy and Ireland). About 85% of arrivals are tourists and the average stay is 9.7 nights. Tourism contributes about 17 percent of the GNP and employs 18 percent of the total workforce.

There are about 4500 beds in the country with an average room occupancy rate of 63%.

In addition to normal holiday spending, visitors pay a nightly room tax of between $2 and $6, always included in published room rates. The 1998 there was an effort to implement a Gold Card for tourists. This has not come to pass. and the only visible tax on visitors is a departure tax of US$40.

Transportation
Land. There are about 280 km (175 miles) of roads of which about 176 km (110 miles) are paved. Most paved roads are on Mahé and Praslin. In 1996 8,460 vehicles were registered. There are no railroads in the country.

Sea. The main, and only international, port is at Victoria, Mahé. Private ferries operate between Mahé, Praslin and La Digue.

Air. Six of 14 airports have hard surfaced runways. Seychelles International Airport (SEZ) is 10km south of Victoria, Mahé. International air services are provided by Air Seychelles, Air France, British Airways, Kenya Airways, Air Mauritius, Aeroflot and Condor. International gateways include London, Paris, Frankfurt, Rome, Zurich, Dubai, Singapore, Nairobi, Mauritius and Johannesburg. There were 2,764 international flight operations in 1996. 53% of all air passengers are non-tourists.

Domestic scheduled services by Air Seychelles run from Mahé to Praslin, Bird, Denis, Desroches and Alphonse Islands. Scheduled service to Silhouette is by Helicopter Seychelles which also operates scheduled and private transfer services between other islands.

Radio & Television
The Seychelles Broadcasting Corporation provides radio and TV broadcasts in Creole, French and English. There are 2 AM and 2 FM radio stations and 2 TV channels. 75-80% of the population can receive TV signals.

Telephone
Country code 248.

SEYTELS and Cable & Wireless team to provide a small, modern telephone system. There are about 18,000 main telephone lines. Cellular service was introduced in 1995 with 4,000 subscribers in 1998. All islands are linked by radiotelephone; for international communications there are radiotelephone connections with mainland Africa plus an Intelsat earth station.

Post Office
The main post office is in Victoria. Airmail to Western Europe normally takes up to a week. To the United Sates, 2 to 3 weeks is typical.

Press
The Seychelles Nation is a government controlled daily (morning) produced in English, French and Creole. Other newspapers include The People (monthly, published by the Seychelles Progressive Front) and Seychelles Review (monthly news review).

A notable feature of the Seychelles economy was the high per capita GDP of US$5,900 in 1992, some fifteen times the average of sub-Saharan Africa. Total GDP was estimated at US$407 million in 1992. Economic growth, which had proceeded at a strong 5 to 6 percent annually since the mid-1980s, resumed in 1992 at an estimated rate of 4 percent.

The major source of economic activity is the tourist industry and tourist-related services in terms of employment, foreign earnings, construction, and banking. Although earnings from the tourism sector are impressive, providing about 50 percent of GDP, they are offset by the need to import large amounts of food, fuels, construction materials, and equipment, costing some 70 percent of tourism income. Gross tourism foreign exchange earnings in 1993 were SRe607 million (for value of the Seychelles rupee--see Glossary). Moreover, the possibilities for expanding tourism are limited, and it is vulnerable to unpredictable shifts in demand, as occurred in 1991 when the Persian Gulf War contributed to a sharp decline from 103,900 tourists in 1990 to 90,000 in 1991. By 1993 there was a strong recovery in the tourist trade, bringing more than 116,000 visitors.

Hoping to avoid overdependence on tourism, the government has attempted to diversify economic activity by encouraging new industries and revitalizing traditional exports. Production of food and other items is being emphasized to reduce the heavy burden of imports needed to sustain tourism. Development of the nation's marine resources remains a principal governmental goal, pursued by expanding indigenous coastal fisheries and by profiting from fees and services provided to foreign fishing fleets operating in Seychelles' EEZ. Small traditional fishing accounted for less than 3 percent of GDP in the early 1990s but provided jobs for about 1,500 persons and growing foreign exchange earnings.

The Seychelles' traditional marketings of copra and cinnamon bark had declined to an insignificant level by 1991. The government's goal of achieving 60 percent self-sufficiency in food has not been realized although its efforts have resulted in increases in fruit, vegetable, meat (mainly chicken and pork), and tea production.

Parastatal (mixed government and private) companies proliferated in many sectors of the economy under the René regime. State-owned and parastatal companies accounted for more than half the country's GDP and about two-thirds of formal employment. The parastatals enjoyed mixed success, and by 1992 the government had begun to divest itself of selected enterprises.

Seychelles traditionally has run a large trade deficit because of the need to import nearly all manufactured and most agricultural commodities. Much of the gap has been covered by revenues from the tourism sector and to a lesser extent by remittances from Seychellois workers abroad and by overseas loans and grants.

Seychelles has been relatively successful in containing inflation. The retail price index, which includes some goods and services whose prices are set by the government, rose by 3.3 percent in 1992 and 4.0 percent in 1993. The generally stable price environment has resulted in part from wage discipline, the weakness in world oil prices, and a policy of importing from countries with low prices, including South Africa, whose currency has depreciated steadily against the Seychelles rupee.

To support its anti-inflationary strategy, the government has pursued a liberal exchange rate policy. Since 1979 the rupee has been pegged to the International Monetary Fund's (IMF--see Glossary) special drawing rights (SDR--see Glossary). The rupee's relative stability has contributed to the stability of domestic prices.

GOVERNMENT ROLE

Under the socialist policies of President René, the government has taken a leading role in developing the national economy. Beginning in 1978, the Ministry of Planning and Development has drawn up very detailed "rolling" five-year development plans, which are updated and extended every year. The Ministry of Finance is responsible for economic decisions and budgetary policy. A separate Monetary Authority supervises the banking system and manages the money supply. Although foreign banks operate branches in Seychelles, the government owns the two local banks--the Development Bank of Seychelles, which mobilizes resources to fund development programs, and the Seychelles Savings Bank, a bank for savings and current accounts.

The expansion of parastatal companies since 1979, when the first such institution was created, has had primary economic significance. By 1988 the number of parastatals had reached thirty-five, but in 1994 there were indications that the government's more liberal economic policy would probably reduce the role and number of parastatals. Among the most important organizations of the public sector is the Seychelles National Investment Corporation, whose role is to promote economic development in areas neglected by private enterprise or to become a major stockholder in private companies that encounter economic difficulties. The most powerful of the state enterprises is the Seychelles Marketing Board (SMB), which is the sole importer of key commodities, exercises controls over other imports, and regulates prices, production, and distribution of most goods and services.

The state-owned Seychelles Timber Company has responsibility for reforestation and for operating the government sawmill at Grande Anse. The fishing Development Company controls industrial tuna fishing and the tuna cannery operated as a joint venture with France. Air Seychelles, a parastatal, flies both international and interisland routes, making a critical contribution to the tourist routes, making a critical contribution to the tourist industry. The Islands Development Company (IDC) was established in 1980 to develop agriculture, tourism, and guano production on ten of the outlying islands-- guano deposits have since been depleted. A hotel complex on le Desroches is among the projects conducted by the IDC. Opened in 1988, the Desroches resort is managed by another parastatal, Islands Resorts. A US$12 million shrimp farming project on Coetivy Island remained in the final development stage in 1992. The high initial investment and heavy transport costs raised doubts about its viability, although a study has indicated that about 8 tons of shrimp could be caught annually in the area.

Despite the government's strong involvement in the economy, it has never imposed a policy of forced nationalization. Rather, the government encourages foreign investment, preferably as joint ventures. Concurrently with the political liberalization in 1992, the government has attempted to strengthen the private sector, announcing measures to attract investment and planning to divest some state-owned companies. Among companies scheduled for privatization are the agro-industrial division of the SMB and Stationery, Printing, and Computer Equipment, to be sold as three separate enterprises. A parastatal holding 65 percent of Seychelles hotel assets reportedly is ready to sell some hotels or to privatize their management. Private investors nevertheless remain cautious because of the continued high level of state economic control.

BUDGET

The government budget for 1993 foresaw total expenditures of SRe1,335.6 million consisting of SRe1,078.7 million in current expenditures, SRe232.5 million in capital expenditures, and SRe24.4 million in net lending. The proposed spending was 6 percent higher than the 1992 level. Total revenues were budgeted at SRe1,186.1 million in 1993, consisting of SRe1,122.6 million in current revenues and SRe63.5 million in grants. The projected deficit for 1993 was SRe149.5 million, compared with a 1992 budget deficit of SRe94.5 million. The 1994 budget projected a 6 percent decrease in expenditures, leading to a surplus of SRe64 million rather than a deficit. The 1994 budget also relaxed import controls and set forth a five-year development plan to increase private sector economic participation, increase employment and foreign exchange earnings, reduce taxation and the inflation rate, and improve social welfare. Interest on the public debt consumed more than 18 percent of current expenditures.

Among other leading components of 1993 current outlays were education (10.7 percent), health (7.0 percent), transportation and tourism (5.6 percent), and subsidies to parastatals (4.3 percent). Defense spending was cut by 35 percent between 1992 and 1993--from 7.8 percent to 5.0 percent of the total budget. The government's contribution to the SPPF--SRe9.6 million in 1991 and 1992--was eliminated in 1993.

The main revenue sources were a trades tax that included taxes on imports (50 percent of total revenues estimated for 1993) and a business tax based on profits (12.4 percent of total revenue). Various fees, charges, dividends and interest, rents, and Social Security Fund transfers made up most of the remaining budget receipts. The government's program of social services, defense spending, and new parastatals had generated growing budget deficits that peaked at 20 percent of GDP in the recession year of 1986. Austerity in public spending and new taxes had resulted in some improvement; by 1992 the deficit was limited to 4.4 percent of GDP but was expected to rise to 6.5 percent in 1993. The continued excess of spending over receipts, combined with lower foreign assistance levels, remains a worrisome problem.

ECONOMIC DEVELOPMENT

The government has detailed its economic development targets in successive five-year plans. The plan for 1985-89 emphasized tourism, agriculture, and fisheries. It proposed to improve the balance of payments by achieving 60 percent self-sufficiency in food and by stimulating tourism. Improved productivity, increased exports, and a lowering of the unemployment level were additional aims. The 1990-94 plan stressed the need to attract foreign investment and the need for greater food self-sufficiency. A tenyear plan for protecting the environment was supported by a pledge of US$40 million from World Bank donors. The total projected investment was SRe4,206 million in constant 1989 prices, of which 26 percent would be funded by the public sector. It was not expected, however, that the investment goals would be realized. Capital spending was aimed at improved living standards--water supplies, waste disposal, and housing. Tourism and related investments were also regarded as priorities.

An ambitious government initiative is the East Coast Development Plan to reclaim land on Mahé for residential and commercial construction. Some 800 new homes are to be built to ease the housing shortage among ordinary Seychellois. In addition, part of the area will be reserved for luxury housing and tourist facilities. In 1993 the government announced that it would seek private sector investment to help complete this major project.

LABOR

The government is the nation's largest employer, providing jobs for 38 percent of the wage-earning labor force in 1991. The parastatal sector employed a further 26 percent, leaving only 36 percent of workers in the private sector. The total labor force was about 29,600 in 1991; some 19 percent were domestic workers, self-employed, or family workers. The remainder were in formal wage employment. Hotel and restaurant workers formed the largest single category (14.1 percent), followed by transportation (13.8 percent), manufacturing (11.2 percent), public administration (10.9 percent), and agriculture (9.1 percent).

The government establishes official minimum wages depending upon job classification, although most jobs are paid at well above the rates set. Average monthly earnings as of mid-1992 were about SRe2,750 in the government and parastatal sectors and SRe2,260 in the private sector. The differential was caused by high 1992 salary increases to government and parastatal workers amounting to 12.3 percent and 14.3 percent, respectively, which the private sector could not match. The Central Bank of Seychelles has noted that wage inflation, which averaged 10.8 percent for the entire labor force, greatly exceeded the retail price inflation of 3.3 percent and could not be justified by corresponding productivity gains. The bank feared that the government's salary awards would add to existing pressures on the country's cost base, its external competitiveness, and its external accounts. , which is controlled by the SPPF. All workers are members because a percentage of their social security contributions are earmarked for union dues. Workers can elect their own shop stewards, but candidates are screened by the NWU executive secretariat, which can dismiss any elected shop steward. Workers can strike only with the permission of the SPPF Central Committee. Nevertheless, two labor disputes occurred in the changed 1992 political environment. Workers in the main electrical generating plant organized a brief shutdown, winning increased allowances in their compensation packages, and stevedores struck for better conditions and higher compensation. To avoid disruption at a critical time for the industrial fisheries sector, the government essentially met the stevedores' demands.

In November 1993, the National Assembly passed the Trade Union Industrial Act, which gave Seychellois workers the right to join and to form their own unions. Any such unions, however, may not compete with the overall NWU. One independent union was formed in late 1993.

In addition to approving collective bargaining agreements and reviewing private wage scales, the Ministry of Employment and Social Affairs can enforce employment conditions and benefits. With many free or subsidized public services, notably education and health, even workers at the low end of the pay scale can sustain their families at a basic level. Even so, many families rely on two or more incomes to deal with the high price structure.

The government has set a legal work week of forty or thirtyfive hours, depending on the occupation. With overtime, the work week may not exceed sixty hours. Workers are entitled to a thirty-minute break each day and twenty-one days of paid annual leave. Comprehensive occupational health and safety regulations are enforced through regular workplace visits.

AGRICULTURE

The Ministry of Agriculture and Marine Resources in 1993 gave up the management of five state-owned farms, which were divided into small plots and leased to individuals. In addition, the agricultural sector consisted of state farms of the Seychelles Agricultural Development Company (Sadeco) and the outer islands managed by the IDC; three other large holdings producing mainly coconuts, cinnamon, and tea; about 250 families engaged in fulltime production of foodstuffs; and an estimated 700 families working on a part-time basis. Many households cultivate gardens and raise livestock for home consumption.

The total cultivable area of the islands is only about 400 hectares. Although rainfall is abundant, wet and dry seasons are sharply defined. Better irrigation and drainage systems are needed to improve food crops. The government has taken various measures to reduce dependency on imported foods, including deregulating production and marketing and reducing the trades tax on fertilizers and equipment. As a result, vegetable and fruit production climbed from 505 tons in 1990 to 1,170 tons in 1992. This increase failed to be matched by a commensurate decrease in imports of fruits and vegetables, which reached 3,471 tons in 1992. Local consumption had apparently increased, and substitution between imported and domestic foodstuffs was possible only to a limited degree. In most cases, imported produce is significantly cheaper in spite of air freight, import taxes, and other costs, necessitating a high import markup by the SMB to prevent disruption of domestic production. Neither rice, a dietary staple, nor other grains can be grown on the islands.

The expansion of livestock production is hampered by encroachment of housing and other development on agricultural land as well as by increased labor and animal feed costs. The number of cattle slaughtered in 1992 (329 head) was virtually unchanged from five years earlier. The slaughter of pigs (4,598) was about 45 percent higher than 1987, and chicken production (439,068) had risen by 60 percent.

The two traditional export crops of copra--dried coconut meat from which an oil is produced--and cinnamon have declined greatly because of the high cost of production and pressure from low-cost competitors on the international market. Vanilla, formerly important, is produced on a very small scale. Tea grown on the misty slopes of Mahé is a more recent plantation crop, serving mainly the local market.

FISHERIES

The fisheries sector is divided into two distinct categories: traditional fishing by a domestic fleet of some 400 vessels; and industrial tuna fishing by foreign vessels, which began to develop in the mid-1970s and has emerged as a major revenue source. The domestic inshore fleet consists mainly of open boats equipped with inboard or outboard engines, operating within a radius of sixteen to forty-eight kilometers of the main islands. Domestic offshore operations on banks surrounding the Mahé group and the Amirantes Isles are conducted by handlines from larger boats with sleeping quarters. Most of the catch is frozen. The fish division of SMB bought and distributed fish landed on the three main islands to avoid serious price fluctuations. An export trade in the local catch developed after the opening of the international airport made possible deliveries to Europe and other markets.

Local consumption of fish traditionally has been high, and has been estimated at eighty-five kilograms per capita annually in the early 1990s. The local catch is also an important menu item at the tourist hotels. The domestic fisheries catch reached 5,734 tons in 1992, about 10 percent of which was accounted for by a new industrial fishing venture, the *Pêcheur Breton* mothership-dory enterprise.

Beyond 100 kilometers from the Seychelles coasts, fishing is conducted by some fifty-five French and Spanish purse seiners based at Victoria. (The Spanish vessels briefly shifted their base to Mombasa in 1992 but returned when the Seychelles government reduced its port charges.) Some 160,000 tons of tuna were transshipped through Victoria in 1992, of which 45,000 tons were reported by the vessels' owners to have been fished within Seychelles' EEZ. The Seychelles authorities had no way of verifying these claims.

In 1991 Seychelles, Mauritius, and Madagascar formed the Tuna Fishing Association to promote their interests. In addition, a series of three-year agreements granted European Community (EC--see Glossary) vessels the right to fish in the Seychelles EEZ. The fourth such agreement, signed in early 1993, was expected to generate US$13.5 million annually. The islands' economy also benefit from the resulting business activity at Victoria in the form of port services, stevedoring, and ship chandling. The Seychelles government had leased one purse seiner to profit more directly from the tuna industry, and is building ten seiners, but the project has encountered financial difficulties.

In 1992 the Seychelles Fishing Authority issued 292 licenses to long-lines fishing vessels mainly from Taiwan and the Republic of Korea (South Korea). These vessels make few calls at Victoria, offloading their catches onto motherships in mid-ocean. Seychelles is unable to carry out naval and air surveillance of possible illegal fishing, especially in more remote parts of the EEZ. There is a strong presumption, however, that unauthorized use is being made of its fishing grounds.

The tuna canning plant opened in 1987, with 70 percent of its capital of Seychelles origin and 30 percent invested by a French cooperative; the plant is designed to process 8,000 to 10,000 tons of fish a year. It employs 425 people, mostly women, and has brought a rapid growth of export earnings, reaching US$12.3 million by 1991. The net gain in balance of payments was less because the operation required some imports, notably the cans, which could not be produced domestically.

OIL

Seychelles depends on imported petroleum to meet its domestic power requirements. Following the increase in oil prices in 1990, fuel accounted for nearly 8.6 percent of the nation's import bill, exclusive of reexports. The possibility of commercially exploitable offshore oil led to the granting of exploration rights in 1977 to a consortium headed by Amoco Oil Company. Amoco later bought out its partners and acquired additional exploration rights but ceased drilling in 1986 when all of its test wells proved dry.

The government embarked on a new program to interest oil companies in exploration in 1985 with technical assistance from Norway in preparing feasibility studies. In 1987 the British Enterprise Oil Company and the United States Texaco Corporation, obtained rights for areas south and west of Mahé. After completing promising seismic studies, Enterprise announced plans to begin drilling in 1995. The Seychelles government retains rights to participate in joint development of the concession if commercial quantities of oil are found. In August 1990, Ultramar Canada, Inc. stated that it had an agreement to search 10,200 square kilometers of seabed northeast of Mahé.

MANUFACTURING

Owing to the small size of the local market and the lack of raw materials, manufacturing occurs on a very limited scale. As of 1991, only 2,563 persons were employed in a total of eightyeight enterprises, twelve of them parastatals. Most employed fewer than ten people, and only five firms employed as many as 100. A number are import-substitution industries (see Glossary), the largest of which is a brewery and soft drink plant. Other firms include cigarette, clothing, paint, plastics, and furniture factories, cinnamon and coconut processing plants, and some handicrafts catering to the tourist industry. To encourage foreign interest in the manufacturing sector, the government has developed a new investment code guaranteeing full repatriation of profits and capital, protection against nationalization, free import of capital goods, and other incentives. The government reserves the right, however, to require that the state share an interest in larger-scale industrial activities.

TOURISM

Tourism is the most important nongovernment sector of the economy. About 15 percent of the formal work force is directly employed in tourism, and employment in construction, banking, transportation, and other activities is closely tied to the tourist industry. Foreign exchange gross earnings from tourism were SRe607 million in 1993. The direct contribution of the tourism sector to GDP was estimated at 50 percent, and it provides about 70 percent of total foreign exchange earnings. Although difficult to measure, the import content of tourism expenditures is high, so net tourism earnings are significantly lower.

The tourist industry was born with the completion of the international airport in 1971, advancing rapidly to a level of 77,400 arrivals in 1979. After slackening in the early 1980s, growth was restored through the introduction of casinos, vigorous advertising campaigns, and more competitive pricing. After a decline to 90,050 in 1991 because of the Persian Gulf War, the number of visitors rose to more than 116,000 in 1993. In 1991 France was the leading source of tourists, followed by Britain, Germany, Italy, and South Africa. Europe provided 80 percent of the total tourists and Africa--mostly South Africa and Reunion-- most of the remainder. European tourists are considered the most lucrative in terms of length of stay and per capita spending.

Under the 1990-94 development plan, which emphasizes that the growth of tourism should not be at the expense of the environment, the number of beds on the islands of Mahé, Praslin, and La Digue is to be limited to 4,000. Increases in total capacity are to be achieved by developing the outer islands. To avoid future threat to the natural attractions of the islands, 150,000 tourists per year are regarded as the ultimate ceiling. The higher cost of accommodations and travel, deficiencies in services and maintenance of facilities, and a limited range of diversions handicap Seychelles in attracting vacationers at the expense of other Indian Ocean tourist destinations.

TRANSPORTATION AND TELECOMMUNICATIONS

Cars and buses are the principal means of transportation; Seychelles has no railroads. The total road network as of 1994 was 302 kilometers, of which 202 kilometers are hard surfaced. Road conditions on the island of Mahé are for the most part excellent. Vehicle registrations consist of 4,072 private cars, 216 buses, 1,105 commercial vehicles, and 102 motorcycles. Between 1983 and 1986, car imports were prohibited to conserve foreign exchange. Under a quota system subsequently introduced, vehicle imports were allowed to rise to 1,070 in 1989.

Mahé has an international airport and a good harbor. A government ferry service links Mahé to the nearby islands of Praslin and La Digue. Private vessels serve some smaller islands, but in the more remote islands service is less frequent and is primarily for loading copra and delivering supplies. In April 1994, Seychelles Shipping Line was founded to provide additional international service.

Seychelles has fourteen airports or airstrips, eight with hard-surfaced runways. The state airline, Air Seychelles, was converted from an interisland to an international carrier in 1983 to offset the effects of termination of air service by British Airways. In 1989 it purchased a Boeing 767, followed in 1993 by a Boeing 757 on a lease-purchase arrangement. The larger 767 flies to northern European cities, such as London, Frankfurt, and Zurich, and the 757 provides service to Johannesburg, Nairobi, Bahrain, Dubayy, Singapore, Rome, Paris and Madrid. The airline also has four de Havilland DHC-6 Twin Otters and one Pilatus Brîtten-Norman Islander. In addition, five international carriers serve the airport on Mahé. Air Seychelles' share of international traffic was 35 percent in 1992, which it hoped to expand to more than 40 percent.

Seychelles has an air traffic control center covering some 2.6 million square kilometers between the east coast of Africa and the Indian subcontinent. The center opened in June 1991 and has taken over some of the responsibilities that Somalia handled; it serves seventeen international airlines.

Seychelles has good telecommunications links with all parts of the world by satellite and telephone service on the islands of Mahé, Praslin, and La Digue. Direct radio communications linked the outer islands to Mahé and to African coastal countries. Some 13,000 telephone lines were in use as of 1994, along with more than 200 telex and facsimile machines. In 1994 some 40,000 radios and 13,000 television sets could receive programs of the government-owned Seychelles Broadcasting Corporation. With the help of three relay stations, television signals are available to between 75 and 80 percent of the population. The television stations carry foreign programming beamed to an Indian Ocean International Telecommunications Satellite Corporation (Intelsat) earth station. There are two amplitude modulation (AM) radio stations, one government and the other a missionary system licensed to broadcast both local and international religious programs.

FOREIGN TRADE

Seychelles has experienced recurrent foreign exchange problems because of its limited export potential and fluctuations in tourist traffic. Growing national income has been accompanied by pressures for increased imports of manufactured consumer goods that cannot be produced domestically. In 1991 the government took measures to restrain imports, and in 1992 it imposed surcharges on luxury goods, in addition to taking other actions to restrict domestic spending.

Until 1987 the nation's principal export was fresh and frozen fish, followed by high-quality copra, for which Pakistan, the leading importer, paid premium prices. Cinnamon bark and shark fins were the only other exports of consequence. Reexports, mainly of tourist-related duty-free items and petroleum products for aircraft and ships, were considerably higher than earnings from merchandise exports. From 1987 onward, canned tuna dominated the islands' export trade. With a value of SRe64.1 million, canned tuna constituted 73 percent of all domestic exports in 1991. Fresh and frozen fish exports brought SRe17.7 million, but copra and cinnamon had shrunk to insignificant levels.

France had been the principal destination of Seychelles exports for many years, sometimes absorbing more than 60 percent of the islands' products. In 1991 the Seychelles trade pattern shifted sharply in favor of Britain (52.7 percent of total exports), followed by France (22.8 percent), and Reunion (13.6 percent). Both Reunion and Mauritius are leading customers for frozen fish.

Seychelles imports a broad range of foods, manufactured goods, machinery, and transportation equipment. The largest single category is petroleum fuels and lubricants, although much of this is reexported through servicing of ships and aircraft. Seychelles' main suppliers in 1991 were

Bahrain, South Africa, Britain, Singapore, and France. Because of its high import dependence, the country's visible trade is always heavily in deficit. In 1991 its total of domestic exports and reexports (SR258 million) was only 28 percent of total imports (SR910 million). Gross receipts from tourism usually cover some 60 percent of imports but fall short of bridging the gap in the balance of payments. In 1993 Seychelles joined the Preferential Trade Area for Eastern and Southern Africa, which should improve its trade because of greater currency convertibility, particularly with Mauritius.

ECONOMIC AND DEVELOPMENT STRATEGY

SEYCHELLES GOVERNMENT BUDGET FOR THE FISCAL YEAR 2019[1]

1. INTRODUCTION

Mr. Speaker, Honorable Leader of the Opposition in the National Assembly, Honorable Leader of Government Business in the National Assembly, Honorable Members of the National Assembly, The People of Seychelles.

Good Morning

Mr. Speaker, ten years ago, our nation embarked on a journey for an economic transformation. It was a difficult choice but as a nation, we opted for a path toward economic sustainability through a macro-economic reform program aimed at restoring macro-stability and putting Seychelles on a path toward fiscal sustainability. Last week, we celebrate ten years of economic reform program and we have seen the progress we have made based on the socio-economic development of the Country. For the past ten years the primary budget balance has been on average above 5% but we are now forecasted a primary budget balance of 2.5% over the medium term. Our economic growth has been above 3% of GDP.

We have remained stable despite the economic pressure from the world market. We have a long list of infrastructure development that need to happen to put Seychelles in the next level of its development.

Mr. Speaker, each Seychellois needs to see his/her development in the progress of the country. One cannot be left behind because of his/her vulnerability. How can we be more productive and responsible as a nation to bring more economic growth for the development of Seychelles and as result the benefit to ourselves. This can only be done through a consolidated effort based on the opportunity that exists. The Government, private sector and civil society will need to work on only one goal, for the development of Seychelles.

Mr. Speaker, in light of this, the theme chosen for the 2019 budget is "***Stability and Progression***"

2. OVERVIEW OF THE ECONOMY IN 2018 AND MEDIUM TERM

[1] Theme: "Stability and Progression" Delivered by: Ambassador Maurice Loustau-Lalanne MINISTER OF FINANCE, TRADE, INVESTMENT AND ECONOMIC PLANNING In the Seychelles National Assembly Ile Du Port, Victoria, Mahe, Seychelles on Monday 5th of November, 2018

2.1. Real Sector

Mr. Speaker, following stable economic activities thus far in 2018, the end of year Real GDP growth forecast remains at 3.6 per cent as per initial estimates. Tourism sector as a whole continues to contribute towards growth despite activities being slower this year compared to the past two years. Visitor arrivals have remained around 1 per cent so far throughout 2018 vis a vis 2017. Tourism earnings on the other hand remain resilient inspite of this. By the end of September 2018, provisional figures from the CBS shows that earnings increased by 8.2 per cent compared to the same period last year. Furthermore, growth is being sustained by the Information and Communication sector. This follows the continuous increase in data usage and the diversifications of products thus increasing competitiveness.

The Manufacturing sector is also on the positive side. In the 'Manufacturing of food' sector, more positive growth is anticipated despite the imposition of the yellow fin tuna quotation. Production statistics from the National Bureau of Statistics reveals that by the end of the second quarter of 2018, a total of 25,653 tons of canned tuna was produced – a record high. This represents a 35 per cent growth when compared to the same period last year. Similarly, greater growth is expected in the 'Manufacturing of Beverages and Tobacco' sector. The level of production has increased for this year compared to last year. Beer, Stout, has increased by 3 and 41 per cent respectively. The rebranding and introduction of new products by the major brewing company is also supporting growth in this sector. However, the production of spirits recorded negative growth of 33 per cent. Finally, new projects such as the dam elevation, ongoing social housing projects by the Government, are boosting the Construction sector.

Global growth, as reported by the IMF July World Economic Outlook, is expected to reach 3.9 per cent in 2018. This is being supported by strong momentum, favourable market sentiments, accommodative financial conditions, and the partial recovery in commodity prices that should allow conditions in commodity exporters to gradually improve. `

Mr. Speaker, in 2019, real GDP growth is estimated at 3.4 per cent – a slight slowdown, driven by steady Tourism growth and this is supported by positive outlooks from the trade and expected increase in flights, sustained ICT growth and a more positive uptake under the Construction sector with new projects as reported by the Seychelles Investment Board. Growth in the 'Manufacturing of food' sector is also estimated to remain resilient following a buoyant 2018.

In the medium term, Seychelles economic growth is anticipated to remain stable with growth averaging to around 3.5 per cent. This is conditional on stable domestic and international factors. Any major shift in these factors can easily influence growth. This mainly include changes in fuel as well as commodity prices and any major crisis in key markets. Mr. Speaker, it is worth to mention that the international fuel price has a direct impact on the cost of living. Medium term growth will be mainly driven by Tourism activities, Information and communication, Financial and insurance activities as well as the Manufacturing and 'Wholesale and retail' sector.

2.2. Monetary sector

In the first quarter of 2018, the cautious loosening of monetary policy stance was maintained as inflation was not forecasted to reach levels that would threaten the Central Bank's primary objective. However, monetary policy has been tightened as of the second quarter of 2018, a position that the Central Bank has maintained for the remainder of the year in a bid to mitigate forecasted inflationary pressures arising from both external and domestic developments. In line with the tightened policy stance, effective April 01, 2018, the interest rate corridor, was revised upwards whereby the standing deposit facility rate, or floor, was raised from 1.0% to 2.0% while the standard credit facility rate, or ceiling, was increased from 6.0% to 8.0%.

Inflation in the second half of the year has been impacted by seasonal effects, key of which being fish prices, albeit with price pressures dampening following a slowdown in the rate of depreciation of the Seychelles rupee. As at September 2018, year-on-year and annualised inflation stood at 3.3% and 3.7%, respectively.

Going forward, imported inflationary pressure is anticipated in view of higher forecasted global commodity prices and sustained domestic demand. The Central Bank remains committed to its primary objective and stands ready to adjust policies to ensure domestic price stability.

2.3. External Sector

The country's external position is projected to remain relatively unchanged in 2018 in comparison to 2017. The current account deficit is estimated to end the year at 19.5 per cent of GDP compared to 19.9 per cent of GDP in 2017 whilst in US dollar terms, the deficit is forecasted to grow from USD 296m in 2017 to USD 305m in 2018.

As at October 26, 2018, the total value of the country's earnings in foreign exchange or inflows into the banking system stood at US$511 million, an increase of 13 per cent relative to the corresponding period of 2017. These primarily represent the contributions from the tourism and fisheries sectors. During the same period, total demand or outflows stood at US$499 million or an increase of 11 per cent. An important share of such demand includes that for the importation of fuel as well as basic commodities.

With regards to the total value of the country's official level of international reserves that are managed by the Central Bank, this stood at US$555 million or equivalent to 3.8 months of imports of goods and services.

3. 2018 BUDGET PERFORMANCE

Mr. Speaker, Government is forecasted to end 2018 with a primary balance of SR 657.4 million or 3.0% of GDP compare to the original budget which was SR 553.6 million or 2.5% of GDP.

As a whole, tax revenue has performed well so far in 2018 with collections up to August standing at 2.6 per cent higher than over the same period in 2017. Total receipts at the end of August stood at SR 4.5 billion accounting for 20.6 per cent of GDP. Tax revenue collections excluding social security tax arrears are estimated to total SR 7.19 billion in 2018.

In comparison to the more optimistic mid-year Budget revision based on receipts up to June 2018, the end of year estimate has been less positive with a 0.6 per cent or SR 42 million reduction to reflect continued under-performances in some lines. This, however, still represents a sizeable increase over the initial Budget estimate of SR 6.85 billion. Further shortfalls under Business tax, which has proven to be less buoyant than in 2017, as well as Excise on imported goods, most notably alcohol, are the main drivers for this downward revision. Stronger than expected Domestic VAT receipts, driven by stronger collections from the tourism sector which is consistent with overall earnings growth as previously mentioned, with positive upside, and a higher outlook for Income tax given certain expected arrears, have done much to offset these under-performances.

Mr. Speaker, we have requested two supplementary budget during the year 2018. The first one was an increase of SR 218.8 million in spending. The second one was a net spending of only SR

196.9 million when we take into account the budget savings for the year.

4. PROJECTIONS FOR FISCAL YEAR 2019

4.1 PRIMARY OBJECTIVES

The principal objective of Budget 2019 is to :

* Consolidate our fiscal position to attain a primary surplus of 2.5% from 2019 to 2021

* Honour our debt obligations and ensure the total public debt is reduce to below 50% of GDP by 2021

* Consolidate the social program of Government

* Invest in infrastructure to support economic growth

* Invest in programs and projects that will improve the lives of our citizens

4.2 REVENUE

Mr. Speaker, in 2019, we are projecting to collect a total revenue including grants of SR 8.95 billion from SR 8.83 billion in the 2018 revised budget. Of this, SR 7.5 billion will be tax revenue, which represents 84% of the total revenue collection. A total of SR 1.25 billion is forecasted for non tax revenue and SR 209.2 million as grant receipts.

4.3 GOVERNMENT EXPENDITURE

For the year 2019, the Government is proposing an appropriation bill of SR 8.46 billion compare to an original appropriation act and the 2018 supplementary motions which give a total revised 2018 expenditure of SR 8.35 billion. This represent an increase of only SR 112.3 million or 1.3% on the revised 2018 expenditure.

Mr. Speaker, the total budget for the Education, Health and Family Affairs portfolios represent SR 3.5 billion or 41.9% of the total appropriation bill. This shows the Government commitment towards access to Education and health care.

Mr. Speaker, before I start I want to highlight again that on the 11th of October 2018, the World Bank has published for the first time a Human Capital Index. This index looks at countries and sees whether the country makes available the conditions that will allow its families to flourish. Do the children born in a country have a good opportunity of succeeding and of meeting their full potential? By looking at health, education and adult survival rates, it assesses the likelihood that a child born in a country will live to realise their full potential. Whether they will live long enough to reach the potential that they would have reached if they had complete education and full health.

Whilst most indices take a look at what a country has achieved, this index compares what the country does achieve to what it could have achieved. Seychelles has come out 43rd of 157 countries. We are first in the region and first in Africa. The next African country is in 52nd place. Our score of 68% means that each new born has a 68% chance of reaching their full potential as an adult. In Singapore, the country which came out first on this index, this figure is 88%.

This shows the Government spending in these sectors have shown results. However, we need to do more to ensure there is more efficiency and more results that directly have an impact on our people. Mr. Speaker, in addition, the Government has started work to relook on its current model in these three sectors to ensure that:

* It is link properly with the labour market

* The costs of ageing are manage prudently and

* Ensure the fiscal costs of the health sector and Agency of Social Protection are sustainable over the medium term

Mr. Speaker as part of the previous announcement, the 2019 Budget will not include the budget for three Government entities. The Seychelles Fisheries Authority (SFA) and the Seychelles National Parks Authority (SNPA) will be operating off budget from 2019. The Public Enterprise Monitoring Commission will have the oversight role on these two entities from January 2019. However, as part of Net Lending vote a total of SR 28.15 million and SR 10.27 million has been allocated for SFA and SNPA respectively as a temporary advance during the first six months in 2019. This will be repaid in full during the year 2019. In addition, SR 47.5 million is budgeted as dividend to be disbursed by SFA.

Mr. Speaker, SR 32.7 million was allocated for Small Business Finance Agency (SBFA) during 2018. As part of the structural reform, for the 2019 budget, SBFA will no longer exist as a separate entity. Government will create a Small and Medium Enterprise Development Fund under Development Bank of Seychelles (DBS). As at 31st of October 2018 the bank balance of SBFA is SR 46.3 million. Therefore, for the 2019 budget, no funding has been provided for SBFA. However, the funds from the bank balance will be transferred into that fund at DBS. From 2020 onwards, Government will allocate SR 20 million per year to the new fund at DBS. Mr. Speaker, the current employees of SBFA will have the option to either transfer to other Ministries, Department and Entities or absorb by DBS into the new portfolio.

Mr. Speaker, during 2019, Government will continue to assess other areas where there could be costs savings measures that can be introduced with the aim of diverting funds into more priority programs.

Mr. Speaker, at present the Environment Trust Fund and Livestock Trust Fund are revolving funds, which are used to finance projects being undertaken by Ministry responsible for Environment and by Ministry responsible for Agriculture respectively, through a separate operating and trading account aside from obtaining budgetary assistance for public sector investment projects. The two funds are managed by a Board.

However, from the January 2019, the Environment Trust Fund and Livestock Trust Fund will be included as part of the budget process.

The Livestock Trust Fund will be allocated under the Seychelles Agriculture Agency budget to be used for capital projects, assistance that will directly benefit farmers as well as funding towards the Agriculture Development Funds under DBS, particularly in line with the following objectives of the fund;

* the research, development and capacity building of the agricultural sector;

* the building of roads, irrigation, water storage and drainage systems for farmers;

* the insurance schemes for farmers;

* part of the slaughtering costs of the abattoirs;

* the government with funds for the Agricultural Development Fund

For, Environment Trust Fund, the projects will be funded under the Department of Environment public sector investment plan. The objectives of the different projects and programs should be as follows;

* to carry out programmes to prevent and reduce pollution;

* to promote environment education and research;

* to clean and beautify Seychelles;

* to do such other things as may be necessary or conducive to the protection, preservation or

improvement of the environment.

In addition, going forward, Government will assess other funds, which their revenues are being sourced into trading and operating accounts as well, to determine feasibility of also applying the same mechanism.

Government will be receiving a grant from the Indian Government of SR 602.6 million to build 27,379 square metres of office space to accommodate several Ministries, Department and Entities. We anticipate that this project will start in late 2019 and we expect a savings of around SR 50 million per year in office accommodation once the project is completed. The offices that Government are currently using will be available to the private sector and we hope that the rental rate will come down.

4.3.1 Wages and Salaries

Mr. Speaker, for the 2019 budget, SR 2.67 billion has been allocated to Wages and Salaries which represents 11.3% share of total GDP forecasted. The total wages and salaries represent 31.5% of the total Appropriation Bill.

Mr. Speaker a total of SR 58.5 million is allocated for revisions or introduction of Schemes of Service.

The following scheme of service will be revised from January 2019; * Retention allowance for Dental and Allied Professional, Health Care Assistant under Public Health Authority

* Doctors revision in supplementation and risk allowance

* Allowances for Library and Archives employees at the Department of Culture

* Road Transport Officers

* Seychelles Revenue Commission adjustment in Basic Salary

* Agency for Social Protection welfare officers

* Veterinary Officers at the National Biosecurity Services

* Department of Employment

* Brassband at the Department of Defense

* Research Officers cadres for all Ministries, Departments and Entities

The following scheme of service will be revised from July 2019;

* Department of Police

* Seychelles Fire and Rescue Services Agency

* Department of Prison Services

* Department of Foreign Affairs Diplomatic Cadre for Headquarters staff

* Attorney General Office

Mr. Speaker, the full year implications for the following scheme of service that has started the implementation during the year 2018 but was not originally in the 2018 budget;

* IT Support Cadre

* Stores and Asset Management Cadre

* Personal Assistant

* Legal personnel for all Ministries, Departments and Entities

Mr. Speaker, during the 2018 budget, Government announced for the introduction of a long service allowance during 2019. The Government will introduce a long service allowance for the public sector non-contract employees from July 2019 as follows:

Number of Years in Service	Monthly Allowance in Seychelles Rupees
5 to less than 10 years	500
10 to less than 15 years	1,000

15 to less than 20 years	1,500
20 to less than 25 years	2,000
25 to less than 30 years	2,500
30 to less than 35 years	3,000
35 to less than 40 years	3,500
More than 40 years	4,000

This will costs SR 50.6 million in the 2019 budget and SR 101.3 million in the 2020 budget. Mr Speaker, this will ensure than staff with more experiences in the Public Service will be compensated for the vast experience. Mr. Speaker, 5,530 staff will benefit on this new incentive and this represent 53% of the total Government workforce. From the total eligible staff for 2019, 69% will receive either SR 1,000 or more than that. The new allowance will also be applicable to the non-core staff like security officers, cleaners cooperative and other maintenance staff working full time on a contract with Government. 382 non-core staff will be receiving this new allowance.

Mr Speaker, Government employed 10,351 staff as per the August 2018 payroll. In addition, the average earnings in the Government sector is SR 14,598 compare to SR 11,318 in the private sector as per the 2018 quarter two National Bureau of Statistics published statistical bulletin. In the same report, it is highlighted that 64% of the total workforce is working in the private sector compare to 21% working in the Government and 15% in the State Owned Enterprises.

Mr. Speaker, President appointed a committee on the 5th of January 2018 to review the Public Service Salary Act, 2013. The committee proposed a 5% salary increase on the base pay as per the Public Service Salary Table. Government has approved their recommendation and this will be implemented from July 2019. A budget provision of SR 42 million has been allocated in the 2019 budget.

Mr. Speaker, I want to re-iterate that as part of the Progressive Income tax system, 54% of the Seychellois workforce are not paying any income tax since the first SR 8,555.50 are exempt from income tax and currently there are 13 exempted emoluments and some of the exempted emoluments are as follows:

a) All compensation payments,

b) All Gratuity payment for long term services

c) A bonus not exceeding an amount equal to 1/12th of the Annual Basic salary

d) Thirteenth month salary as per the Employment Act requirements

e) An end of contract payment limited to 15% of the Total Basic salary earn during the period under contract,

f) Service Charges, and

g) And Overtime payment as per the Employment Act requirements

Mr. Speaker, Government has decided to include allowances such as inducement allowance as per respective scheme of service in the calculation of end of contract payments as of 2019. This will however not include periodic allowances and marketable skills allowances. A provision of SR 5 million has been catered for this in 2019.

4.3.2 Expenditure in Key Sectors

Mr. Speaker, in 2019, a sum of SR 2.82 billion is allocated for Goods and Services and SR 884.7 million is allocated for Capital Expenditure. The total spending under Goods and Services represents 33.3% of the total appropriation bill or 12.0% of GDP. Whereas, the total spending under capital expenditure represents 10.5% of the total appropriation bill or 3.8% of GDP.

Mr. Speaker, apart from the capital expenditure allocated for Ministries, Departments and Entities, there are an allocation of SR 123.1 million and SR 296.4 million allocated under Development grants and Net Lending for Public enterprises respectively. Thus in total this represents an additional of 5.0% under appropriation bill or 1.8% of GDP for capital investment for Public Enterprises.

4.3.2.1 Education

Mr Speaker, a total of SR 1,044 million is allocated for the education sector, which represents 12.1% of the total appropriation bill or 4.5% of GDP. 47% of the total expenditure in the education sector is in wages and salaries since the education sector employed 2,461 employees, which represent 23.8% of the total workforce in the public service. In percentage terms, it represents 18% of the total Government wages and salaries.

Mr. Speaker a total of SR 262.3 million has been allocated in Goods and Services for the Ministry of Education and Human Resources Development. The main spending under Goods and Services are as follows:

* Purchase of Text Books SR 1.5 million

* Exam Costs SR 11.1 million

* Purchase of Stationery SR 3.5 million

* Purchase of Uniforms SR 3.3 million

* Renting of Accommodation for the expatriates teachers SR 43.2 million

* Procure security services SR 34.3 million

* Procure cleaning services SR 44.1 million

* Providing school meal services SR 13.5 million

* Training of teachers SR 9.7 million

Mr, Speaker, the Department of Information Technology and Communication in partnership with Seychelles Cable System Company and the three operators (Cable and Wireless, Airtel and Intelvision) and the Ministry of Education and Human Resources Development are providing substantial internet bandwidth to all state Primary and Secondary schools. This is inclusive of the required network management services and the provision of WiFi access in all schools. All state primary and secondary schools are benefiting from this service except for 4 schools where civil works are required to connect them to the service. It is expected though that these schools will also have service by the end of the year. The provision of these services are at no cost to the Ministry of Education and Human Resources Development. The different parties and the Ministry signed the Memorandum of Understanding associated with the provision of these services in February 2018.

Mr. Speaker a total of SR 90.1 million has been allocated under the capital projects for the year 2019 for the Ministry of Education and Human Resources Development. The main provisions for the year 2019 for the capital projects will be as follows:

* The reconstruction of the La Rosiere Primary school SR 15.0 million

* Ile Perseverance second Primary school SR 15.1 million * Rehabilitation of Anse Royale primary school SR 6.8 million

* Rehabilitation of Belonie secondary school SR 8 million

* Rehabilitation of Grand Anse Praslin secondary school SR 2.5 million

* The reconstruction of the La Digue school will start in 2019 and a provision of SR 5

million has been allocated for the year 2019.

* Construction of a new school for business studies and arts & design SR 18.9 million. This project is being financed by the Chinese Government as a grant.

* The renovation of the Anse Royale Youth hostel SR 4 million.

Mr. Speaker it is to be noted that a total SR 12.4 million has been allocated under the first phrase of the SR 35 million being financed under the Small Development Projects by Indian Government as per the Memorandum of Understanding that was signed between the two Governments during the President Danny Faure state visit in India in June 2018. These projects are as follows:

* Renovation work of the Anse Boileau secondary school SR 2 million

* Renovation work of the English River secondary school SR 2 million

* Renovation work of the Grand Anse Praslin Primary school SR 0.9 million

* Renovation work of the Mont Fleuri secondary school SR 2.5 million

* Renovation work of the Plaisance Primary school SR 2 million

* A provision of SR 3 million for procurement of chainlink fence for state schools

4.3.2.2 HEALTH

In the health sector, today's priority is to address the communicable diseases and noncommunicable diseases, which are affecting our country. Hepatitis C, cardiovascular, diabetes, and cancer are a few example. We will only be able to overcome these challenges if we intensify the prevention programs to change our lifestyle, increase the number and quality of human resources in the health sector, and investing in a modern health system at all level.

Mr. Speaker, for the year 2019 a total of SR 1,024.5 million has been allocated for the health sector. For the first time the budget will be above 1 billion. Most of the spending for the health sector is in Goods and Services with a total of SR 460.8 million which represent 45% of the total spending in the health sector. This represents 16% of the total Government spending in the Goods and Services. Mr. Speaker, 72% under Goods and services are as follows:

* Procurement of Dugs supplies SR 53.1 million

* Procurement of Vaccines Supplies SR 3.8 million

* Procurement of Laboratory Supplies SR 20.8 million

* Radiology SR 6 million

* Hemodialysis SR 55 million

* Entomology SR 57.9 million

* Procurement of other Medical and Laboratory supplies SR 7.2 million

* Specialized Overseas Treatment SR 40.6 million

* Renting of Accommodation for the expatriates health professional SR 27.6 million

* Procure security services SR 16.0 million * Procure cleaning services SR 5.3 million

* Provision of food and rations SR 26.1 million

* Procure of laundry services SR 7.0 million

* Training of health professional SR 5.3 million

The plan to invest in a health information system, which will cost million of rupees is progressing as plan. We expect to launch this project in the coming months and we will continue to invest further during 2019. A good health information system, will help the health sector in becoming more effective in managing its current resources and it will assist the sector in the way its address the prevention program and treatment of diseases. The project has been tendered and a total of SR 36.6 million has been allocated for the year 2019.

Mr Speaker, the Hospital Master Plan is in progress. A total of SR 45.7 million and SR 10.6 million has been allocated under Health Care Agency and Public Health Authority respectively for the other capital projects. The main allocations in the 2019 budget will be as follows :

* Conversion of the Diagnostic Centre into a clinical laboratory SR 5 million

* Construction of the La Digue Logan Hospital SR 5.6 million

* Construction of the Baie Lazare Health SR 5 million

* Renovation of the Baie Ste Anne Hospital SR 1.5 million

* Construction of new Anse Royale Outpatient Unit SR 2 million

* Construction of the Isolation Unit SR 7 million

* Construction of the Public Health Laboratory SR 3.6 million

* Purchase of ambulances SR 3.3 million

4.3.2.3 Agriculture

The agricultural sector is one of the most important pillar of the economy. Over the years some actions have been taken but they were not necessarily targeted towards increasing local production. Mr. Speaker, SR 115.9 million has been allocated in the 2019 budget for the agriculture sector. As part of the comprehensive plan for the agriculture, the Ministry responsible for the agriculture sector has announced new initiatives.

Mr. Speaker, one key project that has been completed during 2018 is the Agriculture new diagnostic centre situated at Grand Anse Mahe. The centre is equipped with various specialized equipment to facilitate research on plants, soil and animals and to timely detect diseases and pests that affect the agriculture sector which can consequently have an impact on the country's economy.

The diagnostic centre consists of various laboratories which will serve different purposes including entomology, bacteriology, parasitology, serology and molecular biology.

The Agricultural sector presently benefits from several incentives, especially tax concessions on importation of equipment. The producers are not necessarily obtaining any incentives regarding the recurrent inputs in the production of chicken especially feed. Therefore, the farmers will start to receive the financial subsidies to assist in curbing their cost of production. The new plan to increase pork production will be as follows;

i. The present concession of SR 4 per kg of chicken slaughtered is maintained. Farmers are presently paying SR 7 per kg of chicken as slaughtering fee to the abattoir.

ii. A further incentive of SR 2.30 per kg of chicken meat is given to farmers to allow for subsidy on the feed. It is established that the total cost of feed to the farmers account for 65 percent of their total cost.

Similarly to poultry, the pork production is facing serious setback since 2008. Up to the year 2007 the country was producing over 50 percent of the consumption. After 2007 it decreased constantly and settling at around 30 percent of national consumption. Today, the sector produces only 429 tons of the total demand of 1,562 tons, thus 27 percent. There are 52 legal pig producers. The Ministry will carry out an assessment and the management of existing farms to ensure the realization of the set target of 50 percent of local pork production over the next 3 years.

i. Those who are in financial difficulties will be called in and a plan will be agreed on.

ii. The farms that are in an abandoned state will be taken back by the government.

iii. Based on calculation, the pork producers make a meagre 4.10 percent of profit. The Ministry believes a reasonable profit margin should be 15 percent. In order to achieve that:

* The government will maintain the financial assistance of SR 200 per head as slaughtering fee at the abattoir.

* The highest cost factor to the production of pork is feed, amounting to around 65 percent. The Government will give an incentive of SR 6.50 per kg of pork produced to each farmer. This is equivalent to 15 percent subsidy on the cost of feed.

Praslin will also benefit with a red meat abattoir for which an amount of SR 2.5 million has been budgeted for this year.

The condition of the present abattoir on Mahe is posing a lot of difficulties to the producers. Certain markets cannot be penetrated because of the inadequacies of the abattoir. The Government will continue with its plan to build the new central red and white meat abattoir at Montagne Posee. It has been approved that the Government will fund the building at SR 15 million and the EU fund will provide equipment worth Euro 180,000.

The Ministry will aggressively promote the use of tropical green houses for the production of crops. The green houses have proven itself in the country as farmers will be able to enjoy relatively same production all year round. It is estimated that a green house of 500 square metres will cost SR 200,000. In addition, the Ministry has identified 100 potential farms for the immediate erection of shade houses and we expect increase in production.

Mr Speaker, the Government has also established that in order to achieve its objectives, it will need to bring in new technology such as hydroponics and an assessment has already been made to allow for two such technologies. One such facility is presently being installed at the Research Centre at Anse Boileau for research purposes.

The Seychelles Agricultural Agency will ensure that agriculture input supplies are consistent in quality and quantity to meet all farming requirements. This will necessitate improvement on existing infrastructure such as the bulk store and sale outlets.

Mr Speaker, under the capital projects the following projects will be financed for the year 2019 for the agriculture sector:

* Building for Vet Quarantine SR 3 million

* Construction of research building at Anse Boileau SR 4.5 million

* Livestock Trust Fund projects SR 17.6 million In addition SR 3 million from the 2019 budget and SR 17 million from the SBFA funds carried forward will be allocated to DBS for the Agriculture Development Fund.

Mr. Speaker, as already announced the gainful occupational permit fees of SR 500 per month will be SR 250 per month for the agriculture sector.

Mr. Speaker, no plan will be realized without proper backbone of human capital, research and development. The Agricultural Institute of Seychelles is a new initiative. The present Seychelles Institute of Agriculture and Horticulture trains only "farmhands". It is for this reason why it has not been attractive to more students of greater academic acumen. The new Agricultural Institute of Seychelles will have the following main objectives:

i. Train students for various fields of agriculture including, crop production, animal husbandry, horticulture and farm management.

ii. Students will acquire a knowledge ready to study at University level.

iii. Carry out research as the present Research Section of the Seychelles Agricultural Agency will be part of the institute.

iv. All the techniques of crop production such as hydroponics, tropical green house and others will be taught.

v. The Agricultural Institute of Seychelles will benefit from all other international support which the agricultural sector is presently benefitting from.

vi. Funds for the Institute are already available through a loan of US$3.7 million from the Kuwaiti Fund for the construction of such an institute.

4.3.2.4 LAND USE AND HABITAT

In line, with the Government's commitment to ensure housing is more accessible with all of our population, this budget has made provision for not only more houses, and infrastructure to make land available, but also more human resources will be available for this Ministry, which include the scheme of service which have started the implementation since 2018. This will complement the work that the Ministry has done and currently doing, to ensure its policies are more transparent and thus, more comfort that the resources that have been made available to the Ministry has been well managed and attaining to its objective.

Mr. Speaker, a total of SR 161.4 million has been provided under the 2019 budget for the different land and housing projects. During the year 2017, Property Management Company (PMC) signed a loan of SR 150 million with SPF and PMC expect to raise another SR 200 million from the financial market during the last two months of 2018. This will ensure that the land and houses target are achieve in the next three years. From all the finances described above, Government expect to deliver 143 and 72 plots of land in 2019 and 2020 respectively. In addition 406 and 32 houses in 2019 and 2020 respectively.

Mr. Speaker, Government has been looking on the different option of ensuring that there are more houses being built in the next six years. As part of the process, Government has engaged with the Government of India to finance the construction of 3,000 houses through a special purpose vehicle. The special purpose vehicle will be created under PMC. The total indicative project cost for the 3,000 houses is SR 3,026 million. The financing from the Government of India will be through a mixture of loan and grants. There will be a grace period of 5 years for the repayment of the loan. The SPV will repay the loan over the years without Government intervention. From this facility, we expect 558 and 506 houses will be available in the years 2020 and 2021 respectively.

Mr. Speaker, SR 102 million that was announced this year a grant from Chinese Government will also be used for housing projects.

4.3.2.5 Local Government

Mr. Speaker SR 57 million and SR 52.1 million has been allocated under the Local Government Goods and Services and Capital Projects respectively. SR 18.8 million and SR 6.9 million allocated in the year 2019 under goods and services are for procurement of security services and maintenance services respectively. In addition, an allocation of SR 4.2 million has been allocated to Local Government for different activities and programs in the districts as follows;

i. SR1.2 million towards the Animateur Scheme: The Scheme is aimed at the identification of potential resource persons interested in developing specific programmes at local level for the benefits of community members.

ii. SR 3 million towards the decentralised Activities: In partnership with other Agencies bring more activities and events at community level.

Mr. Speaker, there have been seven regional councils that were launched in July 2018. A provision of SR 4.6 million has been made in the 2019 budget for the payment of monthly allowances to the seven chairpersons and forty two councillors and SR 772,464 for employment of seven senior office assistants.

The main projects being financed under capital projects are as follows:

* SR 30 million for district small projects

* SR 5 million for extension of Districts Administration office for regional centres

* SR 5 million for upgrading other Districts Administration office

Mr. Speaker it is to be noted that a total SR 11.6 million has been allocated under the first phase of the SR 35 million being financed under the Small Development Projects by Indian Government which will start in late 2018. In the second phase, which will start in the first half of 2019, there will be other projects that will be financed including the construction of a Day Care Centre at Ile Perseverance.

4.3.2.6 Family Affairs and Social Development

Over the years, the Government has hold true to its promise to the people to ensure good education, good health and a good standard of living. However, there is a need to view the social sector with a new perspective.

The social challenges we face today are multi-dimensional. They arise not because of poor education system, nor lack of a good health care system but rather through diverse sub-cultural trends and tendencies that have slowly eroded our social fabric. Seychelles as other countries throughout the world have seen its traditional social pillars eroded.

We know from the last census that 75% of households have 4 or less family members. Who looks after the children if the parents are working and grandparents are far away? This is where we must put in place programmes for children, to provide them with supervised opportunities for growth instead of the dangerous freedom to self-destruction.

The new thinking is to move away from the curative/crisis management/band-aid approach to a more proactive and preventive strategy to address social change. The envelope proposed for the social sector reflects the programmes and services that each ministry have incorporated into their Strategic Plans. There is a need for this sector to have a more coordinated approach in responding to issues affecting our society and families by putting much more resources on prevention and effective programmes.

Government takes cognizance of the need to increase trained social workers, counsellors, and other cadres in the psychosocial field to deliver programmes to pull those who have fallen through the crack and get them to be economically active and productive in society. Revision of schemes of service across the social sector is another step taken to address staff retention and better remuneration package.

The Government recognizes the need to invest heavily in social programmes that will make a difference and in the right services and infrastructures. The vision is to see a performing social sector so that in the long run we can be a country that creates employment and economic opportunities for most of our school leavers and job seekers instead of relying heavily on foreign workers.

Mr. Speaker, another challenge that Seychelles is facing is our demography of our population. Currently our population is made of 22.4% of people below 15 years old and 8.1% of people above 65 years old. But this will be reverse in another 30 years where 16.8% of our population will be below 15 years of age and 19.9% above the age of 65. There is a fiscal costs of this trend and we need to ensure proper policies are put forward to ensure that the country can overcome this challenge.

Mr. Speaker, "The Maison troisieme Age" was one of the many recommendations made by the Senior Citizens associations. Government has finalized the concept with the senior citizens group and private partners. The project is to be located at Ile Perseverance. The project will start in 2020. All CSR contribution from the Public Enterprises will be used to construct this facility. We expect that the total project costs will be SR 22.7 million. Once completed, based on the business plan of the project, it will be self-finance.

4.3.2.7 YOUTH AND SPORTS

Mr. Speaker, 34% of population is under the age of 30. Hence, the youth remains a vital sector of the society that cannot be overlooked. Allocation of budget for the youth is scattered under several ministries, departments and agencies. Whilst the Seychelles National Youth Council is the main body to implement the newly revised National Youth Policy, empowering the youth will remain the focus for the year 2019. A provision of SR 2 million has been allocated for the different youth programs for 2019.

Sports are embedded in the Seychelles culture as a mean to enhance healthy living and develop physical and sporting skills in order to bolster personal, social and personal development. Mr. Speaker to ensure that this happens; the main emphasis in 2019 will be to decentralize sporting activities and bring sports to the districts and regions for the greater benefit of the populace.

Mr. Speaker, we all know how the good performance of our athletes instils pride and foster unity among our people. Government will need to invest for the preparation and participation of Team Seychelles in the Indian Ocean Island Games to be held in Mauritius in 2019. During the year 2018, all Corporate Social Responsibility Tax contributions from our Public Enterprises were used to finance the housing projects. During the year 2019, the same collection will be done from the Public Enterprises and the funds will be used for the preparation of our athletes in the Indian Ocean Islands Games. Thus, a total of SR 24 million is anticipated for the Indian Ocean Island Games preparation and participation. This will complement the SR 10 million that was allocated in 2018. Additionally, a sum of SR 4.5 million has been budgeted for the 2019 All Africa Games.

Mr. Speaker, Government will continue to support the Contribution to sport federation and sport clubs with an allocation of SR 3.2 million.

4.3.2.8 National Security

The Department of Police has been allocated with a budget of SR 405 million. Mr. Speaker, Government with the assistance with the Government of India will finance a Police Headquarters building at Ile Du Port. This facility will be occupying 100 employees and it will include the Forensic Laboratory. The main allocations for the 2019 budget in the capital projects, are as follows;

* Renovation of the La Digue Police Station SR 3.5 million

* Upgrading of other Police Stations SR 2.1 million

* New Police Academy SR 1.1 million

During the year 2018, procurement was done for fingerprint Equipment, Chemicals, and Equipment for the Crime Laboratory.

Mr. Speaker, external threats to our small island nation which impose serious challenge to our sustainable development is an insecure environment due to Illicit drug trafficking, illegal and unregulated fishing activity and piracy, all of which adversely affect the pillars of our economy. Since the threats are unconventional, the Department of Defense requires national support and holistic approach to operate in synergy with SMSA, SCAA, SFA, Police and the Ministry of Health. The Department of Defense will receive an allocation of SR 316.3 million for the 2019 budget.

Mr. Speaker, a major project that Government will start in 2019 is the Biometric Passport system. The existing system analysis conducted on the current National Passport Issuance System has indicated that the system has become very old. Most countries have moved to or is in the process of transiting to e-passports. It is expected that the transition to e-passports to ensure cross border security will become a mandatory requirement by ICAO (International Civil Aviation Organisation). As thus, the Department of Immigration will start developing a new passport system for the Seychelles that will have the enhanced security features and which will also contains an embedded chip that store biometric information as per ICAO standards. The budget provided for the year 2019 is SR 16.5 million for the project.

4.3.2.9. Attorney General Chamber

A provision of SR 33 million has been allocated for the Attorney General's Chamber for 2019. This is significant increase compare to SR 25.4 million in the 2018 revised budget and SR 19.1 million in the 2017 actual spending. The Attorney General's Chamber has been allocated funding to recruit a total of 10 additional posts in drafting, prosecution and litigation. Mr. Speaker, Government will receive a grant from the Indian Government for the construction of a new office block for the Attorney General Chambers on Ile du Port. The proposed office block will have a total built area of 4,157 square metres, which will allow the Attorney General Chamber to have sufficient space for its future needs and the location will be more convenient since it be will closer to the main courts for more efficient delivery of its services.

4.3.2.10. Constitutionally Appointed Authorities and Statutory Bodies

Mr. Speaker a total of SR 172.3 million has been allocated for the constitutional appointed authorities in the 2019 budget compare to SR 146.4 million in the revised 2018 budget and SR 119.4 million in the 2017 actual spending. The allocations will be as follows:

* The Judiciary SR 94.5 million

* The Legislature SR 43.1 million

* Office of the Auditor General SR 20.5 million

* Office of the Ombudsman SR 3.7 million

* Office of the Public Service Appeals Board SR 1 million

* Constitutional Appointments Authority SR 2.1 million

* Electoral Commission SR 7.5 million Mr. Speaker, SR 1 million has been allocated for the Seychelles Human Right Commission. The Anti-Corruption Commission has been allocated SR 14.2 million in the 2019 budget compare to SR 12.3 million in the 2018 revised budget and SR 7.0 million the actual 2017 spending.

5. DEVELOPMENT IN KEY SECTORS

5.1 Environment and Energy sector

Protection of our environment remains one of the key of Government priority, and with the 2019 budget, Government will continue to invest SR 238.8 million to Landscape and Waste Management Agency to ensure a number of small contractors benefit from the cleaning contracts. In line with the Government waste management policy, the recycle activities and the investment for the removal of plastic products will be encouraged.

Government will continue in 2019 with its measures against using plastics products, for example on the 1st of January 2019, there will be a ban on importation and using plastic straws. By mid of

2019, people will start receiving refund of SR 1 on glass bottle. Early 2019, the Government intention to launch an expression of interest for any local or international companies to provide their idea on the waste to energy.

As a Small Island Developing State (SIDS), Seychelles has already embarked on the path to embrace renewable energy for its sustainable development. One important initiative to facilitate this process is the formulation and adoption of the Energy Act. So, the Energy Act has created a more dynamic market for stimulating energy efficiency and encourages the import of more efficient appliances into Seychelles. This has allowed the private sector to fully participate in the production and supply of clean and renewable energy. Individual is able to produce their own electricity using renewable energy technology.

Solar energy offers a clean, climate friendly and inexhaustible energy resource with an unprecedented opportunity to bring energy security to our peoples and improve their lives. Seychelles, therefore, has embarked on a serious solar energy implementation programme to help us achieve our target of renewable energy of 5% by 2020 and 15% by 2030.

To achieve these targets, we have launched the following important initiatives in 2018 and will continue in 2019:

'Smart Energy in Public Spaces' programme of which the Government of India provided US$3.24m to focus on installing rooftop PV solar panels on the State House, which houses the Office of the President, the National Assembly building, home to the country's parliament, and the Palais de Justice which comprises the law courts, the three branches of Government will lead by example.

'SMART Energy in Homes and Businesses' programme has also been launched where the Public Utilities Corporation has tendered two contracts to companies to build the first two solar farms on Ile Romainville. A 5MW PV solar farm financed by IRENA and the Abu Dhabi Development Fund. In addition, a contract was awarded to an Indian Company in January of 2018 for a 1 Megawatt solar photo voltaic democratisation farm. This is also

being financed by the generous grant of 3.4 million US Dollars from the Government of India. This project will provide free energy to 500 Seychellois families that are currently receiving social assistance from the Government.

Seychelles plans to light up the road network with LED lights with 9,000 lights of 22 – 30 watts and 1,000 lights of 140 – 150 watts. Further, about 5,000 – 10,000 lights would be required for replacement of the existing less efficient lights.

Public sector and the Government buildings use 4% of national electricity generated in Seychelles. In order to increase the renewable energy portfolio in the energy mix, Government has decided to set up roof-top solar PV units on 22 public buildings to a total capacity of 2.2 MW.

The two 1.0 MW solar PV plants to be installed on Praslin and La Digue Islands would be provided with energy storage facility to counter unexpected fluctuations in solar power generation and smoothen the power output.

Mr. Speaker, Seychelles Islands Foundation (SIF) installed PV on Aldabra Island 7 years ago. On the 1st of November 2018, President officially launched the renewable energy project on Alphonse island. This project has modern technology, which will ensure Alphonse island produce 90% of its energy needed on the island with solar. This will be managed by Island Development Company (IDC). IDC anticipate to install this project on other islands like Farquhar, Desroches and Astove.

PUC will be investing in some major projects in 2019 and over the medium term are follows;

* Two 8MW generator sets at Roche Caiman Power station

* 33KV Network at Ile Du Port

* Baie Ste Ane Power Station

* Water supply and network projects on Mahe, Praslin and La Digue

* Sewerage projects

5.2 Fisheries Sector

Mr. Speaker, the Seychelles Fisheries Authority is to be renamed as Seychelles Fisheries Authorities and to operate as a Financially Autonomous Institution as from 1st January 2019. The entity will pay dividend to Government at the end of 2019.

Construction has started on Seychelles Fisheries Authority Research and Development Centre at Ile Du Port for an estimated project cost SR 30 million.

The authority will launch the Aquaculture sector plan and introduce the Aquaculture Regulations that establishes licensing and investment frameworks/ opportunities for locals and international investment. In addition, SFA will start Brood-stock Acclimatization Quarantine Facility Phase 2 at Providence Fishing Port and compassing a fish hatchery and office spaces at a proposed project cost of EURO 700,000.

Mr. Speaker, the main fishing ports development projects during 2018 have been as follows; * The completion of the extension Providence Port Phase 2 – additional 200 m quay, shed, ice plant and access road.

* Completion of La Digue Fish Market and Gear store

* Construction of fish processing and value addition facilities for tuna and tuna like species at Providence fishing port and Ile du port.

* Starting of operations for Bel Ombre processing plant and value addition facilities for artisanal fish and fish products.

In addition, SFA will explore the potential for the development of dedicated industrial long line fishing port and its on-shore support facilities. In regards to Praslin, SFA has initiate the development project for artisanal fisheries infrastructure facilities at Baie Ste Anne and Grand Anse Praslin.

Mr. Speaker, the development of seafood value chains is expected to deliver long-term growth, jobs, and food security. However, the expansion and diversification of value chains must be aligned with improved governance to prevent changes in demand or price signals translating into greater pressure on marine resources and ecosystems. To achieve this complementarity, categories of investments in the seafood value chains are dependent on milestones being met in fisheries management and marine spatial planning

The expansion of seafood processing facilities has been a strategic focus area since 2007. New facilities at Providence and Bel Ombre have created added capacity for the processing of semi-industrial and artisanal catch, and an emerging opportunity to handle purse seiner bycatch. The newly commenced development of the Common Central Cold Store (CCCS) at Ile du Port substantially will add to the services offering with facilities to sort, store and tranship 12,000Mt of industrial fisheries catch and value-add a further ±4,800Mt.

5.3 Employment Sector

Mr. Speaker, the unemployment rate remained below 5 per cent and in first quarter 2018 it was

4.2 per cent similarly to first quarter 2017 at 4.7 per cent. To note the average national unemployment rate for the year 2017 was 3.9 per cent with females' unemployment rate being slightly higher at 4.0 per cent compared to males at 3.9 per cent.

There has been a decrease in the youth unemployment rate which was 11.3 per cent in Q1 2018 compared to 12.7 per cent in first quarter 2017. As at second quarter 2018, there were 448 graduates from the Professional Centres out of 661 registered (68%) under the My First Job scheme, who have been placed in employment in various sectors of the economy.

The Department of Employment has continued to enrol unskilled and inexperienced young jobseekers on the Skills Development Programme. As at second quarter 2018, approximately 223 trainees were active on the programme including cohorts from 2016 to 2018.

As at second quarter 2018, there were 428 welfare recipients registered on the Unemployment Relief Scheme (URS), out of which 126 were placed in employment. A total of 30 employing organizations are registered under the URS.

Mr. Speaker the challenge remains the growth rate of the economy versus the supply of labour market. The Government, will ensure that the Seychellois receive the require skills so that they can be promoted where there is a foreigner in the post. I take the opportunity to remind the employers of the advantage of the tax incentives that exist today if they provide training to their employees.

5.4 Micro, Small and Medium Enterprises (MSME) and Investment Climate

Mr. Speaker, the Micro, Small and Medium Enterprises or MSMEs makes up more than 80% of the total number of businesses in Seychelles contributing to a spectrum of sectors from Child Minding Services to Creative Industries and Light Manufacturing activities. They are the major source of job creation in any modern day economy. There is no doubt that Government has always been committed to creating an enabling business environment for MSMEs through the establishment of various Agencies, Facilities, Financing Schemes just to name a few.

For the year 2018 the following support and initiatives have been furnished to this sector:

* *The establishment of the Enterprise Seychelles Agency or ESA to replace SEnPA*; ESA is shouldering and elevating the responsibilities and functions of SEnPA to meet the exigencies and realities of the MSME sector as well as, provide them with institutional support.

* *Provision of business training to an additional 300 entrepreneurs;* this has only been possible with the outstanding collaboration with, the African Development Bank, SENPA and the Guy Morel Institute. It is vital to note that this initiative brings us to a total of 800 trained entrepreneurs thus far. Efforts will continue to be made through the industrialization policy to enhance capacity and encourage MSMEs to go into manufacturing or higher productive activity, integrate production technology to drive the diversification of the economy, hence increase the share of the manufacturing output to GDP.

Mr. Speaker, Government continues its effort to put forward new initiatives for the MSMEs sector and in 2019 this will be as follows;

* The establishment of the Prompt Payment Policy and Bill; many businesses, particularly the MSMEs experience considerable difficulties from their customers failing to pay their purchases on time. Delaying payment puts financial pressure on MSMEs particularly, putting their liquidity and sustainability at stake. This policy and proposed law aim to promote best commercial transactions payment practices, improve cash flow between suppliers and purchasers in commercial transactions and instil more financial discipline in the national payment culture. The Bill will be presented to the National Assembly during 2019;

* Amendment of the Seed Capital Grant Scheme; Following a Monitoring and Evaluation exercise launched by the Department of Industry and Entrepreneurship Development, the Scheme has been further improved to make it a "walk in" Seed Capital Grant Scheme. A provision of SR 5 million has been allocated for the 2019 budget.

* The establishment of a Land Allocation points system for Industrial and Commercial Land: This points system ensures organized and better management of industrial and commercial land. It sets out Government's priorities and optimized land as a scarce resource.

Mr. Speaker, Government will allocate funds to the Industrial Estate Authority for the following investment;

* SR 8.8 million for the Infrastructure Development on Zone 20

* SR 5 million for the Infrastructure Development on Eve Island

* SR 2.2 million for Road Improvement on the Industrial Estates

During the year 2018, the Department of Investment has focused its attention on improving the Investment Framework to facilitate investment and business operation in the country.

One of the major milestone this year has been the launching of the Investment Policy. The principles driving the investment policy are:

Creation of a conducive and transparent environment to attract investment and operate businesses

Modernization of the legal framework for investment

Application of international best practices and standards for investment

Respect for the environment and sociocultural fabric of the country

Another important emphasis of the Department of Investment this year, has been the drive to review the procedures and requirements one needs to follow to start and eventually operate a business.

The intention is to now move the onus for compliance to the investor/operator. For this to happen, it is necessary that the person has access to the policies, laws, requirements and standards so that all plans may be designed in accordance with the same.

In this light, Government has revived the High Level Ease of Doing Business Committee, which is chaired by the Vice President and groups Ministers and representatives of the private sector. This committee looks at the plans of action of the related public agencies in relation to the eleven parameters used in the Ease of Doing Business Index as well as other business related matters.

The Department is also engaging the various regulatory bodies to review the actual procedures one follows to start a business with the aim of designing more direct and simple procedures thus allowing the starting of a business to be much simpler.

In addition, Government, with the Seychelles Chamber of Commerce, jointly held the Seychelles Business Forum, the recommendations from which have been presented to the Cabinet of Ministers. A committee has been established which made up representatives from the private sector to ensure proper follow up on the recommendations.

5.5 Information, Communication and Technology

Mr. Speaker, over the past year, we have observed an increase in the usage in ICT services, especially data service on mobile and fixed network. We have noted that this year, both the operators are providing 2G, 3G and 4G mobile service to more than 90% of our population. We have seen further revision in the price of broadband services offered by operators. Thus, increasing the affordability, value, and choice of such services to customers. This is a positive trend. These are evidence of market forces at play, but it is agreed that more needs to be done to cater for especially for the lowest income earners of the population.

The Government will continue to facilitate the development of the ICT sector with the introduction of conducive policies and legislations and through engagement with all the stakeholders in the sector. The Communications Tower and Antenna Policy has recently been approved by Government and comes into effect. The policy will guide the installation of towers by operators, to facilitate sharing of those towers and mitigate some of the concerns that the general public has in relation to installation of towers.

In the coming months, it is anticipated that the Broadcasting and Telecommunication (Quality of Service) Regulation will be enacted. This regulation will set minimum standards, which operators would have to comply. Most importantly, it places obligations on the operators to publish information about quality of services offered to the public so that customers are well informed about the service quality offered by operators.

The Department of ICT and the mobile telecommunication operators has started the process to introduce Mobile Number Portability (MNP). The introduction of MNP is expected to catalyze competition among the mobile operators, increase consumer choice, improve customer service and network quality, drive innovation and efficiency, and eventually make mobile services more affordable. In addition, the offering of Mobile Number Portability will further enhance consumer's right.

Underpinning the development and performance of the telecommunications and broadcasting sector is the legislative framework. The new Communications Bill that will replace the prevailing Broadcasting and Telecommunications Act, 2000, is in its final phase of drafting. This legislation will provide for better oversight of the sector and encourage development and competition in the sector. It will also provide for the setting up of an independent regulator that will be separate from the DICT.

The country is also set to be connected by its second submarine cable in 2020. The signature of agreements and contracts between the Seychelles Cable Systems Co Ltd. or SCS (the SPV, Special Purpose Vehicle, put in place to build the first submarine cable) and Chinese companies involved with the PEACE system; means that Seychelles will be connected by a branch to the PEACE system which is set to become operational in 2020. Connectivity to PEACE will complement the connectivity provided by SEAS (current submarine cable linking the country). The second cable link will ensure the security of international connectivity of the country and mitigate significant negative economic impact that would otherwise result from any disruption in the operation of SEAS (e.g. a cable cut). The cost for this second submarine cable link is USD 20 million. As a PPP initiative, SCS has been a successful one and it is now in a position to arrange the financing of this new project without having recourse to its shareholders for equity investment or security. The shareholders of SCS are Government, CWS and AIRTEL. It is to be noted that the second submarine cable was one of the national strategic infrastructure projects identified by the President in his SONA of 2017 and can now be considered will be achieved in 2020.

As part of its E-Government initiative; focus continues to be placed on putting in place the means for citizens and businesses to interface and transact through electronic channels with Government. The regulation relating affixing of digital signatures issued under the ETA (Electronic Transaction Act) was enacted in April 2018. This allowed the use of digital signatures and their legal recognition in Seychelles. In conjunction with the use of electronic payments means; this allows doe end-to-end electronic processing of services to be undertaken fully electronically and paperless. The processing of Planning Applications is the first service that is delivered end-to-end in this manner and which makes use of digital signatures. Several other applications and e-services are also being upgraded to support the use of digital signatures.

New systems along with their associated e-services are also being implemented and it is expected that some of the key ones such as the Collateral Register and the Credit Information system will be operational by the end of the year. The deliveries of these are aligned with initiatives supporting the ease of doing business.

Mr. Speaker, the World is changing fast into the fourth industrial revolution. Seychelles needs to create a dynamic environment that will ensure we have a digital economy that will embodies changes to its infrastructure, regulations, skills and finance. We need to ensure that we review our current planning process so that it incorporates digitalization in everything we do. Therefore, Mr Speaker, during the 2019, the Government and private sector will work together to have a Digital Economy Strategy in place.

5.6 Blue Economy The Government is now implementing the Third South West Indian Ocean Fisheries Governance and Shared Growth Project (SWIOFish3), following two years of project preparation. The SWIOFish3 project, which is financed by a $5m World Bank loan and $5.3 m

GEF grant, is supporting Seychelles in strengthening its policy and governance framework for a transition to sustainable fisheries and the expansion of the fisheries value chains.

Mr. Speaker, I am pleased to announce that the world's first sovereign Blue Bond was issued by the Government and launched on the 29th of October 2018, with the proceeds to be used to support the objectives of SWIOFish3. The proceeds of the Blue Bond ($15 million) will capitalise a Blue Grants Fund ($3 million) administered by the Seychelles Conservation and Climate Adaptation Trust (SeyCCAT) and a Blue Investment Fund ($12 million) administered by the Development Bank of Seychelles (DBS). The targeted beneficiaries of grants and loans under these two funds encompass individuals (fishers, distributors, processors, and business-small, medium or large in size), fisher associations, government agencies, academic institutions, locally registered NGOs, community-based groups and civil society, among others. A wide range of opportunities are eligible under this Bond and these include:

* Community-based management of sustainable-use zones and implementation of fisheries co-management plans; * Adoption of new technologies and platforms (e.g. apps) for accessing markets and supporting monitoring activities; * Adoption of sustainable fishing practices as market-based incentives through label and

certification schemes; * Scientific and logistics services to the fisheries sector; * Restructuring of fishing fleet capacity, for example by vessel refitting for other

underexploited fisheries or tourism activities; * Expansion and development of fish processing and value addition for sustainable value

chains (e.g. tuna fishery by-catch); * Energy and waste efficiencies to improve performance in fish processing; * Small and medium-scale aquaculture.

The Blue Grant Funding through SEYCCAT will be as follows:

a) Small and medium grant concept up to SR 100,000 b) Large grant concept from SR 100,000 to SR 1 million DBS will offer a loan up to US$ 3 million for a particular project with an interest rate of 4% and repayment up to 15 years.

5.7 Financial Sector Development

Mr. Speaker, as per the announcement in the 2018 budget speech, the Central Bank of Seychelles amended the Financial Institutions (Bank Charges and Fees) Regulations on 26th February 2018 to ensure the following:

* that first home acquirers be charged a maximum processing fee of SR 2,500 on housing loans below SR 1.5 million. * For the remaining loan amount above SR 1.5 million, the first home acquirers will be charged a maximum of 0.5% as processing fee on the balance.

In addition, the amendment was done to ensure that the banks shall not impose a penalty interest of more than 5 per cent per annum and shall be calculated on the default instalment excluding the interest payable thereon.

Mr. Speaker, the financial services sector regulatory framework continues to be modernized to ensure that the sector diversifies and remains compliant to international best practice. This includes work on Base Erosion and Profit Shifting (BEPS) and the adoption of the common reporting standards.

The National Risk assessment against Anti-Money Laundering and Combating Financing of Terrorism (AML/CFT) risk was finalized in October 2017, and the Mutual Evaluation by the Financial Action Task Force (FATF) regional body Eastern and Southern Africa Anti-Money Laundering Group (ESAAMLG) was completed in August 2018. The report on Seychelles will be available on the ESSAMLG and the Seychelles authorities' website during November 2018. The report includes a number of recommendations, which should lead to strengthening the AML/CFT regulatory framework. In particular, a new AML/CFT law will be submitted soon to the National Assembly after additional review, including by the IMF legal Department. The law will establish a high-level national committee to oversee AML/CFT enforcement, and an independent board will be created to supervise operations of the Financial Intelligence Unit (FIU). The FIU will adopt a risk based operational framework to guide its activity, and its inspection staff will be increased. Memorandum of understandings will be established to improve cooperation on AML/CFT issues between the three regulators, the CBS, the Financial Service Authority (FSA) and the FIU.

Further to the launching of the National Financial Education Strategy, the authorities have deemed it equally important to formulate a roadmap at the national level with the ultimate objective for all stakeholders to cooperate in a coordinated approach in promoting a more effective and efficient process to enhance financial inclusion in the Seychelles. Particular emphasis is being placed in addressing issues regarding the efficient use of financial services including innovative financial services, reduction in the use of cash for payments, SMEs' access to finance and competition in the financial sector. In this context, the Central Bank also has as objective to work in collaboration with the Ministry responsible for Finance to enhance the efficiency of Government payments as well as the remittance market.

Digitalising the economy is an item that is high on the Central Bank's agenda. The Bank is in the process of designing a modernisation plan to further develop the payments infrastructure, to allow for a wider choice of e-payment/digital channels for financial services consumers. The modernisation plan of the payments infrastructure includes the implementation of a Central Security Depository (CSD), a Real Time Gross Settlement (RTGS) and a national payment switch, which is scheduled to begin in 2019. CBS is further collaborating with the Ministry responsible for Finance to digitise government payments and enhance the use of e-payment facilities in the country in the effort to drive the move to a digital economy.

Work is ongoing to enhance the current Credit Information System and also to promulgate the Credit Information System Act. The latter is to make provision for extension of the coverage of credit information to allow for better assessment by banks of the credit worthiness to support risk-based pricing of credit. The project is expected to be finalized by December 2019.

The authorities have identified that Financial Technologies (Fintech) can enhance financial sector development especially in areas identified in the Financial Sector Development Plan. It has therefore been approved for a National Strategy for Fintech to be formulated to provide for a coordinated approach as regards to the adoption of Fintech for both the onshore and offshore financial sector of the country, whilst considering the associated risks. The strategy is to further take into consideration the national initiatives to digitise the economy and the potential of Fintech being an enabling factor to achieving a digitised economy. The strategy is expected to be finalised by first half of 2019.

The Central Bank and the FSA are liaising with the Attorney General's Office to promulgate a Financial Consumer Protection law by the end of 2019. The aim of the Financial Consumer

Protection law and its supporting Regulations is to give the competent authorities explicit mandate to address financial services complaints, provide consumer redress and make provision for equitable and fair treatment of consumers. In conjunction with the promulgation of the law, the competent authorities are equally working towards establishing a framework that aims at preventing possible violations of market conduct rules that would in turn increase consumer trust in financial products and services.

5.8 Transport Sector

The Seychelles Civil Aviation Authority continues to make progress with capital development efforts in order to meet the growth in traffic demands at Seychelles international Airport. The new Mahe Domestic Terminal will fully open for business by December 2018 following a total investment of SR 87 million.

In the year ahead, much needed development will be undertaken to extend the handling capacity of the international airport's terminal concourse, at an investment value of SR12 million, with the aim to position our facility in line with international standards for aviation security and safety, as well as uplifting the passenger experience. The concourse project will start in 2019 and continue in 2020.

Mr Speaker, in 2018, Seychelles has embarked on a major project to extend and modernize the Commercial Port. The present port infrastructure has become too small for the expanding trade demands of our country and it has become outmoded for the more advanced types of container ships that are plying the Indian Ocean. Port Victoria must expand and modernize in order for Seychelles to remain a competitive and viable port of call for the new generation of cargo vessels. Financing arrangements for the port project were signed in April 2018 between Seychelles Port Authority and a consortium of international lending institutions, namely the European Investment Bank Euro 12.5 million, the Agence Francaise de Developpement Euro 16.5 million and a grant of Euro 5.0 million from the European Union (EU). If all goes according to plan, the project is expected to complete in 2022.

Other than the expansion and modernization of the Commercial Port, the SPA has several other capital projects in line for implementation in 2019. These include:

* During the last quarter of 2018, construction shall begin of 150 metres of Passenger Jetty opposite the Eve Island cargo terminal on Praslin with a capacity to accommodate four inter island ferries and 500 passengers simultaneously. The jetty will also be able to accommodate a small inter island cruise ships. The project will cost SR 19 million and is expected to complete mid 2019.

* To complement the Passenger Jetty project, at a cost of SR 40 million, a modern Passenger Terminal building with adequate seating capacity for 500 passengers, proper sanitary facilities, ferry ticket offices, baggage handling and other essential facilities shall also be built.

* In 2018, the Seychelles Port Authority commissioned two warehouses containing a total of 12 units that have been constructed at Ile Du Port to consolidate the position of Port Victoria as a logistics center for the industrial tuna fishing activity. At a cost of SR 10 million, these units shall

be available to serve small and medium entrepreneurs in the field of professional marine electro / mechanical works.

Mr. Speaker a total of SR 68.2 million will be invested for the different road infrastructure projects. One main one is the Construction of new motorable road from Pasquere to Grand Anse Praslin Via La Plaine Holandaise which has been estimated at SR 46.5 million.

5.9 Tourism Sector

Mr. Speaker, the tourism sector still remains as the main pillow of the economy. The total tax collection from the tourism represents 31% of the total tax collection. The Department of Tourism will continue to ensure quality assurance in the tourism industry through constantly assisting tourism businesses to strive and maintain desirable standards and offer value for money through, constant monitoring, inspecting and regulating of all tourism businesses so that Seychelles can maintain its position as an up-market however, affordable destination that will continue to contribute to the country's economy so as to keep enhancing the standard of living of all Seychellois people.

With the aim to establish quality standards within the accommodation sector the Tourism Department has over the past 3 years worked on a hotel grading programme, this has involved development of criteria, advisory visits and pilot tests at hotels, consultative meetings, workshops and finally the drafting of a Tourism Development Bill. The initial stage of this programme is coming to an end and the Department prepares itself through the 2019 budget for implementation of this programme which seeks to establish a greater degree of standardisation and increase professionalism within the tourism industry.

The Seychelles Sustainable Tourism Label programme that was initiated in 2012 has steadily gained interest over the years with 17 hotels presently certified and a number of hotels working towards certification. The programme has gained international recognition when it achieved the GSTC recognised status. Through the 2019 budget the Department of Tourism will continue its work to mainstream sustainability within the sector by increasing the number or certified products, increasing the visibility of these responsible products to potential clients and showcasing the financial benefits of being certified through case studies of our certified hotels.

Mr. Speaker, the Government has remain committed to the marketing undertaking by the Seychelles Tourism Board. A provision of SR 91.7 million has been made for the 2019 budget for the Seychelles Tourism Marketing.

5.10 Arts, Culture and Heritage

Mr. Speaker, arts, culture and heritage has received a total of SR 171.2 million to different departments and entities compare to only SR 119.3 million in the revised 2018 budget. This shows the great importance for this sector in the 2019 budget. There are potential for this sector in the development of our economy. From the total SR 46.2 million or 25.8% is for capital projects and some of the large investment are as follows;

* SR 2.1 million for the renovation of Carnegie

* SR 1.7 million for the renovation of theatre des palmes

* SR 16.68 million for the renovation of national library

* SR 5 million renovation of the admin block close to annex of the ex-supreme court

* SR 1 million renovation of National Arts Council Building

* SR 1.5 million renovation of National Theatre

* SR 1 million construction of the administration block for the Seychelles Heritage Foundation

* SR 3 million for the repair of roof at the International Conference Centre

* SR 5 million for the Music Stadium

* SR 5.9 million for the construction work on a new administrative block for the creole institute and the renovation for the current building

6 2019 BUDGET FOR SOCIAL PROGRAMS

In the 2019 budget, Government will maintain its commitment to finance Social Programs targeting the most vulnerable people in our society. The budget for the various programs are as follows:

* SR 40 million for Social Safety Net by the Agency for Social Protection (ASP),

* SR 240 million for Home Carers which include their 13th Month pay,

* SR 8.5 million for Home Improvement/Re-roofing Scheme for Pensioners through HFC,

* SR 10 million for Vulnerable Home Repair Scheme through ASP,

* SR 18 million for housing finance Subsidy Scheme,

* SR 4.2 million for dedicated funds for Schools

* SR 6.7 million for Daycare Scheme, and

* SR 3.2 million for Foster Care Scheme In 2019, Government will also offer budget support to the various business schemes.

* SR 5 million for Youth Employment Scheme (***My First Job Scheme***),

* SR 1 million for the Youth Entrepreneurship Scheme (***YES***)

* SR 16 million for the Small Medium Enterprises Scheme (***SMEs Scheme***)

Mr Speaker, a sum of SR 17.3 million is allocated for the Post-Secondary student's bursary. This will be needed for Government to continue providing support to the students as follows;

* First Year Student SR 850 per month

* Second Year Student SR 950 per month

* Third Year Student SR 1,050 per month Praslin and La Digue students in post-secondary institutions receive an additional SR 1,400 per month for all three years of study and SR 200 is deducted for the utilities for the Youth Hostel.

Mr. Speaker, SPTC has started to implement a new scheme of service from July 2018 that will have a full year impact during 2019. In addition, SPTC has started to exit some of the contract services and let these contracts to the private sector operators. During the year 2019, Government will undergo a thorough assessment of SPTC's operation and assess different options with the private sector to see areas that they can come in. To that effect, a budget provision of SR 30 million has been provided for subvention for SPTC and SR 28 million for SPTC travel concessions for the elderly and students.

The Office of the Secretary of State for Poverty Alleviation has the mandate of defining a National Anti-poverty Strategy for Seychelles, including a clear poverty definition in the Seychelles context. While at the same time, identifying people living in dire conditions, alerting relevant agencies for immediate intervention and collaborating with those same agencies to ensure adequate and efficient follow-up actions. This is being done through an innovative and targeted approach which touches not only revenue, but all the dimensions of poverty: In other words, a multidimensional approach. Programs have included the following;

* Poverty profiling surveys to identify who is poor and which will result in a National Poverty Index which will then serve a data base of people living in poverty, their causes and remedies applied according to their deprivations;

* Meeting with those identified as poor through public clinics and community visits; and

* Rapid response by means of effective Inter-agency partnership.

To that effect, a provision of SR 20 million has been allocated under the Ministry of Habitat, Infrastructure and Land Transport public sector investment programme to support cases as identified by the Office for Poverty Alleviation.

7 CONTINGENCY

Mr. Speaker, during the year 2018 we are paying part of the compensation to the staff of the Department of Culture in regards to the Fungus problem. The balance will be paid in 2019. In addition, we have put some funds for the compensation of the La Misere water pollution cases. This is why a provision of SR 50 million has been allocated for the 2019 budget compare to the normal SR 20 million provision in recent years.

8 NEW POLICES FROM THE 2019 BUDGET

8.1 Increase in Minimum Wage

As per announcement made in the 2018 State of the Nation address, the minimum wage will increase by 5% effective 1st of January 2019. This will be equivalent as follows:

* From SR 33.30 to SR 34.97 per hour for all workers other than casual.

* The rate for casual workers will be raised from SR 38.38 to SR 40.30 per hour.

The Salary Increase by 5% for full time Home Carers will come into effect as of 1st of January 2019. The Home Carers on part time basis will be pro-rata.

8.2 Increase in Benefits and Approved Programs of Agency and Social Protection

Mr. Speaker, the following benefits will be increased as follows:

* Retirement Benefits from SR 5,050 to SR 5,250

* Invalidity and Disability Benefits from SR 5,050 to SR 5,250

* Funeral Benefit from SR 1,700 to SR 2,000

8.3 Increase in stipend for students in the tertiary education institutions

Mr. Speaker, with the aim of ensuring that our overseas students are binding to the visa requirement and align the stipend to the costs of living index in those countries, Government will from February 2019 increase the stipend for all the students studying overseas.

In addition, the students studying for a degree at the University of Seychelles will also receive an increase. The details of the increase will be given by the Agency of National Human Resource Development.

8.4 Review of Housing Subsidy and Personal Contribution through HFC for Praslin and La Digue Residents

The Government has taken note of the cost of construction on Praslin and La Digue in view of the higher cost on materials taking into account the transportation cost element. Mr. Speaker, currently all HFC applicants will need to contribute 7.5% personal contribution for their housing loan. From 1st of January 2019, all Praslin and La Digue residents, the personal contribution will reduce from 7.5% to 5%.

Currently through the budget, there is a housing subsidy scheme for all housing loans applicants with income brackets of SR 25,000 or below. Government is in the process of reviewing the current scheme after 5 years of implementation to ensure that it is better targeted. Government will look into reviewing the formula for calculation of the subsidy entitlement for Praslin and La Digue Residents, to ensure that the higher cost of construction materials on these two islands is taken into consideration. This will be effective from 1st of April 2019.

8.5 Remove VAT on canned tuna

Mr. Speaker there are currently over 500 specific goods or targeted categories imported into the country that are exempted from VAT. In our combined effort to reduce the prices of canned tuna on the local market for the average Seychellois, IOT has managed to re-look at its costing models and the supply chain distribution, and has managed to reduce its price of canned tuna in the local market. To complement the reduction on price, the Government has decided to remove the 15 percent VAT on canned tuna. This will be applicable as from 1st of January 2019.

Mr. Speaker, as canned tuna has become part of our staple diet for the general households in Seychelles and a good source of protein, we hope to see an increase in consumption of canned tuna in view of health nutritional benefits and reduction in price.

8.6 Immovable Property Tax

During the 2018 budget speech it was announced the Immovable Property tax on foreign property to be applicable on all foreign-owned residential and company owned properties. After further discussion with all stakeholders, Government has reconsidered that the Immovable Property tax will be only on all foreign-owned residential properties.

The rate will still be at 0.25% as announced last year. The Government will finalize the bill to ensure the implementation will start on the 1st of April 2019.

8.7 Sugar Tax

Mr. Speaker, the Ministry of Health incurs huge expenses for the treatment of diseases which are linked to lifestyle risk factors. One of these risk factor is obesity which result from the high consumption of sugar sweetened beverages. An approximate of SR 83.3 million is spent per year, an amount which excludes the indirect costs incurred for treatment of diseases partly caused by obesity.

Approximately 11% of the adult population are suffering from diabetes and 30% with hypertension. It is estimated that only about 50% of these patients seek treatment and abide to it. According to the Ministry of Health, medications for diabetes and hypertension amount to an approximate SCR 18.25 million per year, whilst the costs involved for medical consultations and haemodialysis is estimated to amount to SCR 65 million per year.

Mr. Speaker, in 2019, Government will impose a tax on beverages that contain sugar. This is Government effort to encourage people especially our children, to reduce considerably on the consumption of sugar sweetened beverages. As a result, this will reduce the risk of obesity, diabetes, and other non-communicable diseases. Research has shown that this strategy works and this has been recommended by World Health Organisation, as well.

The sugar tax will apply to all beverages (including alcoholic beverages) of which the sugar content exceeds 5g per 100ml, at a rate of SR4 per litre. Freshly squeezed fruit juices shall be exempted from payment of the tax.

Noting that those products would now be excisable, all manufacturers will be required to be registered with the Excise Unit in the Customs Division and to comply with all provisions of the Excise Tax Act 2009, before the date of entry into force of these regulations, which will be on the 1st of April 2019. In addition to other relevant information it will now also be compulsory for importers to declare the sugar content in imported beverages.

8.8 Excise Tax on Tobacco

Mr. Speaker, to deal with the scourge of excessive tobacco consumption, the effects that these have on society, and the significant costs to the budget for treatment of tobacco-related diseases, Government will, as of January, 2019, increase the rate of excise tax on these products. We will implement a 10 percent increase on all tobacco products. These increases will apply on both imported and local products. The new excise tax rates all tobacco will apply on all manufactured tobacco products.

8.9 Revised Rates for the Poultry Levy and Introduction of a Levy on Pork

Mr Speaker, with a view of supporting the growth of the livestock sector, the Government will increase duty on imported pork and poultry meat, as of 1st of January 2019. This would be a short term measure to re-energise the industry and provide some further leeway against the more competitive imports.

The new rate of pork will be 15% + SR 3/KG.

The new rate of poultry will be 15% + SR 5.92/KG

8.10 VAT refund on Local Purchases by businesses engaged in Agriculture and Fisheries

Mr. Speaker, the VAT regulation makes provision for persons engaged in farming, fishing and supporting activities to be exempted from payment of VAT on importation of goods and equipment approved by the Ministry responsible for Agriculture and Fisheries.

The Government is amending the VAT regulations to allow registered farmers and fishermen to be eligible for VAT refund on locally purchased goods/equipment (*excluding motor vehicles, except specialized motor vehicle as certified by the Ministry responsible for Agriculture and Fisheries which also benefit with Excise Tax concessions*) solely for use in their business. The list of purchased goods and equipment will be stipulated under an exemption schedule. The procedure for VAT refund would be as follows:

The farmer/fisherman purchases a good or equipment locally through a VAT invoice and requests for a receipt after purchase;

The VAT Invoice and receipt are taken to the Seychelles Agricultural Agency/Seychelles Fishing Authority for endorsement;

The endorsed VAT Invoice and receipt are then taken to the Seychelles Revenue Commission in order to process the refund.

A legislation is being proposed for such refund mechanism, similar to an existing refund mechanism, for VAT refund at airport. The legislation would also prevent any possibilities of abuse.

8.11 Legislative amendment Governing Excise Tax for fuel concession

Mr. Speaker, before the transfer and consolidation of all the categories of businesses and persons entitled to fuel concessions and exemption under the Excise Tax (Fuel concession/Exemption) Regulation in 2018 -(S.I 27 of 2018), the provisions for fuel concessions and exemptions was segmented under various legislations. One such legislation was the Tourism Incentives Act (TIA) introduced in 2003, which granted various fiscal incentives to tourism related entities to boost development of the tourism sector. It allowed entities such as Licensed accommodations, Restaurants, Dive centers/operators, Tour Guide operators, Hire Crafts, Ferry services, Yachts and Liveaboard operators to benefit from: special Business Tax rates, reduced GOP fees, special deductions or allowable deductions on taxes for certain expenditures, and

Trades Tax (on minor operating items, vehicles, and capital equipment) and also Tax concessions on fuel. Entities who benefited with these incentives (including Tax concession on fuel) have in their possession a TIA certificate (valid for 5 or 10 years) that served as proof of entitlement. Most of these certificates will expire in 2018.

The fuel concession has been costing SR 364.4 million and SR 411.8 million for the years 2016 and 2017 respectively. This include all concessions that exist under the fuel concession regulation which include PUC and SPTC.

The proposed review was intended to involve public consultations and subsequently the removal of entities (certificate holders) benefiting under the TIA, whereby the concession and exemption would be completely removed making them liable to full taxes on fuel purchased. Public consultations were done during 2018 and the Government will be undergoing the reform as follows;

Maintained as per the rates in schedule 1 of the fuel regulation for entities or categories such as PUC, SPTC, SFA, Companies mandated by Government to undertake development activities on outer islands, Domestic Air Transportation, Boat owners, Fuel concessions under signed agreements with Government of Seychelles, Licensed Ferry services Operators for cargo.

The licensed accommodations, which are not connected to the PUC grid, that use fuel to generate their own electricity will be maintained. However, once PUC is ready to include them in the grid the concessions will no longer applicable.

A phase out approach to remove fuel concession for TIA Licensed Operators in Hire Craft, Dive Centre, Tour Operator, Cruise Ship, Yacht/Live aboard Operator. These concessions will be gradually reduced until 2020 when they are liable to full taxes on fuel purchased.

From January 2019, the concessions will be reduced from 50% to 25%

From January 2020 from 25% to nil

A phase out approach to remove fuel concession for TIA helicopter services Licensed Operators. These concessions will be gradually reduced until 2020 when they are liable to full taxes on fuel purchased.

From January 2019, the concessions will be reduced from 25% to 12.5%

From January 2020 from 12.5% to nil

8.12 Business Tax Reform

Mr. Speaker, during the 2018 budget, several measures were announced for the reform in the business tax act. The bill in regards to the Base Erosion Profit Shifting has been gazetted and is before the National Assembly to be tabled for the second reading once we complete the budget process. The proposed amendments that are before the National Assembly are to make clear that only income sourced in Seychelles is liable to tax in Seychelles, that is a territorial business tax system.

In reference to the Base Erosion Profit Shifting, there are other amendments in other legislations that need to be done before 31st of December 2018. The following legislations are before the National Assembly to be tabled after the budget process;

* Companies (Special Licences) (Amendment) Bill, 2018

* Securities (Amendment) Bill, 2018

* Mutual Fund and Hedge Fund (Amendment) Bill, 2018

* International Business Companies (Amendment) Bill, 2018

* Insurance (Amendment) Bill, 2018

* International Trade Zone (Amendment) Bill, 2018

Mr. Speaker, in addition, currently the taxable business income generated from the offshore banking is being taxed at 3%. This provision under the business tax act will continue to apply until 31st December 2018. From the 1st of January 2019, the normal business tax rate applicable to the banks will apply.

Mr. Speaker, in line with our commitments we will have to bring our preferential tax regimes, containing geographically immobile activities (i.e. manufacturing, processing, light assembly and redistribution activities under the ITZ Act), in line with the EU requirements by December 2019. This will be discussed with the industry during the first quarter of 2019.

Mr. Speaker one main amendment being proposed in the current Business tax amendment bill is the issue of the capital gains from the sale of business assets. The amendments make it clear that that any surplus obtained from the sale of an asset is not subject to any taxes. This will be limited to the amount claimed for tax depreciation.

In addition, one other amendment that has been discussed with the Bills committee is that any income that has been subject to withholding tax will be consider as the final tax paid on this assessable income.

Mr. Speaker, another amendment that has been included in the proposed bill is the withholding tax rate of 5% for any remuneration paid in respect of a performance in Seychelles by a non-resident entertainer or sports person.

The Government intention is to reduce the business tax rate from 2020. In addition, tax holidays will be provided to businesses in particular sectors, for example, any businesses exporting large amount of their products in the international market, businesses invested heavily in capital equipment. These are few examples but Government will undergo these discussions with the business community during the first half of 2019 to ensure new amendments are presented to National Assembly for the 2020 budget.

Mr. Speaker several announcements were made in the 2018 budget speech. These will be postponed until the new business tax regime will be discussed with the stakeholders with the implementation to be from 2020. The amendments that will be delayed until further discussion will be as follows;

* A flat fee of SR 3,000 for businesses deriving a Turnover of not more than SR 500,000 per year.

* A flat percentage of 3% for businesses deriving Turnover above SR 500,000 but up to SR 25 million,

* The removal of the Accelerated depreciation and 200% allowable deduction for marketing and promotion costs for the tourism sector.

* The reduction of business tax on residential dwelling from 15% to 3%.

Mr Speaker, the Pay As You Go specified business which certain businesses were liable to deduct 5% of their income at source will no longer exist as from January 2020. These businesses are Building Contractor, Maintenance Contractor, Mechanic, Hirer or Operator of Plant and Equipment, Hirer of Omnibus.

The second phase of the Business Tax reform will continue with discussion with the business community. The intension is for the Government to work with the private sector to find a simpler option. It would also aim to simplify the operations of Seychelles Revenue Commission and reduce our heavy reliance of taxes to fund the budget as well as a huge pressure to recruit more tax personnel.

8.13 Definition of Turnover under the Corporate Social Responsibility Tax Act, 2013 and Tourism Marketing Tax Act, 2013

The main issue being faced today is that for certain businesses, to levy the CSR Tax on the 'gross receipt' in the strict interpretation of it would have an adverse effect on the business. Reference is being made particularly to Bureaux de Change, Travel Agents, Tour Operators in Seychelles and other companies that operate on a commission basis. This is because the income derived by these businesses does not necessarily belong to them and they would normally act as agents in order to receive a commission.

Under the Business Tax Act, 2009, there is a definition of assessable income which is quite similar to the definition of 'turnover' under the Corporate Social Responsibility Act, 2013, however, it is restrictive in the sense that it is more detailed in the income it will capture.

Mr Speaker, from January 2019, for consistency purposes, the Government will align the definition of "turnover" under the Corporate Social Responsibility Act, 2013 and Tourism Marketing Tax Act, 2013 with the definition of "assessable income" under the Business Tax Act, 2009.

8.14 Enforcement of Payment of Royalties to Seychelles Authors and Composers Society (SACS)

The Copyright Act 2014 allows the Seychelles Authors and Composers Society (SACS) to collect and distribute royalties on behalf of their members for the commercial use of musical works.

However, SACS was encountering difficulties in respect of collection of royalties from entertainment establishments such as hotels, discotheques and public bars that are making commercial gains through the use of musical works. In this regard, SACS and the Seychelles Licensing Authority (SLA) undertook to develop a Memorandum of Understanding to ensure that the SLA includes, as a condition of license, compliance to the Copyright Act 2014, which confers the power unto SACS to collect royalties from such establishments.

After numerous deliberations and approval from the Cabinet of Ministers on 14th March 2018, amendments to the Licences (Liquor and Outdoor Entertainment) Regulations 1998 and the Licences (Accommodation Catering and Entertainment Establishments) Regulations 2011 to include the license condition which compels entertainment establishments and persons holding an outdoor activity licence to pay the required royalties to SACS prior to the renewal or issuance of these respective licenses. It is expected that the Regulations will be promulgated in 2019 followed by the signing of the MOU.

8.15 Introduction of a Prescription Fee in the Health service

Mr. Speaker, for the past 40 years there has been no contribution from any Seychellois for the health services. However, over the past 10 years the budget for the health sector has increased from SR 315.2 million to SR 1.02 billion. Mr. Speaker, as a country we will need to re-think how we continue to sustain such an investment in the future. Everybody will need to start to take care of their own health. Therefore, the time has come for Government to charge a prescription fee of only SR 25. Mr. Speaker, the medicine will still be available free of charge. The children under the age of 18 years, full time students, elderly and patient with chronic diseases will be exempt from this prescription fee. This will be implemented in the first quarter of 2019.

8.16 Revision in Fees and Charges

The Seychelles Maritime Services Authority (SMSA) Bill has been approved by Cabinet and is expected to go before the National Assembly in last quarter of 2018, which will turn SMSA into an autonomous body. This will empower SMSA in 2019 to tackle the various maritime issues; making it mandatory for all vessels to be registered (including fishing vessels) and surveyed. This will promote safety and seaworthiness of vessels. This will include new revision in fees and charges since the fees have not been revised for the past 20 years.

The National Bio Security Agency has done a review to improve the Schedule of fines, fixed penalties and fees under Regulation fees and charges under the Animal and Plant protection Act (2014). The keys elements of the proposed revision are;

* Simplify and Reduce the Existing Number of Biosecurity Fees from 90 to 70

* Remove the Multiple Import Permit option valid for 3 or 6 months because phytosanitary conditions in many of the exporter countries change frequently. Only the Single Import option will remain as it is already the case in other countries such as South Africa

* Remove all Inspection Fees and Others Fees based on time in office and out of office because it was difficult to apply and not used and replace by a flat fee.

* Update biosecurity fees with current cost level as per performance programme based budgeting of the National Biosecurity Agency to improve cost recovery

8.17 Legislative review of national laws relating to intellectual property

In 2018, the National Intellectual Property Committee discussed the need to review both the Industrial Property Act 2014 and the Copyright Act 2014 given recent developments. One of the outcomes of a project funded by the Commonwealth, was recommendations for the amendment of the Industrial Property Act 2014 in certain areas. Additionally, due to potential accessions to IP related Protocols and the creation of the single IP Office, a thorough review of the current national laws will need to be undertaken to ensure conformity with international best practices. It is expected that this review will be finalised during 2019.

8.18 Trade Remedies Process of enactment of legislations and Phase Two on the implementation

Mr. Speaker, the Ministry of Finance, Trade, Investment and Economic Planning is in the process of developing the necessary legislations to allow for the imposition of trade remedy measures in Seychelles. This is expected to provide our domestic industries with a recourse in instances where the domestic industry has suffered injury following certain market conditions resulting from the effects of trade liberalisation. For example, it may be applied in cases where there are surges of imports, dumping and highly subsidised imports affecting a domestic industry producing the same products. These legislations are being developed with the assistance of a consultant procured under the SADC Trade Related Facility.

The legislations is expected to include an enabling Act and its supplementary instruments, dedicated to each of the three trade remedies measures, that is, safeguards, anti-dumping and countervailing measures.

It is expected that the trade remedies legislations will go to the National Assembly for their consideration and approval during 2019.

Additionally, it is expected that the second phase of the trade remedies project focusing on the implementation will commence by first quarter of 2019.

9 REVENUE MANAGEMENT REFORMS

9.1 Seychelles Licensing Authority

Mr. Speaker, work has started to review the Seychelles Licensing Authority act, 2010 and its regulations. A consultant was recruited and has done an analysis to identify the strengths and weaknesses of the current system and assess opportunities for improvement in the context of the risks to Seychelles. The objective of the analysis was to reduce the administrative burdens and to improve the business enabling environment while maintaining standards to protect public safety, health and protect the environment. The analysis has identified license categories that could be removed. It has also considered the cost of licensing, periods for renewing licenses and the procedures followed in the issue and enforcement of licenses. Finally, the assessment has involved a review of the functions, powers and duties of the Seychelles Licensing Authority. A stakeholder's consultation was done on the 26th of September 2018. This will be presented to cabinet of Ministers in early 2019 so that the revised legislations are tabled during 2019.

Mr. Speaker, at present, sports entertainment is not legislated by any law. Sport entertainment activities are types of spectacle that presents a competitive event using a high level of adrenaline for the purpose of entertaining an audience or competition. Given the nature of these activities, it is necessary to have a framework to cater to these activities. Taking note of the genre of the sports, safety, the level of investment, oversight, and enforcement, such could be properly captured under a licensing framework. Government is finalizing the licensing framework for the sports entertainment activities.

9.2 Transfer Pricing and Common Reporting Standards

Mr. Speaker, since September 2017, the Seychelles Revenue Commission has been exchanging information such as bank account information with their overseas counterpart. This is as per the requirement of the Revenue Administration (Common Reporting Standards) regulations. The information exchanged is financial information on all non-tax resident persons that have an account with a financial entity. Such information received by Seychelles Revenue Commission will assist in audits of resident persons of Seychelles who have directed payments for goods and services through an overseas bank account or overseas entity and not declared these income in their tax return. Common Reporting Standards would therefore reduce possibility/risks of tax evasion through offshore bank accounts or investment and ensure that all Seychelles tax resident pay their fair shares of taxes to the State. Thus, I urge all resident persons or entities in Seychelles, which are transacting through their overseas bank account, to ensure that all required information/income are being provided/declared to the Seychelles Revenue Commission.

Mr. Speaker, another issue that has been discussed previously which remains a concern is transfer pricing with the multinational enterprises. Transfer pricing consistently ranks among the top concerns for tax authorities. Emphasis in relation to transfer-pricing is expected to increase globally in the coming years.

Mr. Speaker, in line with that, as per requirement of OECD in line with the BEPS initiative, the Government is finalizing a regulation which will require Multinationals Companies with a turnover above 750million Euros operating in Seychelles or having a subsidiary in Seychelles to fill their returns to SRC. Mr. Speaker, we will work with the Seychelles Revenue Commission to increase focus on transfer-pricing audits.

Nonetheless, for MNE's or companies below the 750million Euros operating in Seychelles or having a subsidiary in Seychelles, a team from the IMF will be in Seychelles early in 2019 to assess the current situation and build capacity of our tax auditors in view that OECD requirements is above 750 million.

9.3 Informal Sector

Mr. Speaker, today, there is renewed interest in the informal economy worldwide. This is because the informal economy is growing in many contexts and appearing in new sectors. The informal sector consists of all activities operating outside the official legal and fiscal system, with a resulting lack of reliable statistical information. Mr. Speaker, there is no single overarching policy intervention to address the concerns associated with the informal economy, a range of interventions need to be considered and implemented. Further, these interventions need to be tailored and targeted to meet the specific constraints, needs and risk of the different groups in the informal sector. As such during 2019, the World Bank will assist the Government with a study on the Informal Sector in Seychelles. Once the study is completed, we will ensure policy responses are appropriate to the constraints and risks faced by the informal sector.

9.4 Seychelles Revenue Commission Tax Arrears

Mr. Speaker, as at 30th of September 2018, Seychelles Revenue Commission tax debt is at SR 850.6 million broken as follows:

* Primary Tax SR 417.8 million

* Penalty SR 432.8 million However, the figures that Seychelles Revenue Commission are able to pursue is only SR 424.3 million because of the following reasons;

* SR 95.7 million has been amended after new information have been provided by the tax payers

* SR 260.0 million objection cases which are being handled by the legal section of the Seychelles Revenue Commission

* SR 46.7 million are being persecuted

* SR 20.6 million is written-off cases since some of the tax payers have passed away and their businesses have been liquidated.

* SR 3.3 million is before the Revenue Tribunal Mr. Speaker, an immense effort is being done by the Seychelles Revenue Commission to collect the outstanding debt using different strategies amongst which include:

* Garnishee Notice * Passport Restrictions * Departure Prohibition Order * Prosecution of companies through company directors based on Attorney General's advice.

10 INVESTMENT OPPORTUNITIES

Mr. Speaker, Government has had to review its privatization strategy based on the current economic conditions. We will not be privatizing SEYPEC as previously announced. However, the Government owes 60% shares in the Seychelles Commercial Bank and the account holder holds 40%. We will need to bring Seychelles Commercial Banks on the next level to ensure that the account holders receive more dividend. Thus, the Government will offer 50% of its share to a strategic partner by July 2019.

Mr. Speaker, the Government will provide the support necessary to establish the country's first investment fund, for which through an indirect mode of financing, would contribute towards addressing the country's impending infrastructure needs. The intermediary approach would present several advantages including:

i. mitigating several of the risks associated with the direct method of raising capital; The indirect form of raising capital would also provide a channel for a larger and more sustainable investor base to participate in public private partnership arrangements for infrastructure projects.

ii. providing access to funding from a larger base of investors with a wider range of risk appetites and investment needs, by pooling of resources in a fund; and
iii. diversify investment risk and increase economic efficiency.

11 PUBLIC DEBT MANAGEMENT

Mr. Speaker, as at September 2018, the total debt as a percentage of GDP was 59.6%. As a Government, we remain committed to reduce the total public debt to 50% of GDP by 2021. For the first time we have include a fiscal risk statement with the 2019. This enables the disclosure of fiscal risks emanating from State Owned Enterprises. As such, Government has disclosed all guarantees and any other explicit commitments of State Owned Enterprises.

Mr. Speaker for the year 2019, the Ministry of Finance, Trade, Investment and Economic Planning and in collaboration with CBS will be launching three long term bonds; 3 years, 5 years and 7 years bonds. This will provide additional facilities for the Seychellois to invest in and also in ensuring, we extend the maturity of our domestic debt.

12 RESULT BASED MANAGEMENT FRAMEWORK

After the strong fiscal and public sector reforms, Seychelles is now moving towards second-generation public sector reforms to spur inclusive growth. These reforms are at the center of the President's principles of transparency, accountability and good governance. Cabinet has approved the results-based management (RBM) policy to lay the foundation for these performance reforms. It aims at strengthening the results-focus across government to enhance public sector efficiency, effectiveness, transparency and accountability with the ultimate objectives to enhance growth, economic diversification, and social inclusion across sectors.

Mr. Speaker, the 2019 budget will be fully on Program Performance Based Budgeting methodology. This process started with the 2015 budget where the first pilot Ministries were the education portfolio and agriculture and fisheries portfolio. Five years later, we have a comprehensive budget with clear performance indicators for all Ministries, Department and Agencies. Mr. Speaker, for the 2020 budget, the budget ceiling will be allocated by portfolio and the Ministries, Departments and Agencies will need to discuss and agree the individual departmental ceiling within their portfolio. This will be based on the priorities within the portfolio and the targeted results that need to be achieved.

However, the next phase is to link the sectoral strategies with the Program Performance Based Budgeting so that we can see more results oriented. Mr. Speaker, on the 2nd of November 2018, the draft Seychelles Vision 2033 was discussed with all stakeholders. The aim is to launch the National vision in January 2019. In addition, during 2019, the Government will ensure we complete all sectoral strategies and ensure the strategies are consistent with the national vision.

Mr. Speaker, the other pillar that we have started to pilot is the Monitoring and Evaluation. The design and adoption of a performance monitoring and evaluation policy and guidelines has been finalized. The implementation has started in two sector pilots and is now proceeding in two other pilots. The Public service reforms are led by the Department of Public Administration. Reforms under the fourth pillar have now become more urgent to ensure the Government can deliver its services effectively and efficiently. These reforms address increasing concerns with public service management, both regarding the size and performance of the public service. Mr. Speaker, Government is to complete the full reform of the Results Based Management Framework by end 2021.

13 CIVIL SOCIETY ENGAGEMENT

Mr. Speaker, the Government has remained committed to work with the civil society. A budget provision of SR 3 million has been allocated to CEPS for the year 2019. In addition, a budget allocation of SR 19.1 million for different programs under Social Programs of Government for different community based programme and organisations under for civil society. As part of the memorandum of understanding that was done during the year 2018 between Government and CEPS, it was agreed for both parties to be partners in ensuring support to the civil society.

During September 2018, the grant process was launched for the civil society organizations to submit their application form. The Ministry of Finance, Trade, Investment and Economic Planning were previously doing the process. However, this process is being done through a national committee, which include CEPS, and the committee is assessing all the applications through a transparency process.

In addition, the Registrar General is working with CEPS to ensure there is a review of the current legislations that regulate the framework that the civil society organizations operate within. This process will be completed during the year 2019.

14 CONCLUSION

Mr. Speaker, last week on the 31st of October 2018, we celebrate a decade of economic reform program. We know that it has not be an easy process but as a small islands state we need to ensure that we are resilient and ready for any adverse pressure based on the World Economy.

We would like to stress to all Seychellois on the need to work even harder and that we must remain united in the wake of any storm.This stance and our unity will remain key to our success.

Mr Speaker, it is for this reason that the 2019 budget is one to sustain our economic progress.

I would like to thank the President of the Republic for his guidance and support for the people of Seychelles and Seychelles. I would also like to thank my colleague ministers and their respective teams.

I thank my staff in the Ministry of Finance, Trade, Investment and Economic Planning for their teamwork, steadfast professionalism and motivation to succeed for the Seychelles economy.

I would like to congratulate members of the private sector and civil society who are truly making

their presence felt for the country and its people. Thank you for your collaborative spirit. I would like to thank the international community who has work with us during the past few years to ensure that our socio-economic development is benefiting each and every Seychellois.

In addition, thank you to all the members of the National Assembly and yourself Mr Speaker.

I would like to thank the people of Seychelles for their confidence in the economic direction of Seychelles. I now commend the Appropriation Bill 2019 amounting to SR 8,463,947,478 for the approval of

the National Assembly. Thank you, Mr. Speaker.

INVESTMENT AND BUSINESS CLIMATE - STRATEGIC INFORMATION AND CONTACTS FOR STARTING BUSINESS

Contact for More Information

Shariff Jathoonia
Economic Specialist
4th Floor, Rogers House, John Kennedy Ave, Port Louis, Mauritius

+230 202 4464
JathooniSX@state.gov

An island nation, Seychelles is located off the eastern coast of Africa in the middle of the Indian Ocean. Seychelles is an upper middle-income country with an estimated population of 90,000. Years of centrally-planned economic policies led to rapid economic development immediately after the socialist coup of 1977, but also created serious economic imbalances. These problems included large fiscal and external deficits and mounting debt arrears, which contributed to persistent foreign exchange shortages and slow growth that plagued Seychelles in the first decade of the 21st century. In October 2008, facing the near depletion of official foreign exchange reserves, Seychelles defaulted on interest payments due on its USD 230 million Eurobond, issued two years previously, severely damaging its credibility as a borrower. The government of Seychelles (GOS) subsequently turned to the International Monetary Fund (IMF) for support. In an attempt to meet the conditions for a stand-by loan, they implemented a program made up by radical reforms. These included a fundamental liberalization of the exchange rate regime, involving the devaluation and floatation of the Seychellois Rupee (SCR) and the elimination of all foreign exchange controls.

Seychelles' implementation and completion of this five-year reform program in late 2013 received praise from the IMF and was helped by ongoing market-based reforms. Seychelles welcomes foreign investment. However, while the country's investment policies encourage the development and utilization of Seychelles' natural resources, the improvement of its national infrastructure, and an increase in productivity levels, the GOS also stresses the paramount importance of achieving this in an environmentally sound and sustainable manner.

While the GOS has attempted to diversify the economy, it remains primarily focused on two sectors; fishing and tourism. Seychelles' vast Exclusive Economic Zone (EEZ), which encompasses 1.3 million square kilometers of the western Indian Ocean, is viewed as a potential source of untapped oil reserves and represents potential business opportunities for U.S. entities. Seychelles also has a small, but growing, offshore financial sector. There is also scope for U.S. investment in renewable energy as Seychelles seeks to reduce its heavy dependence on imported fossil fuels while preserving its naturally beautiful environment.

1. OPENNESS TO, AND RESTRICTIONS UPON, FOREIGN INVESTMENT

Attitude toward Foreign Direct Investment

Seychelles welcomes foreign direct investment. The government's objective is to promote economic and commercial relationships to sustain its tourism and fishing industries, which are currently the main drivers of economic growth, as well as to diversify the economy. However, certain types of businesses have been classified by the GOS as reserved for domestic investors only:

Accommodation of up to 10 rooms (excluding luxury villas)

Liveaboard (overnight scuba services up to 2 boats)

Travel Agent

Tourist Guide

Car Hire Operator (foreign franchises must be maintained by Seychellois)

Tour Operators

Boat Charter

Taxi Operator

Diving Centers (excluding dive operators)

Water Sports

Cottage Industry Projects

Video Shops

Internet Reseller

Public Exhibition of Films

Employment Agency

Building Contractor (with limited exceptions)

Artisanal Fishing

Small Enterprises (except where the project introduces or ventures into an area never before invested in, or introduces new technology that has never before been applied in Seychelles).

Other Investment Policy Reviews

Seychelles has recently completely its accession into the World Trade Organization (WTO) at the end of 2014. To date, Seychelles has not been scheduled for a WTO, Trade Policy Review. Likewise it has not conducted an investment policy review through the Organization for Economic Cooperation and Development (OECD), or the United Nations Conference on Trade and Development (UNCTAD).

Laws/Regulations of Foreign Direct Investment

Foreign direct investment in Seychelles is governed by the Seychelles Investment Act of 2010. Since the financial crisis of 2008 and under the auspices of the IMF reform program, Seychelles has made great strides to attract and protect foreign direct investment in the country, despite a lingering perception among the local population that well-connected foreign investors or government personnel receive special treatment in investment disputes. The Seychelles Investment Board (SIB) serves as the investment promotion agency for Seychelles and can advise all foreign investors of the laws, regulations, and procedures for their activities in Seychelles. SIB's website is found at www.sib.gov.sc.

Industrial Promotion

Seychelles' economy is heavily dependent on fisheries and tourism. In an effort to diversify its economic base, the government of Seychelles seeks investment in the following areas:

Agribusiness

Food processing and packaging

Eco-tourism and health/medical tourism

Renewable energy

Marine technology, including oil exploration

Ocean industry support services

Environmental technologies, including, solid waste management and recycling

Seychelles' Exclusive Economic Zone (EEZ) is viewed as a potential source of oil reserves. Initial exploration has already begun to the immediate north of the main inner island grouping (Mahé, Praslin, and La Digue), and there is potential for further exploration in other areas. Petro Seychelles, which was established in 2012, is responsible for the upstream sector of the oil industry, including the promotion and supervision of oil exploration activities in Seychelles' waters.

There is also scope for investment in the renewable energy sector as Seychelles seeks to reduce its heavy dependence on imported fossil fuels while preserving its near-pristine environment. The government is working closely with several donors, including the International Finance Corporation (IFC), the Abu Dhabi Fund for Development, and the United Nations Development Program (UNDP) to encourage cleaner energy production and energy efficiency investments.

Limits on Foreign Control

Seychelles does not place limits on foreign ownership or control of resident companies. While SIB and the government of Seychelles encourage foreign investors to collaborate with a local partner, there is no formal requirement.

Privatization Program

The GOS remains a major player in the local economy although the private sector is expanding, especially into the tourism and services sectors. A key aspect of the government's reform program relates to increasing the economy's market orientation and supporting private sector development. In this context, the government worked closely with the IMF and the World Bank to accelerate its privatization program and improve the business climate through a comprehensive review of the legal and regulatory framework. At present, there are no plans for further privatization of major government enterprises such as Public Utilities Corporation or the Seychelles Housing Company. There are no formal legal barriers to foreign investors participating in privatization.

Screening of FDI

The Seychelles Investment Board (SIB) is a one-stop shop for all matters relating to business and investment in Seychelles. SIB's main function is to promote investment and facilitate the investment process in line with the administrative, policy and legal framework. SIB also assists in screening potential investment projects in cooperation with other government agencies. The government of Seychelles is particularly keen to ensure that no business activity is undertaken at the expense of Seychelles' natural environment. In order for a business to be operational, all prospective investors need to apply for a license from the Seychelles Licensing Authority (SLA).

Competition Law

SIB reviews all transactions for competition-related concerns (whether domestic or international in nature).

Investment Trends

The Seychelles' economy is dominated by tourism and fishing, with the real estate development of reclaimed islands having also emerged in most recent years. Due to the oversupply in the hotel industry, however, most current investment is focused on seafood processing.

Table 1

Measure	Year	Index or Rank	Website Address
TI Corruption Perceptions index	2014	43 of 175	transparency.org/cpi2014/results
World Bank's Doing Business Report "Ease of Doing Business"	2015	85 of 189	doingbusiness.org/rankings
Global Innovation Index	2014	51 of 143	globalinnovationindex.org/content.aspx?page=data-analysis
World Bank GNI per capita	2013	USD 13,210	data.worldbank.org/indicator/NY.GNP.PCAP.CD

2. CONVERSION AND TRANSFER POLICIES

Foreign Exchange

Since the IMF reform package of 2008-2013, there are no restrictions or limitations placed on foreign investors converting, transferring, or repatriating funds associated with investment. Funds are freely converted. Seychelles maintains a floating exchange rate for the Seychelles Rupee, which has mostly fluctuated between SCR 12 and SCR 15 to USD 1 over the past five years.

Remittance Policies

All foreign exchange controls were also removed in 2008 and foreign investors are free to repatriate their profits and other incomes. We do not know of any planned changes to remittance policies, time limits on remittances, or use of any legal parallel market. According to the Department of State's Bureau for International Narcotics and Law Enforcement Affairs Money

Laundering and Financial Crimes database, Seychelles is currently listed as a country/jurisdiction "of concern."

3. EXPROPRIATION AND COMPENSATION

The Lands Acquisition Act 1978, last amended in 1990, states that in the event of compulsory acquisition or taking of possession of any property by the government, the latter should pay prompt and full compensation for the property. The GOS may expropriate property in cases of public interest or for public safety. Following the 1977 coup, the new GOS engaged in expropriation of land for redistribution or for use by the state. With the return of a multi-party political system in 1992, the GOS compensated some of those who had lost land to expropriation/redistribution in the late 1970s. There have been no expropriations since the 1990s aside from public works and infrastructure projects. We see no indications of possible major expropriation in the future and no pattern of discrimination against U.S. persons.

4. DISPUTE SETTLEMENT

Legal System, Specialized Courts, Judicial Independence, Judgments of Foreign Courts

Seychelles has a unique mixed jurisdiction legal system; English common law, influences of the Napoleonic Code and customary law. Civil law is governed by a Civil Code of Seychelles, which is derived from the French Napoleonic Code. The civil code covers contractual and tort matters. Criminal law is substantially based on British criminal law. Procedural law is based on British common law. The sources of law are mainly through legislation. The supreme law of the land is the Constitution. Commercial Law is based on English Common Law. The highest court is the Court of Appeal. Seychelles does not maintain a specialized commercial court. The judicial branch is independent of the executive branch; many Seychellois believe that well-connected individuals receive special treatment in the courts.

Judgments of foreign courts are governed by the Foreign Judgments (Reciprocal Enforcement) Act of 1961, Section 3.

Bankruptcy

Bankruptcy in Seychelles is governed under the Insolvency Act of 2013. According to the Act, an individual may be discharged from bankruptcy 3 years from the date of its declaration. Bankruptcy is not criminalized in Seychelles. According to the World Bank's Doing Business Report, Seychelles ranks 68th out of 189 countries on the Resolving Insolvency index.

Investment Disputes

Parties involved in investment disputes are encouraged to resolve their disputes through arbitration and negotiation. The Seychelles Investment Act of 2010 provides for an Investment Appeal Panel to which aggrieved investors may appeal for a review of a decision made by a public sector agency with regard to their investments or proposed investments in Seychelles. In addition, investors may appeal to the Supreme Court (Court of Appeal) in the event they are not satisfied with the decision of the Investment Appeal Panel.

International Arbitration

Due to Seychelles' small size and relatively short recent history with foreign direct investment, there is no precedent for international arbitration in Seychelles, although the legal framework exists through the Seychelles Investment Act of 2010.

ICSID Convention and New York Convention

In 1978 Seychelles became a member state to the International Centre for the Settlement of Investment Disputes (ICSID Convention). Seychelles is not a signatory to the Recognition and Enforcement of Foreign Arbitral Awards (1958 New York Convention).

Duration of Dispute Resolution

The court system in Seychelles in general is slow. Business disputes litigated in court can last three to five years before finally reaching a judgment; minimal financial and personnel resources, as well as the possibility of multiple appeals, all contribute to a significant backlog of cases. If and when resolved, however, court decisions are generally enforced. The government of Seychelles and the Seychelles Investment Board encourage arbitration through the Investment Appeal Panel as detailed in the Seychelles Investment Act of 2010.

5. PERFORMANCE REQUIREMENTS AND INVESTMENT INCENTIVES

WTO/TRIMS

U.S embassy is not aware of the GOS maintaining any measures inconsistent with the Trade Related Investment Measures requirements. The Seychelles National Assembly ratified World Trade Organization (WTO) accession on March 23, 2015. Seychelles become the 161st member.

Investment Incentives

Seychelles provides incentives for investment in several sectors, including: the fisheries sector under the Fisheries Incentives Act; the tourism sector under the Tourism Incentives Act; investments in the International Trade Zone under the Seychelles International Trade Zone Act; and fiscal incentives under the Investment Code. Incentives under these Acts most often take the form of tax credits, tax holidays, duty-free access for the import of materials required for the initial investment, and expedited work permits for foreign employees that move to Seychelles.

Research and Development

We do not know of any barriers to U.S. or other foreign firm participation in government/authority-financed research and development programs. Seychelles welcomes collaboration from foreign partners in research, technology transfer, and development of new sectors.

Performance Requirements

Investors operating in Seychelles are expected to abide by the following obligations:

> To comply with the provisions of the governing laws on investment procedures and to carry out investment activities correctly in accordance with the relevant approvals granted. This includes the responsibility of the investor for the accuracy and truthfulness of the contents of investment proposals and registration; and of the lawfulness of document on certification;

To discharge fully their financial obligations, including taxation, in accordance with the law;

To carry out the provisions of the laws on accounting and auditing;

To carry out the provisions of the laws on registration of companies and other legal entity;

To carry out the provisions of the employment laws and regulations.

The government of Seychelles does not mandate local employment. There are no local employment mandates for senior management or directors. Visa, residence, and work permit requirements are not excessively onerous.

Data Storage

Information not available.

6. RIGHT TO PRIVATE OWNERSHIP AND ESTABLISHMENT

Foreign and domestic investors are able to own and hold lands subject to the provisions of the Immovable Property (Transfer Restriction) Act of 1963.

In March 2014, the sale of freehold estates to non-Seychellois was stopped and the GOS introduced a policy on Alienation of Land and the Management and sale of state land as well as a Villa Policy. Non-citizens can still buy land freehold from private owners.

Foreigners can obtain long term leases of state land. Before leasing land from the government, a foreign investor must submit a project proposal to the Seychelles Investment Board for approval. Foreign nationals or companies engaging in foreign participation must obtain permission from the Ministry of Land Use and Housing before completing a purchase. The investor will need to use a notary or attorney to manage the transfer of ownership when buying land from a private individual or company, which will then need to be registered at the Registration Office.

In practice, the government engages in leases ranging from 60-99 years for commercial or industrial activities and has stopped selling state land.

7. PROTECTION OF PROPERTY RIGHTS

Real Property

Yes, interests in property are enforced. Mortgages and liens exist and are enforced; the land registrar is reliable and in use for the resolution of land disputes going back generations. All lands in Seychelles are either publicly or privately held. According to the World Bank's Doing Business Report, Seychelles ranked 78th out of 189 countries in the Registering Property index in 2014.

Intellectual Property Rights

The Republic of Seychelles respects intellectual property rights, and regards laws and other measures to protect them as crucial for long-term economic development. Efficient and effective protection of Intellectual Property Rights is considered vital by the government for promoting foreign investment, the transfer and dissemination of technology, and protecting local businesses and artists as well as facilitating the integration of Seychelles' into the regional and global economies. Seychelles joined the World Intellectual Property Organization (WIPO) in March 2000. In addition, the country became a contracting party to the Paris Convention for the Protection of Industrial Property and the Patent Cooperation Treaty (PCT) in November 2002. Seychelles is also a member of the African Regional Intellectual Property Organization (ARIPO). In 2013, an Intellectual Property Office was established to enable the registration of patents, trademarks and copyrights.

The Copyright Act, the Trade Marks Decree and the Patents Act contain provisions that lay down the procedures and measures dealing with infringement of intellectual property rights. All foreign nationals and Seychelles citizens are treated equally in regard to IP laws. Seychelles legislation will not discriminate between nationals and foreigners, following WTO principles. Enforcement of IPR protection laws is limited due to the fact that very few international brands and trademarks have local or even regional representatives.

While no statistics are publicly available, the Seychelles Revenue Commission's customs officials monitor incoming shipments for counterfeit goods. However, their focus is on counterfeit products that pose a public health risk, such as medications and electrical appliances. Counterfeit (or unlicensed sale of) apparel, CDs, and DVDs are generally available.

Seychelles is not listed on USTR's 2014 Special 301 report or the Review of Notorious Markets Report. For additional information about treaty obligations and points of contact at local IP offices, please see WIPO's country profiles at http://www.wipo.int/directory/en/.

Resources for Rights Holders

Patrick Koucheravy
Economic Officer
U.S. Embassy to Mauritius and Seychelles
Port Louis, Mauritius
+230 202 4410

KoucheravyPE@state.gov

A list of available attorneys practicing in Seychelles can be found at http://seychelles.usvpp.gov/list_of_attorneys2.html.

8. TRANSPARENCY OF THE REGULATORY SYSTEM

Although the government has made considerable efforts to liberalize the economy, Seychelles continues to suffer from overregulation. Concerns over government corruption have focused on the lack of transparency in the privatization and allocation of government-owned land and businesses. While the legal and regulatory framework is in place for transparent governance, many Seychellois believe that those well-connected to the government of Seychelles, whether foreign or local, receive preferential treatment.

In an attempt to promote greater transparency in the public procurement system, Seychelles' National Tender Board publishes all its tenders on its web site and local newspapers. It also publicizes the contracts that have been awarded, including the name of the successful bidder as well as the bid amount in all local newspapers. The government has also set up a Procurement Oversight Unit, which serves as a public procurement policy and monitoring body.

Proposed laws and regulations are published in the Official Gazette on a monthly basis, but often such legislation is voted into law by the National Assembly before the Official Gazette notifying the public of proposed legislation has been made publicly available.

9. EFFICIENT CAPITAL MARKETS AND PORTFOLIO INVESTMENT

Seychelles' financial services sector is regulated by the following laws: Financial Institutions Act 2004, Anti-Money Laundering Act 2006, Data Protection Act, Mutual and Hedge Fund Act 2007 and Central Bank Act 2004. In addition to the Central Bank of Seychelles, there are eight commercial banks: Bank of Baroda, Barclays Bank, Habib Bank, Mauritius Commercial Bank, Nouvobanq, Seychelles Commercial Bank, BMI Offshore Bank, and Bank of Ceylon. Seychelles also has two non-banking financial institutions, the Seychelles Credit Union and the Development Bank of Seychelles, which provide flexible financing for businesses and projects to promote economic growth and employment.

A wide range of financial services such as checking (current) accounts, savings accounts, loans, transactions in foreign currencies, and foreign currency accounts are available in the banking system. The government established a securities exchange at the end of November 2012 as part of its efforts to diversify the financial services sector.

Seychelles welcomes foreign portfolio investment. Portfolio investment in Seychelles is limited by the small size of the economy and banking sector; the entry and exit of sizeable positions may have an outsized impact on the Seychelles Rupee and the economy in general. Existing policies do facilitate the free flow of financial resources in and out of the economy. The government of Seychelles respects IMF Article VIII by refraining from restrictions on payments and transfers for current international transaction. Foreign investors are able to obtain credit on the local market and through the Seychelles banking system; a variety of credit instruments are available to both local and foreign investors.

Money and Banking System, Hostile Takeovers

Seychelles has a two-tier banking system separating the central and commercial bank functions and roles. The commercial banks, both domestic and foreign, are regulated and supervised by the Central Bank of Seychelles. According to the Central Bank of Seychelles Act 2004, the CBS is responsible for the formulation and implementation of the Seychelles' Monetary and Exchange Rate policies. The Central Bank of Seychelles is the only administrative body responsible for receiving applications for banking licenses, whether domestic or offshore, and issuing the corresponding licenses.

The Seychelles banking sector is generally healthy, although it is limited by its small size and is reliant on correspondent bank relationships. According to the Central Bank of Seychelles in February 2015 nonperforming loans to total gross loans in the Seychelles banking sector stood at 7 percent, net foreign assets stood at SCR 9.5 billion (USD 708 million), and net domestic assets stood at SCR 5.9 billion (USD 440 million).

Foreigners and foreign/offshore firms must establish some residency or proof of business registration in order to obtain a bank account.

10. COMPETITION FROM STATE-OWNED ENTERPRISES

Seychelles is one of 14 countries participating in the State Owned Enterprises (SOE) Network for Southern Africa, which was launched in 2007 to support, in collaboration with the OECD, the southern African countries in their efforts to improve the performance of SOEs. The government has shares in a number of enterprises, including Air Seychelles, the Indian Ocean Tuna Company, Seychelles Commercial Bank, and Seychelles Broadcasting Corporation. Seychelles' SOEs are active in housing, civil aviation, tourism, banking, import/export, retail, and public utilities. There is no standing list of Seychelles SOEs or parastatal entities, but they are audited on a rotating basis by the Office of the Auditor General. SOE structure varies by sector and mandate. The Seychelles economy is so small and focused on fishing, tourism, and offshore finance that there is often little space for more than one major operator, whether it is private or public. SOEs are free to purchase and/or supply goods and services from private sector and foreign firms, depending on the sector and situation. There is a growing concern in the business community that SOEs such as Seychelles Trading Company have been allowed to exceed their explicit mandate and compete unfairly.

In March 2007, the government presented its National Development Plan - Seychelles Strategy 2017 - with the overarching objective of reducing the commercial activities of the State and stimulating private sector development.

OECD Guidelines on Corporate Governance of SOEs

The governance of SOEs varies depending on their purpose and structure. Seychelles' SOEs do not adhere to the OECD Guidelines on Corporate Governance for SOEs. Most SOEs and parastatal bodies both maintain a board of directors and make regular reports to the corresponding Minister/Ministry. Seats on the boards of many Seychelles' SOEs are appointed by the President.

Sovereign Wealth Funds

Seychelles does not maintain any sovereign wealth funds.

11. CORPORATE SOCIAL RESPONSIBILITY

Seychelles has a great awareness of corporate social responsibility, especially in environmental protection and social programs, but CSR is generally regarded as a function of government. Since 2013, the Seychelles Revenue Commission collects a CSR tax of 0.5 percent on monthly turnover for businesses with an annual turnover of SCR 1 million. Officially, there are no waivers available for foreign investors with regard to labor, employment rights, consumer protection, or environmental protections. The Citizens Engagement Platform Seychelles, an umbrella organization for Seychelles' NGOs, provides a summary list of NGOs active in the country on an annual basis to the Ministry of Finance, who then decides which organizations would benefit most from the CSR tax revenues. The areas recently targeted under CSR include: the environment; waste and coastal management projects; health and wellness, including sports and leisure; training and capacity building; small enterprise development; community development; child and youth development; and arts and crafts.

OECD Guidelines for Multinational Enterprises

Seychelles is not an adherent to the OECD Guidelines for Multinational Enterprises.

12. POLITICAL VIOLENCE

The People's Party, commonly known as Lepep, has governed Seychelles since the 1977 coup and has won every election since they introduced multi-party democracy in 1992. The constitution provides citizens the right to change their government peacefully, and citizens exercise this right in practice through periodic elections based on universal suffrage. Seychelles has not experienced large-scale political violence since the late 1970s.

13. CORRUPTION

While Seychelles provides a legal framework for combatting corruption, they have taken little action in response to allege corruption and still many Seychellois believe that those with close connections to government received preferential access and treatment.

In 2003, the government of Seychelles published the Public Service Code of Ethics and Conduct, the stated purpose of which is to provide guidance to public sector employees on the standards of behavior required of them and "to provide a basis for more detailed codes that are required to meet the particular circumstances of individual public sector organizations." The Public Officer's Ethics Act of 2008 prohibits personal enrichment through public office, defines and outlaws bribery, provides guidelines for avoiding conflict of interest, and mandates declaration of financial assets for public officials.

The government does not require private companies to establish internal codes of conduct. There is no dedicated anti-corruption unit in the Seychelles. The constitution provides for an Ombudsman, but in practice the Office of the Ombudsman has not been proactive in rooting out corruption and investigating allegations in collaboration with the police. We do not know of any NGOs investigating corruption in Seychelles.

UN Anticorruption Convention, OECD Convention on Combatting Bribery

Seychelles signed the UN Convention against Corruption in February 2004 and ratified in March 2006. Seychelles is not party to the OECD Convention on Combating Bribery of Foreign Public Officials in International Business Transactions.

Resources to Report Corruption

Dora Zatte
The Ombudsman
Office of the Ombudsman
Room 306, Aarti Chambers, Mont Fleuri, Mahé
+248 225147
ombuds@seychelles.net

14. BILATERAL INVESTMENT AGREEMENTS

Seychelles has not signed a treaty or agreement with the United States.

Bilateral Taxation Treaties

Seychelles signed Double Taxation Avoidance Agreements with China, South Africa, Oman, Botswana, Mauritius, Thailand, Malaysia, Vietnam, Cyprus, Belgium, Indonesia, the United Arab Emirates, Barbados, Kuwait, Qatar, and Zimbabwe, Bahrain, Kenya, Sri Lanka, and Guernsey. Seychelles has signed Bilateral Investment Treaties with Cyprus, Egypt, China, and India.

15. OPIC AND OTHER INVESTMENT INSURANCE PROGRAMS

Seychelles and the United States signed an OPIC investment agreement in 2012: https://www.opic.gov/sites/default/files/docs/africa/Seychelles-signed-02-03-2012-entered-into-force-10-05-2012.pdf. Due to the small size of the economy, there is little potential for OPIC programs in Seychelles, although Seychellois firms and investors may seek OPIC financing or insurance for joint ventures elsewhere in Africa and Asia.

16. LABOR

Seychelles' labor force is estimated at 52,000, out of which about 70 percent are employed by the private sector. Foreign migrant workers, who comprise about 24 percent of the labor force, are mainly employed in the construction and commercial fishing sectors. The unemployment rate is estimated at 3 percent, nearly full employment following the five-year IMF reform program.

Seychelles has been a member of the International Labor Organization (ILO) since 1977, and has ratified all of the International Labor Organization (ILO) fundamental conventions. Under Seychellois law, all workers, with the exception of police, military, prison, and firefighting personnel, have the right to form and organize unions of their own choosing, to participate in collective bargaining, and to conduct legal strikes. However, such right is limited or restricted by other provisions of law. Although collective bargaining is legal it rarely happens because the law gives the right to the government to review and approve all collective bargaining agreements in both the private and public sector. Strikes are illegal in Seychelles unless all other arbitration procedures have been exhausted. Furthermore, the Public Order Act of 2014 defines an illegal protest as the gathering of more than one person, unless the protesters have received permission from the Seychelles Police.

Seychelles has a government-mandated minimum wage of SCR 4,050 (USD 300) per month based on a 35-hour work week. In the event of layoffs where there is no employee misconduct, the employer must provide the worker with one month's notice or the equivalent of one month's salary. Additionally, for workers that have been employed for five years or more, the employer is obligated to pay a day's pay for each month that the employee has worked for the employer. There is no distinction between layoffs and firing with severance.

The government of Seychelles introduced the Occupational Safety and Health Decree in 2012 and the Prohibition of Trafficking in Persons Act in 2014. Seychelles Police and customs personnel have traveled to USG-led training at the International Law Enforcement Academy in Gaborone, Botswana. However, there are very few health or labor inspectors in Seychelles and they are limited by meager public resources and the vast ocean distances they are expected to cover.

In November 2011, Seychelles and the ILO signed the 2011-2015 Decent Work Country Program, which seeks to address such issues as employment creation, consolidation and protection of workers' rights, enhancing social protection, and strengthening social dialogue.

17. FOREIGN TRADE ZONES/FREE PORTS/TRADE FACILITATION

The Seychelles International Trade Zone (SITZ) Act of 1995 provides for the establishment of international trade zones, which aim to combine the benefits of a free port and an export processing zone. So far a number of locations have been declared International Trade Zones. A wide range of business activities is permissible provided they are export-oriented.

The concessions available to license holders in SITZ include the following:

Exemption from customs duties on capital equipment to be used in SITZ;
Exemption from Business Tax, Trades Tax and Withholding Tax;
Exemption from social security contributions;
Exemption from fees with respect to work permits;
Entitlement to full foreign ownership.

18. FOREIGN DIRECT INVESTMENT AND FOREIGN PORTFOLIO INVESTMENT STATISTICS

Table 2: Key Macroeconomic Data, U.S. FDI in Host Country/Economy

	Host Country Statistical source*		USG or international statistical source		USG or International Source of Data: BEA; IMF; Eurostat; UNCTAD, Other
Economic Data	Year	Amount	Year	Amount	
Host Country Gross Domestic Product (GDP) ($M USD)	2013	1,410	2013	1,443	www.worldbank.org/en/country
Foreign Direct Investment	Host Country Statistical source*		USG or international statistical source		USG or international Source of data: BEA; IMF; Eurostat; UNCTAD, Other
U.S. FDI in partner country ($M USD, stock positions)	2013	N/A	2013	N/A	Note: no data available from host country. BEA data indicates non-zero figure between -$500,000 and $500,000.
Host country's FDI in the United States ($M USD, stock positions)	2013	N/A	2013	N/A	Note: no data available from host country. BEA data indicates non-zero figure between -$500,000 and $500,000.
Total inbound stock of FDI as % host GDP	2013	N/A	2013	161.4%	Source: UNCTAD World Investment Report 2014

*Seychelles National Bureau of Statistics

Table 3: Sources and Destination of FDI

Seychelles and Mauritius have both in recent years focused on developing their offshore financial sectors. A significant amount of FDI in the region is intended for other countries/economies in the region.

Direct Investment from/in Counterpart Economy Data
From Top Five Sources/To Top Five Destinations (US Dollars, Millions)

Inward Direct Investment			Outward Direct Investment		
Total Inward	1,080	100%	Total Outward	N/A	100%
Mauritius	438	41%			
Cyprus	228	21%			
Russian Federation	127	12%			
United Kingdom	55	5%			
United States	43	4%			
"0" reflects amounts rounded to +/- USD 500,000.					

ADVANTAGES OF SEYCHELLES

Seychelles is an established and reputable offshore jurisdiction offering international businessmen and investors a range of sophisticated offshore products that meet the increasingly demanding criteria of flexibility as well as adaptability. The regulatory environment has been carefully developed, in a public/private partnership, to adhere to international obligations of global best practices, which at the same time take into account the expectations and demands of the offshore market. Other key reasons for choosing Seychelles as an International Financial Centre include:

no Exchange Controls
fiscal Incentives
expanding Double Taxation Avoidance Treaty Network
a skilled, professional and bilingual population
modern communication network
reputable jurisdiction
sophisticated, modern & flexible offshore structures

This is complemented by the business approach and strategy adopted by government with the further development of the offshore industry.

Key elements are: (i) flexibility; (ii) adaptability; (iii) security; (iv) confidentiality; (v) professional services through automation, training and regulations; and (vi) networking.

The Seychelles represents a bigger market for Britain than is suggested by its small population of barely 80,000. At present (December 2000), Seychelles' purchasing power is at an all time low, due to a chronic shortage of foreign exchange, which is being made worse by a depreciating Rupee. Thus, in recent years, Seychellois importers have increasingly had to look to cheaper sources such as South Africa and the Far East. From being second largest exporter to Seychelles two years ago with approximately £20million, Britain settled for fourth position with sales of £14.2m. in 1999.

However, there are as always pockets of opportunity for British business, particularly in the Tourism sector. A number of `five star' hotel developments by groups such as the Banyan Tree, Beachcomber, Sun International, Sofitel have been proposed/ are already underway. In order to capture the higher end of the tourism market to Seychelles, the Government has set up a number of incentives schemes, which includes the operation of foreign currency accounts. The ability for the major hotels to transact in foreign currency, without having recourse to the local bank's foreign currency pipelines is an obvious advantage. The construction of these resorts present any opportunities for British suppliers of goods and services.

There is talk locally of IMF/ World Bank rescue packages which would include cash injections on the one hand and devaluation on the other, as well as privatisation - all of which would have obvious effects in different market sectors in 2001.

Overseas Press and Media Association
C/o Powers International Ltd
517-523 Fulham Road
London
SW6 1HD

Website: http://www.opma.co.uk/
Tel: 020 7630 9966
Fax: 020 7385 5555

The print media is the main mode of advertising in Seychelles, as Television is limited to only one national channel with very few commercials.

Advertising is done mainly through:

Seychelles Nation: The official daily newspaper
Website: www.seychelles-online.co.sc
E-mail: nation@seychelles.net
Tel: 225775 Fax: 321006)

As well the Regar (Tel: 224507/ 224987) and The People (Tel: 224455/225070) which are weekly newspapers;

Other publications, such as the following carry corporate advertisements.

Seychelles Review, Tel: 323700,

Seychelles Today, Tel: 225619
E-mail: seyunltd@seychelles.net,

Chamber of Commerce newsletter, Tel: 323812, Fax: 321422
E-mail: scci@seychelles.net,

A growing number of local companies, particularly retail outlets, are finding the popular local Radio Station - Paradise FM, E-mail: sbcadmin@seychelles.net, a useful advertising tool.

Direct mail, cinema and outdoor advertising have for various reasons not caught on in Seychelles.

There are no more than 5 advertising agencies operating in Seychelles.

Meanwhile, word of mouth remains an important force in this tiny market.

SELLING PRODUCTS AND SERVICES

SALES PROMOTION

It is important for price lists to be included, because many local companies may not make the effort to find out more about products in the brochures, instinctively assuming (often wrongly) that UK prices are higher than elsewhere. Due to the foreign exchange constraints, local firms are increasingly turning to the Far East and South Africa.

INTERNET / E-COMMERCE

Though the internet is fast catching up with fax as a business tool, e-commerce still has quite some way to go in Seychelles. Nonetheless as a second ISP has recently come on the scene, it is very likely that internet use will escalate in the coming year.

COUNTERTRADE

Where cash-based trading is difficult, countertrade offers the best chance for securing a deal. Our Countertrade pages can give further information on this.

TERMS OF PAYMENT

In view of the ongoing shortages of foreign exchange in Seychelles, it is advisable for UK suppliers to demand cash against documents. There is no debt collecting agency and all litigants have to go through the courts.

EXPORT FINANCING AND INSURANCE

The Trade Partners UK Export Finance team encourages the availability of competitive export finance to all UK companies seeking to export goods or services or invest overseas. For further information on how we can help you, please see the Export Finance pages.

Export Credits Guarantee Department (ECGD)
Can provide insurance or arrange medium/long-term finance packages in a wide range of markets worldwide for UK exporters of capital goods and projects. They can also provide contacts for private sector insurance for UK exporters of consumables. For more information on how ECGD may be able to help you visit the ECGD website or contact their helpline: E-mail: help@ecgd.gov.uk Tel: 020 7512 7887

Insurance for short-term credit
A number of companies provide insurance for short-term credit to guard against non-payment, such as:

Tel: 029 20824000
Fax: 029 20824003
Tel: 020 7512 9333
Fax: 020 7512 9186
Tel: 020 7623 9043
Tel: 020 7325 7620

GETTING YOUR GOODS TO THE MARKET

The British International Freight Association's New Importer / Exporter Initiative aims to provide specialist help and assistance to companies who are new to exporting. This service, available through selected BIFA registered members, offers up to one day's free consultancy to advise companies on such matters as modes of transport, distribution methods, costing, documentation and payment terms. They can be contacted on 020 8844 2266.

The Delmas Line serves Felixstowe to Victoria once a fortnight while the Maersk Line does the same route every 18 days. The local agents are Hunt Deltel & Co. Ltd
P.O Box 14
Trinity House, Victoria
email: hundel@seychelles.net
Tel: 380300
Fax: 225367

Port Victoria is equipped with four mobile cranes of up to 41 tonnes capacity and has storage space of 6,600 square metres. Up to 6 ships can be accommodated in the outer harbour area at one time and the 370 metre quay can handle 2 ships at any one time.

COMMUNICATION

INTERNET / EMAIL

There is growing use of email in Seychelles, though not all businesses are on-line. There are two ISP's in Seychelles, with their two respective cyber cafes situated in Victoria. The 2 companies are:

ATLAS:
E-mail: Atlas@seychelles.net

KOKONET:
E-mail:Kokonet@seychelles.sc

The major hotels have business centres with internet facilities.

TELEPHONE

International Direct Dialling is available in Seychelles. The area code to the Seychelles is 248.

There are two telecommunications companies operating in Seychelles: Cable & Wireless (Seychelles) Ltd and Telecom Seychelles Ltd (Airtel). In addition to fixed lines telephones and fax, the following telecommunication services are available in Seychelles: fixed bills or prepaid mobile phones/ voicemail/ international roaming, ISDN and PABX systems. Mobile phones are widely used and are available for purchase or hire. Public payphones are available in Victoria and suburbs in most villages, hotels, public buildings and other places in Mahe, Praslin and La Digue.

Cable and Wireless (Seychelles) Ltd is the largest and longest established of the two. It's rates to the UK are as follows:

Peak rate : R8.89 per minute

Off-Peak: R6.95 per minute

Peak hours: 0700hrs-1900hrs: Mondays to Fridays Off-Peak hours begin 1900hrs Fridays- to 0700hrs Mondays and all day on public holidays.

Emergency numbers

Fire Brigade, Police, Ambulance : 999

Important numbers

International Operator - free call (Cable and Wireless):
151 Victoria Hospital: 388000
Dr Haresh Jivan (Private GP): 324008

Dr Alan Nimmo, Specialised Dental Clinic: 225822
Central Police Station: 288000
Pointe la Rue Airport: 384000/ International Flight enquiries: 384400 Meteorological Office: 383377

FAX

This is the most frequently used method of doing business with overseas - it is widely available (in all hotels and most businesses) and charged at the same rate as telephone calls.

POST

Exporters are advised to use airmail which can take as little as three days to reach addressee in Seychelles; surface mail can take up to 2 months. For local mail, next-day delivery is almost always guaranteed.

The Central Post Office in Victoria is open Monday to Friday (0800 –1600hrs) and on Saturday (0800 – 1200hrs).

COURIER SERVICES

Two companies operate courier services in Seychelles. They are:
1-DHL
Hunt Deltel & Co. Ltd
P.O Box 14
Trinity House, Victoria
email: hundel@seychellesnet
Tel: 380300
Fax: 225367

2- TNT Express Worldwide
Shipping House
P.O Box 336, Victoria
email: maheship@seychelles.net
Tel: 380500
Fax: 322978

REGULATIONS

LOCAL REPRESENTATION / AGENTS AND DISTRIBUTORS AGENCY LEGISLATION

There is no legislation governing local agency appointments.

State trading organisations / privitisation role and contacts / trade promotion organisations

The Seychelles Marketing Board (SMB) is a parastatal which acts as the Central Procurement Agency. It has the monopoly on the import of a number of categories of staple goods into Seychelles, and a virtual monopoly on many more.

SMB
P.O Box 634
Victoria
Tel: 285000
Fax: 224735
Email: smb01@seychelles.net

STANDARDS AND TECHNICAL REGULATIONS

Technical Help for Exporters (THE) is a service provided by the British Standards Institution (BSI) to provide information and advice on compliance with overseas statutory and other technical requirements.

THE produces a wide range of publications and provides a special updating service of information in some product fields. THE can supply detailed information on foreign regulations; identify, supply and assist in the interpretation of foreign standards and approval procedures; research and consult on technical requirements for a specific product; and provide translations of foreign standards, items of legislation and codes of practice.

Fees vary according to the amount of work involved.

For further information visit the British Standards Institution (BSI) website or e-mail: The@bsi-global.com

The Seychelles Bureau of Standards advises on local standards requirements (British standards are widely used):

P. O Box 953
Victoria
Tel: 375333
Fax: 375151
Email: sbsorg@seychelles.net
Website: www.seychelles.net\sbsorg

LABELLING AND PACKAGING REGULATIONS

As a rule of thumb, packaging which complies with UK regulations will be acceptable in Seychelles. Markings may be in English.

Enquiries regarding specialist packaging and labelling should be directed to:

Seychelles Bureau of Standards
P. O Box 953
Victoria
Tel: 375333
Fax: 375151
Email: sbsorg@seychelles.net
Website: www.seychelles.net\sbsorg

PATENTS AND TRADEMARKS

The UK Patent Office supplies information on Patents, Designs, Trademark and Copyright, including free information packs. For further information e-mail: enquiries@patent.gov.uk or contact the **Central Enquiry Unit** on 08459 500 505.

All enquiries about patents and trade marks should be addressed to:

The Registrar General
Department of Legal Affairs
Rm 8, Kingsgate House
P.O Box 142
Victoria
Tel: 224904

Seychelles is signatory to WIPO

EXCHANGE CONTROLS

In theory, there are no official restrictions on foreign currency transfer in and out of Seychelles, provided one can prove that the currency was obtained by legitimate means ie. Through banks and not the (ever growing) black market.

In practice however, the chronic shortage of foreign currency is a restriction in itself. Banks take many months to process payments owed overseas.

IMPORT CONTROLS

An import permit must be obtained from the Ministry of Finance for all imports which are usually issued within 48 hours of application. The 2 main categories of restrictions on imports are `dangerous goods' and the `essential items' that are the preserve of the Seychelles Marketing Board. Each company is allowed an import quota (financial quota) and import permits have to be sought for each consignment within the quota before ordering goods. This measure was put in place due to the ongoing shortages of foreign exchange.

Refer to:
Import Permit Section
Ministry of Finance

Oceangate House
Victoria
Tel: 382092
Fax: 225265

EXPORT CONTROLS

The Government maintains export controls to prevent the export of goods, including technology, for a variety of reasons including:

- the collective security of the UK and its allies in NATO
- national security and foreign policy requirements
- international legal obligations and commitments
- non-proliferation policy
- concerns about terrorism
- internal repression
- other human rights violations

If goods or technologies are subject to UK export controls, a licence is required to gain the legal authority to export them. The Department of Trade and Industry is the licensing authority.

The DTI's Export Control Organisation's Helpline is the first point of contact for information on export controls. The Helpline provides advice on many issues, including how to establish whether or not specific goods need an export licence, the different types of export licences, how to complete export licence application forms and how long they take to process. The Helpline is also the point of contact for Export Control Organisation publications and licence application forms.

The Defence Export Services Organisation (DESO) can provide information concering the export of defence related equipment.

For information concerning export controls on antiques and works of art, please visit the Department for Culture, Media and Sport website.

DOCUMENTATION

The Simpler Trade Procedures Board (SITPRO)
SITPRO is the UK's trade facilitation agency. It is dedicated to encouraging and helping business trade more effectively and simplifying the international trading process. Its field is within the procedures and documentation associated with international trade.

SITPRO manage the UK aligned system of export documents and license the printers and software suppliers who sell the forms, laser and export document software. SITPRO's other services, many of which are free of charge include:

- a trade efficiency help desk
- an extensive library of briefings covering topics from general export to payment and finance advice and individual country information
- management guidelines booklet for traders
- Letter of Credit (L/C) checklists
- quarterly newsletter and comprehensive seminar programme.

For further information contact:

Simpler Trade Procedures Board (SITPRO)
Tel: 020 7467 7280
Fax: 020 7467 7295
E-mail: info@sitpro.org.uk

A `Bill of Entry' is required for all goods imported into Seychelles that are subject to the control of the Trades Tax Import Division (of the Ministry of Finance).

When lodging a Bill of Entry, the following documents are required by the Trades Tax Import Division:

- 4 copies of Bill of Entry (First copy original)
- 2 copies of import permit (First copy original)
- 2 copies of Bill of lading (First copy original)
- 2 Copies of insurance certificate, packing list, letters and other documents showing the value of the goods at the place were they were purchased together with freight, and other charges on the goods, plus authorised letters from importers for any person or agent clearing them.

Enquiries to (and Bill of Entry forms to be collected from):
The Trades Tax Import Division Head Office
1st Floor, Liberty House
Independence Avenue
Victoria
P.O Box 408
Tel: 382000
Fax: 225768

CUSTOMS DUTIES

HM Customs and Excise can help you locate your local Customs Advice Centre and your local Excise and Inland Customs Advice Centre who are the first line of enquiry for routine tariff classification advice down to the 6 digit Harmonised System subheading level, used worldwide.

The Customs Classification Helpline can also provide advice on tariff classification numbers. The Helpline is open from 09.00-16.30. Tel: 01702 366 077

Tariff information for many countries is available from the Market Access Database.

A Trades tax (imports) is applied to all items imported into the domestic economy. It is very similar to customs duty in that it is based on the CIF value of the item landed in Seychelles. Rates of tax vary but the average rate is 25%.

The payment of Trades Tax may - at the discretion of the Ministry of Finance- be exempted on imports of capital equipment by new businesses, raw materials and industrial throughputs and personal effects of individuals taking up residence in Seychelles, excluding passenger vehicles.

Goods for transhipment and re-export are exempt from Trades tax.

A manual containing the Trades Tax Act as well as a schedule of rates may be purchased from the Ministry of Finance:

Trades Tax Import Division Head Office
1st Floor, Liberty House
Independence Avenue
Victoria
P.O Box 408
Tel: 382000
Fax: 225768
Email: sezcus@seychelles.net

ADDITIONAL TAXES

No additional taxes are levied on imported goods.

ANTI DUMPING AND COUNTERVAILING

Dumping is not a consideration as very little is manufactured locally.

DRAWBACK AND BOUNTIES

- Drawback: These considerations apply in respect to International Trade Zone (SITZ) companies involved in re-export (More details can be obtained from the Seychelles International Business Authority (SIBA, P.O Box 991, Victoria, Tel: 380800, Fax: 380888, email: siba@seychellles.net, website:www.siba.net),

- Bounties are not paid on locally produced goods.

COMMERCIAL SAMPLES AND TEMPORARY IMPORTS

Consideration is made for tax free/ tax remissions. Application for exemption must be made to the Comptroller of Trades Tax

The Trades Tax Import Division Head Office
1st Floor, Liberty House
Independence Avenue
Victoria
P.O Box 408
Tel: 382000
Fax: 225768
Email: sezcus@seychelles.net

SEICHELLS DEVELOPMENTS

ENVIRONMENT MANAGEMENT PLAN OF SEYCHELLES

Seychelles embarked on its first environment management plan in 1989, with the support of UNDP, UNEP and the World Bank. The Environment Management Plan of Seychelles (EMPS) 1990-2000, raised pledges of over 40 million USD, and after a decade of implementation was a successful programme. Key highlights were the expansion of the Department of Environment; training of environment professionals; enactment of a modern Environment Protection Act; introduction of Environmental Impact Assessment;

implementation of national effluent quality standards; the elimination of the turtle shell industry and construction of the Greater Victoria sewerage system.

The success of the EMPS 1990-2000, prompted Government to embark on the preparation of a second generation action plan; the EMPS 2000-2010. With the support of the World Bank, the EMPS 2000-2010 was prepared through a national multi-stakeholder consultation process and national expert input. The EMPS 2000-2010 was also further closely aligned to environment and sustainability principles emerging following the UNCED Rio Summit held in 1992. EMPS 20002010 therefore also incorporated major global environmental issues such as climate change and biodiversity loss. Although the EMPS 2000-2010 was successfully implemented, efforts at improved

monitoring and evaluation of the benefits were limited. In 2009, a review of the EMPS 2000-2010 revealed that 85% of the EMPS 2000-2010 action plan was effectively implemented despite serious economic difficulties experienced during this period. Some objectives were not attained in relation to capacity and the report made suggestions to improve the institutional mechanism for effective steerage of the EMPS.

1.2 SEYCHELLES COMMITMENT TO SUSTAINABLE DEVELOPMENT

Small Island Developing States (SIDS) forms a distinctive group which shares many characteristics and whose vulnerability and special situation has been recognized by the international community. The sustainability of SIDS, in particular, drew the attention of the international community in 1989 when the United Nations General Assembly (UNGA) adopted a resolution (GA 44/206) on SIDS, which later became enshrined in Agenda 21, Chapter 17G (1992). This was further recognized by the 1994 Barbados Programme of Action for Small Island States (BPOA) and the 2005 Mauritius International Meeting of the Small island States. However, despite a global consensus on sustainable development, its translation into practice has not been so straightforward. Efforts by the United Nations have been driven mainly by global summits every 10 years, three global environmental conventions (the CBD, the UNFCCC and the UNCCD) and one major global financing mechanism, the Global Environment Facility (GEF).

Seychelles, being a Small Island Developing State, has played a leadership and active role in this process. It was one of the initial signatories to the three Rio global environmental conventions and has been instrumental in driving sustainable development at the national and international level. Indeed, the development of the EMPS 1900-2000 and EMPS 2000-2010 are hinged on the premise that Seychelles wishes to be a global leader in sustainable development. This national drive, endorsed by the Head of State at various international meetings, in particular the United Nation General Assembly, is testimony to this commitment. The Constitution of the Republic of Seychelles (1993) makes reference in the preamble on the need to '...participate in the sustainable economic and social development of our society.' Furthermore, Section 38 (Right to safe environment), Part (b) of the Constitution also states the intention '...to ensure a sustainable socio-economic development of Seychelles by a judicious use and management of the resources of Seychelles.'

The President of Seychelles James Michel, in a statement to the UNGA in 2008, stressed that 'Despite our small size, we shall continue to lead. And we shall lead by example. By our example, we have shown and will continue to show to all that sustainable development is achievable in our present generation.'

1.3 THE SEYCHELLES SUSTAINABLE DEVELOPMENT STRATEGY (SSDS) 2012-2020

The overall objective of the EMPS 1990-2000 and EMPS 2000-2010, was to promote, coordinate and integrate sustainable development in Seychelles. In line with the Agenda 21 (in particular Chapter 17), and outcomes of the BPOA, the need to transform the EMPS into a strategy for national sustainable development is of importance and merit. This is particularly crucial as many of the issues tackled in the previous two EMPS's are closely linked to development and social issues. There is also the need to cater for the increasing complexity of ongoing and emerging environmental concerns and threats. The institutional dimension of the EMPS also needs to shift from being seen as exclusively an environmental matter to become a national matter of prime importance for the future prosperity and security of the Seychelles people.

The rationale for shifting from an environment plan to a Sustainable Development Strategy is derived from extensive multi-stakeholder consultations associated with the review of the EMPS 2000-2010, and consultations in preparation for this new plan (See Annex 1). A survey undertaken during the review of the EMPS 2000-2010, found that 3 out of 5 people agreed that the EMPS is about sustainable development rather than only environmental management. The same review concluded that the EMPS is 'still the reference strategic document for sustainable development programmes in Seychelles.' Furthermore, stakeholders recommended that sustainable development principles form a core part of the new strategic plan, which should be reflected in the vision and overall objective of the new strategy and plan.

In the EMPS 2000-2010 Review national experts were of the view that a sustainable approach was required to tackle many of the issues, in particular: population growth; agriculture; land use; coastal management; fisheries; and addressing climate change adaptation and mitigation. It was highlighted that efforts were necessary to further link biodiversity conservation and development which would entail a close implementation of the sectoral development plan within a coherent sustainable strategy framework. The role of education and its links to sustainable development was also emphasized. Therefore, there was wide consensus that the next generation of the EMPS should be reviewed and emphasized to develop into the Seychelles Sustainable Development Strategy. This entails an improved national institutional framework, with enhanced inter-ministerial influence, effectiveness and wider stakeholder buy-in and participation. Those recommendations have been incorporated in the SSDS.

2 BACKGROUND TO THE SSDS 2012-2020

The Seychelles Sustainable Development Strategy (SSDS) 2012-2020 is an approved national instrument which incorporates national priorities for sustainable development and lays out a roadmap for the implementation of those priorities. Both the priority setting and development of the roadmap is a result of consultations with various stakeholders and groups, including community groups. The drafting of the SSDS 2012-2020 has been supported with the financial assistance of the Regional Programme for the Sustainable Management of Coastal Zones in the Indian Ocean Countries (ReCoMaP) and the UNDP-GEF Capacity Development for Improved National and International Environmental Management in Seychelles (CB2) Project. The entire project is being supported administratively by the Department of Environment and the Joint Seychelles-UNDP–GEF Project Coordination Unit.

The drafting of the SSDS 2012-2020 was undertaken by a team of Seychellois experts, with input from thirteen thematic teams (See Annex 2). These teams consulted a wide range of stakeholders to identify constraints and gaps, identify national priorities and then developed an action strategy to address those priorities. In addition the various thematic stakeholder consultations, two national multi-stakeholder consultation workshops were organized to specifically determine (i) the approach to stakeholder analysis, (ii) guidance on engaging stakeholders, (iii) key cross-cutting themes and issues, (iv) integrated approaches and systems thinking, and (v) the identification of various institutional models for the implementation of the SSDS 2012-2020.

3 THE SEYCHELLES 2020 SUSTAINABLE DEVELOPMENT VISION

VISION

To contribute to the realisation of the nation's economic, social and cultural potential through an innovative, knowledge-led approach, being mindful of the need to conserve the integrity of the Seychelles natural environment and heritage for present and future generations.

The vision for the SSDS 2012-2020 emanates for a series of exchanges between national stakeholders. It reflects the vision of the country to become a knowledge-based society and to manage its natural resources in a sustainable manner.

The approach is based upon knowledge development and creation – a critical, strategic resource for sustainable development. Innovation transcends all levels and elements of sustainable development. It is not only about technology, but includes thinking, practice, solutions and removal of barriers. The vision reflects the determination of a nation to embrace modernity with a penchant on maintaining a high quality of life based upon a green economy, low pollution and a rich biodiversity environment. Achieving balance or the triple bottom line is fundamental to maximizing the effectiveness of polices

The vision comes with the recognition that Seychelles cannot exist without its natural and unique environment, and champions the preservation of the environment as an asset for today's and tomorrow's generation.

4 SEYCHELLES SUSTAINABLE DEVELOPMENT OUTLOOK 2020

The 2020 Sustainable Develop Outlook is a compilation of observations from experts involved in the preparation of the SSDS 2012-2020. The outlook provides a qualitative perspective on key drivers of environmental change in the coming decade. Deficiencies such as unavailability of trend data and lack of a defined national assessment process of indicators, limits the merit of this outlook.

The document does however still provide important insights into key challenges. The outlook also provides critical areas in which policies and actions will be needed to address principal sustainable development challenges. It also demonstrates that the effective tackling of present-day and emerging development challenges is feasible and can be addressed by measures outlined in this plan. The impact of climate change on the potential level of implementation of these sustainability objectives is also explored.

The Seychelles economy is very sensitive to external economic perturbations. The economic growth for 2010 was 6.2 %, despite a global economic downturn, largely as a result of high FDI inflows especially in the tourism industry. The challenge to government and the private sector is to ensure there is sustainable growth in the goods and services sector so as to maximize job creation and social development as well as minimise the negative impact of industrial development, resources consumption and associated degradation on the environment.

The Seychelles population increases at a birth rate of 18.1 per 1000 persons per year and the pressures of human development on the fragile and limited resource-base of the country is expected to increase significantly by 2020. Accelerated growth in tourism arrivals will also contribute to increased pressure on local resources such as land, beachfront property, water, food and energy.

However, significant investment in tourism can yield benefits for the management, rehabilitation and restoration of these natural resources. This will indeed be a determining factor for long-term sustainability of the tourism industry in Seychelles, since the same tourism is highly dependent upon the quality of the natural environment. Global economic turmoil may affect the performance of these local activities, especially if there is a reduction in tourism receipts.

Seychelles has met all its MDGs with more than 95% of the population having access to drinking water and electricity, but it is evident that existing infrastructure will not be adequate to meet present trends until 2020. Food security will remain an issue in view of the country's dependence on imported food, and increased pressure to further convert existing agricultural land. There is an increasing trend towards consumption that creates ever larger ecological footprints, including increasing generation of wastes in the midst of weak efforts for energy, water and other forms of resource conservation. Progress in changing people's behaviour may be achieved, provided there is adequate policy and institutional reforms coupled with increased education, sensitisation and awareness at all levels. Water and energy demands are expected to increase by 2020. Whilst infrastructure investments in utilities can be prohibitively costly, integrated approaches such as using waste-to-energy technologies are likely to become more common. The risk of outbreaks of certain infectious diseases, for example dengue and chikungunya, are expected to increase, in spite of efforts to prevent entry through border control and reduction of local prevalence. Of concern is also the emergence of global pandemics and other globally infectious diseases.

Coastal development and urban sprawl are expected to increase as the country aims to further develop the reclaimed zones and densify certain rural areas of the main islands. Mahé has already one of the densest coastal populations, especially along the east part of the island. Further expansion of industries, tourism and fisheries will augment further pressure on coastal resources. Conflicts will more likely arise if the highlighted institutional weaknesses and adequate consultations on development projects are not addressed. Sea level rise, extreme storm surges and other impacts associated with climate change will affect existing coastal infrastructure, beaches and other coastal environments.

Seychelles' unique and diverse biodiversity is under threat primarily from intense tourism development pressure, environmental degradation and pollution. Impacts of climate change are likely to become more evident in the next ten years. The sustainable management of protected areas, both terrestrial and coastal/marine, will remain a challenge in view of stakeholder expectations and problems of access to resources involved. It is however expected that the area of protected areas will increase. Fishery pressure is expected to increase as well as demand for forestry products. Endemic and rare species will continue to be threatened by natural and human related hazards such as environmental degradation from development, the spread of alien invasive species, land use change and effects of climate change in the next decade.

The Seychelles is economically dependent upon its fishery resources with measures in place to ensure sustainability. However, with an EEZ of 1.44 million km^2, maritime security and enforcement of illegal and unreported fisheries will remain a major challenge. The uncertainties with respect to the impact of climate change on fisheries will attract a good deal of scientific attention. Coastal fisheries will continue to be threatened from overfishing and other impacts on fish habitats. The fisheries industry is expected to expand and other fish species may be commercially exploited.

The outlook shows that the cost of doing nothing would be very high on the fragile national ecosystems and ultimately on the society of Seychelles.

Seychelles Sustainable Development Outlook

Macro-indicators	Positive Trend	Welcome Trends	Warning Trends
Economic	• Increased inclusion	• Macro-economic	• Reduced investment
Development	of environmental issues in finaning development	reform programme • Sustainable debt levels	in environment/ resource management & rehabilitation
Social well-being	• Low population growth • Good education & employment possibilities	• Land use plans • Improved solid waste management • Focus on national food security	• Increased urbanisation • Over-consumption • Disease epidemics
Institutions/Education	• Reforms to increase involvement of NGOs and private sector	• Improved policy coherence and networking	• Poor enforcement of existing laws
Pollution	• Investments in water/waste treatment technologies	• Maintain environment quality standards	• Pollution for highly urbanized areas • Lack of monitoring
Utilities (energy, water, waste)	• Continuous expansion of water & sanitation network	• Recycling of some types of wastes • Water harvesting initiatives • Pricing which encourages conservation	• Increase in waste output • Lack of water during dry season • Increased in electricity consumption • Increase in vehicles

Biodiversity	• Reducing risk of threatened endangered species • Private sector in volvement • Protected area increased • Conservation of key species	• Improved management and financial sustainability of protected areas • Mainstreaming biodiversity • Restoration of key degraded habitats • Education for conservation and bio-safety	• Degradation of coral reefs • Threat of invasive species • Loss of critical habitats • Encroachment by development
Climate Change	• Institutional and policy reforms focused on adaptation • Investments in Renewable Energy	• Reduction of GHG emissions • Energy, water & resources conservation	• Coastal damage, coral bleaching, extreme droughts, forest fires

5 ADDRESSING THE CHALLENGES OF SUSTAINABLE DEVELOPMENT

The wide acceptance of sustainable development as a guiding principle for the future of humanity, its well-being and surrounding environment has gathered enormous pace at the international level, especially after the recent global economic crisis and hikes in the price of oil. Indeed the adoption of Agenda 21 in 1992, and subsequent adoption of the Programme for the Further Implementation of Agenda 21 in 2002, has stimulated the global community, as well as national governments and institutions to address current environmental, social and economic problems within a framework of sustainable development. The next section will elaborate the number of elements or principles necessary for the integration of sustainable development in all forms of planning and in addressing current national challenges.

In the preparation of this SSDS a number of key challenges were highlighted by stakeholders:

The challenges of implementing sustainable development are varied and complex, but 'no action' is not an option for consideration by Seychelles. Seychelles' unique position as a small island state implies that it is particularly vulnerable on all fronts. With an economy based primarily upon tourism and fisheries, which are in turn linked to global perturbations, Seychelles remains highly vulnerable to external economic upturns and downturns. Similarly, the Seychelles has a very fragile natural environment, meaning that any environmental stress arising from over-exploitation or global phenomena, such as climate change, is immediately translated into impacts on livelihood and ecosystem health. The Seychelles has a very advanced social development network (for education, health, welfare and housing), but this could be seriously undermined by poor economic performance and environment degradation. Linking sustainable development with economic policies in the form of incentives or disincentives has been shown to be an effective approach in the implementation of sustainable development. There is also the need to especially address the growing lacuna of financing for sustainable development.

The overall vision of achieving sustainable development should be re-enforced at the national level in terms of political commitment and ensure that clear linkages are indentified for better inter-thematic action. The SSDS 2012-2020 has been endorsed by the Cabinet of Ministers (Government of Seychelles) and each action plan (in Volume 2) features a section on interlinkages and elaborates an implementation framework for sustainable development. In addition, each thematic chapter has a section on cross-sectoral issues which highlight potential linkages across thematic sectors. In fact, the SSDS should not be seen as an 'environment' document but one that seeks to mainstream environmental and sustainability issues into all the thematic sectors, policies and other institutional frameworks of the country. All stakeholders and institutions should feel part of the SSDS in such a way that they are ready to take ownership of it. A change in approach to development at all levels is an essential prerequisite to the success of the SSDS 2012-2020. The SSDS provides strategic direction and guides other national development plans. It should be seen as a guidance document on the overall national sustainable development vision and be a reference point (in terms of sustainable development) for ongoing and future development plans of Seychelles, whether it be in infrastructure development, technology transfer or market expansion, such as in tourism.

The SSDS 2012-2020 should also acknowledge and respond to the limited human capacity in Seychelles for implementation. In the action plan (Volume 2) 'Policy, Institutional and Regulatory' thematic sector a number of strategies toensure effective implementation given resource and capacity constraints are proposed. In particular, synergies and linkages will need to be clearly identified to

Addressing the Challenges of Sustainable Development reduce duplication of effort and activities, and encourage partnerships and collaboration to achieve joint goals.

The SSDS supports the role and involvement of NGO's, CBO's and other organizations, including efforts to build capacity in those institutions. Indeed, Chapter 6 of Agenda 21 specified that countries should set priorities for action based on cooperative planning by various levels of government, nongovernmental organisations and local communities.

The effective establishment of systems of governance is primordial to the implementation of sustainable development. In the context of Seychelles this should primarily focus on transparent and responsible action by all parties, effective and non-discriminatory enforcement of policies and regulations, efficient delivery of services and adequate platforms for public expression of views and participation in decision-making. The SSDS should also adopt an organizational approach to capacity building, implying that capacity building should become more institutionalized rather than limited within projects and initiatives. This approach will provide long-term sustainability and support for the implementation of sustainable development in Seychelles.

Indeed these challenges have been reflected in the action plan (Volume 2) and seen as major issues to be resolved to ensure effective and efficient implementation of the SSDS.

6 PRINCIPLES OF SUSTAINABLE DEVELOPMENT

Sustainable development is governed by a set of principles developed through several decades of global discourse and research. It is not the objective of this section to discuss all these principles, but rather highlight those that that are relevant to the implementation of the SSDS 2012-2020.

Detailed and specific principles of sustainable development are presented in each of the thematic chapters. Judging from the vision and objectives of first two environment management plans (EMPS), it is evident that the Seychelles wishes to pursue an ecologically-driven approach to sustainable development. Recognising the fragility of the Seychelles environment and its relative vulnerability, this approach to sustainability is widely accepted by the Seychelles community and stakeholders and impregnated in ongoing government policy and action. Ecologically sustainable development is especially important for Seychelles in view of its high dependence on tourism and fisheries as main sources of economic prosperity.

6.1 EMERGING ISSUES: RIO+20 (UNITED NATIONS CONFERENCE ON SUSTAINABLE DEVELOPMENT)

The publication of the SDSS 2012-2020 dovetails into the preparatory process for Rio+20. It is therefore expected that issues agreed upon by contributors to this global process on sustainable development will not be adequately represented in the present version of the SDSS 2012-2020. However, a few key issues likely to dominate the Rio+20 negotiations include: the concept of the green economy; the clustering and binding implementation modalities of MEA's; the role of international environmental arbitration – such as an international environment court, and other recommendations to reform or create a UN environment organization. The concept of the green

economy is of specific significance to the SSDS.

Principles of Sustainable Development

6.1.1 THE GREEN ECONOMY

The Green Economy has taken many forms of definitions:

UNEP – 'one that results in improved human well-being and social equity, while significantly reducing

environmental risks and ecological scarcities. In its simplest expression, a green economy can be thought of as one which is low carbon, resource efficient and socially inclusive.'[1]

WRI – 'as an alternative vision for growth and development; one that can generate growth and improvements in people's lives in ways consistent with sustainable development. A Green Economy promotes a triple bottom line: sustaining and advancing economic, environmental and social well-being.'[2]

In practical terms these concepts will need to be linked to both national, regional and global economic policies and regimes. It has implications for trade, alleviation of poverty, management of the world's resources as it is simply not a 'greening of the brown economy' but an alternative path. However, the use of the word green economy has created concerns among SIDS, and other developing countries, during various regional Rio+20 preparatory meetings[3]. Some of the concerns include whether use of the term could potentially be used to justify the imposition of trade conditionalities on the basis of environmental standards as well as protectionist measures to insulate countries' own green industries. Whichever the outcome of Rio+20, it is recommended that the Seychelles continues with the green economy approach (as per the definitions above), as a pathway towards sustainable development and thus an important underpin to the SSDS.

[1]http://www.unep.org/greeneconomy/AboutGEI/WhatisGEI/tabid/29784/Default.aspx (accessed 15th Oct 2011) [2]http://www.wri.org/stories/2011/04/qa-what-green-economy (accessed 15th Oct 2011) [3]http://ictsd.org/i/news/biores/117254/ (accessed 15th Oct 2011)

7 ASSESSMENT OF PROGRESS IN SUSTAINABILITY DEVELOPMENT

The criteria adopted for sustainable development emanates from the work undertaken by a group of experts on the assessment of progress towards sustainable development[4]. The study suggests ten aspects which can be used to assess progress from the beginning of the SSDS to its completion. Indeed, the tools to measure such a complex developmental process are still in their infancy. However, there is much innovation and lessons to be learned if a dynamic and learning process is adopted. The table below presents a set of 'diagnostic' questions for proposed evaluation of this SSDS.

Criteria	Key questions
Guiding Vision & Goals	Are the goals set-out in Volume 2 contributing to the overall vision of the SSDS? Can these be measured in quantitative terms?
Holistic Perspective	Has a systems approach consisting of the social, ecological, and economic sub-systems been considered in the implementation of each of the thematic sector of the SSDS? Has consideration been given to the inter-relationships, linkages and potential synergies among the thematic sectors?
Essential Elements	Has consideration of existing and future trends in ecological and resource conditions been further researched and discussed in the implementation of the various thematic sectors? Has an in-depth evaluation of existing policies, institutions and stakeholders been undertaken and recommendations addressed in subsequent projects?
Adequate Scope	Has a long enough time horizon been given to capture both human and ecosystem time scales in the project implementation? Has issues outside the immediate locale been considered?
Practical Focus	Is there a prioritisation of action and a plan which explicitly inks vision and goals to verifiable indicators?
Openness	Is the entire planning and implementation process accessible to all stakeholders?
Effective Communication	Is it designed to be understandable by all stakeholders and appropriate for adoption at all levels? Is there a communication plan/strategy developed and implemented?
Broad Participation	Has it obtained broad representation from all levels of society? Does it ensure the participation of decision-makers and other stakeholders?
Ongoing Assessment	Are there plans to develop capacity for ongoing assessment of progress and trends?
Institutional Capacity	Have appropriate governance mechanisms been discussed and agreed upon by stakeholders? Have responsibilities been clearly assigned and ongoing support identified?

[4]Hardi, P & Zdan T. 1997 Assessing sustainable development. IISD, Canada.

8 MAINSTREAMING SUSTAINABLE DEVELOPMENT IN SEYCHELLES

Mainstreaming sustainable development involves the informed inclusion of sustainability concerns into national development policy and plans. Mainstreaming involves better and more coherent national policies. More efficient planning fosters technological innovation and seeks novels ways to improve productivity, resilience and the adaptive nature of human systems. Such mainstreaming depends upon a change in mindset, in approach, with more stakeholders working together towards the vision and seeing how linkages may be achieved to bring about the desired outcome with the best possible benefits to society and the environment.

The SSDS seeks to promote the mainstreaming of sustainable development. Such willingness has been demonstrated between various government authorities and departments, as well as the role played by non-government organizations. This may take the form of 'upstream' changes such as influencing policy, a decision or a new development plan, or 'downstream' changes such as change in consultative approaches, behaviour and mindset. Mainstreaming is considered a critical component in the implementation of this SSDS.

Whilst there is no standard approach to mainstreaming[5], some practical steps are recommended following the adoption of this SSDS:

1. Convene a multi-stakeholder group to steer the mainstreaming process
2. Map institutional roles and responsibilities for each of the goals outlined in Volume 2
3. Identify associated institutional, governance and capacity – and changes required
4. Identify entry points for environmental mainstreaming in key decision-making processes
5. Establish or use existing forums and mechanisms for debate and consensus
6. Install criteria/indicators and accountability mechanisms to ensure monitoring and continuous improvement in environment-development integration

[5]Dalal-Clayton B. & Bass S. (2009) The Challenges of environmental mainstreaming. IIED, London, UK.

9 CRITICAL SUCCESS FACTORS

9.1 INTRODUCTION

One of the findings of the EMPS 2001-2010 Review process was that for some sector objectives, the performance indicators was inadequate to successfully measure progress made. The SSDS provide in addition to improved indicators, Critical success factors (CSFs) to effectively measure the success of the SSDS. These CSFs are important areas of activity that should receive constant and adequate attention from the institutional authority mandated to implement this plan. CSFs are built upon the goals and objectives of SSDS and were elaborated through an iterative process organized as part of the stakeholder consultation process in the preparation of this plan.

The critical success factors are:

1. Political support– the government has an important role to play and it is vital that all ministries and departments see the plan as part of the national strategy for develoment, rather than just an 'environment' document. The SSDS should be used as a primer for national development and

international financing for its implementation

1. Ownership by stakeholders – maintaining a long-term relationship and commitment with the plan is an important part of fostering ownership. Benefits derived should be shared in

an equitable manner and transparent systems should be established to enable active participation by all stakeholders. Stakeholders should, in the same spirit, recognise their responsibility to engage in the process.

2. Effective implementation framework – an institutional framework which enables the goals and objectives to be implemented effectively is an important component of this plan. It is discussed in detail in the next section.
3. Capacity – is critical to the implementation and the success of the outcome of SSDS. It is important to develop and retain trained human resources able to implement programmes to a high level of competences.
4. Integration into national planning process – This is critical, especially when the country is developing its own development plan for 2020. Efforts and measures to integrate sustainable development principles into those projects is paramount at the onset of the planning process.
5. Periodical Audits – previous EMPS could not be evaluated in terms of their true worth and effectiveness due to lack of an effective system of review. A specific monitoring and evaluation function will need to be established.

10 OVERVIEW OF THE POLICY AND INSTITUTIONAL SETTING

10.1 AT THE NATIONAL LEVEL

There is an extensive legislative and policy framework which covers all sectors is in place at the national level for environmental management in the Seychelles. These include provisions in the Constitution of the Republic, a large collection of laws and regulations, as well as specific institutional frameworks to implement those policies and laws. Within each thematic chapter key policies specific to that sector are listed. However, a specific undertaking to evaluate the present policy and institutional setting led to several important conclusions useful for the successful implementation of the SSDS. As part of this evaluation a SWOT (Strength-Weakness-Opportunity -Threat) analysis was conducted with stakeholders and is summarized in the matrix below and addressed in the thematic chapter on 'Policy, Institutional and Regulatory' in Volume 2 of the SDSS.

Strengths	Weaknesses
Signed/ratified the majority of international conventions	Insufficient knowledge/ awareness of stakeholders.
related to sustainable development	Insufficient capacity to implement policies and regulations.
Wide range of environment legislation/policies in	Poor research and monitoring framework.
place.	Some legislation are outdated and not coherent.
Key strategies – biodiversity, climate change, capacity	Enforcement of legislation is weak.
building, land-based sources of pollution have been	
developed.	
Opportunities	Threats
To incorporate sustainability issues into national	Lack of political support for proposed enhancement
development strategies and plans.	of policy, legal and institutional framework.
Use of indicators to monitor progress and identify	Poor buy-in from stakeholders in driving the necessary

gaps.	institutional reforms.
Create better synergies among legislation and policies.	Lack of financial support to implement required institutional
Better integration of issues across sectors.	reforms.
Institutional reform to implement SSDS.	

10.2 AT EMPS IMPLEMENTATION LEVEL

The EMPS 2001-2010 institutional framework focused on a coordinating secretariat nested within the Ministry responsible for the Environment. Guidance for the operation of this secretariat emanated from a broad-based Steering Committee under the joint chairmanship of the Principal Secretary responsible for Environment and the Foreign Affairs counterpart. The Steering committee comprised of representatives of government, the civil society and the private sector. The EMPS 2001-2010 was supported by a unit created within the Ministry responsible for Environment. Although the structure was implemented as recommended, the Review of the EMPS 2001-2010 raised a number of issues:

• The EMPS Steering Committee was too cumbersome for steering and not balanced in terms of representativeness. Participation waned and discussions were dominated by a few members. As to its function, it was recognised as being more an information exchange platform rather than performing its steering role. Participation was also driven by availability of funds for project implementation and willingness of partners to report on progress in implementation. Despite efforts it was concluded that the committee as structured could not effectively implement and monitor the EMPS 2001-2010.

• The Coordinating Unit was weak in terms of capacity and ability to impart any influence on partners. The Review concluded that the unit failed to implement 60% of its mandate as stipulated in its terms of reference; reasons being lack of appropriate human capacity, lack of dedicated budget to implement activities, lack of cooperation with partners, and poor guidance from the EMPS Steering Committee. Without a proper framework, the unit was also inefficient in establishing monitoring and evaluation systems for the management plan.

• Institutionally, the implementation of the EMPS remained a sectoral or organizational matter, with little input or coordination from either the Steering Committee or the Coordinating Unit. Some projects en dorsed or funded by government, and being implemented by both Government and NGOs, did not have the oversight of the institutional structure. Such deficiencies resulted in lost opportunities for synergy, linkages and measurement of performance. Although the EMPS 2001-2010 was implemented with a measurable success, the institutional coordination and oversight remains a challenge.

11 INSTITUTIONAL FRAMEWORK FOR SSDS 2012-2020

Based upon the recommendations from (i) the Review of the EMPS 2001-2010, (ii) the various stakeholder workshops, (iii) the potential outcome of Rio+20 on institutional frameworks for sustainable development and (iv) Cabinet decision it is proposed that a Secretariat under the Ministry responsible for Environment is established to implement the SSDS.

The SSDS-Secretariat (SSDS-Sec), as it shall be called, will be responsible for the implementation and coordination of the SSDS and will report to the Minister responsible for Environment. For practical purposes the establishment of the Secretariat shall be undertaken in phases, as it will involve a review of the existing UNDP-GEF Project Coordination Unit and the

EMPS Coordinating Unit, both of which are currently under the responsibility of the Department of Environment.

The SSDS-Sec shall be:

1. to act as coordinator of the SSDS 2012-2020
2. to monitor and evaluate progress in the implementation of the SSDS 2012-2020
3. to provide independent policy advice to the government on sustainable development and other relevant issues
4. to drive the building of capacity, awareness and management to achieve the sustainable development vision of the Seychelles

The SSDS-Sec shall have a three tier-level of governance to ensure adequate and effective participation and also make provisions for the out-sourcing of capacity to implement the SSDS 2012-2020.

11.1 THE SCOPE AND MANDATE OF THE SSDS-SEC IN RELATION TO PROJECT APPROVAL, ENDORSEMENT AND FINANCING

The SSDS-Sec shall coordinate, in relation to the SSDS, and where appropriate, the implementation of (i) government financed projects, (ii) projects with significant government involvement and (iii) those requiring counterpart government funding.

Projects by organizations outside of government shall not require prior approval or endorsement of the Secretariat for implementation, unless sources of funds include government and agencies in which government have commitments or substantive interests in. In some cases government endorsement may be required, for example the Global Environment Facility (GEF). Projects with research objectives will still be subjected to other requirements, such as permits for export of samples.

Other organizations not dependent upon government funding, endorsement or counterpart financing shall have the option of working with or without the oversight and support of the SSDS-Sec.

In cases where endorsement is required from multiple government agencies, the SSDS-Sec shall act as a one-stop shop for these endorsements and approvals.

The Secretariat shall be financed through a core government budget and a percentage of project

funds being implemented through the SSDS. The use of a percentage of the funds will apply to (i) all government financed projects, and (ii) projects requiring counterpart government funding.

This arrangement shall also be subject to the approval of the funding agency.

11.2 THE STRATEGIC-POLICY LEVEL

At the strategic and policy level, a Council chaired by the Minister responsible for Environment shall be established. It shall provide direction and oversight of the work of the National Coordinator and the Secretariat. It will also act as a facilitator for project approval and implementation. The Council shall have broad and balanced representation from government, private sector, non-governmental organizations, academic institutions and community representatives. The Council shall have no more than 13 members, as follows: the chairman, the National Coordinator, five representatives of government (from the Ministries of Finance, Foreign Affairs, Environment, Social Affairs and Culture), five representatives of the civil society (Environment NGO, Social NGO, Private Sector, LUNGOS,

Community NGO), plus academia and the Chair of the Seychelles Sustainable Development Intersectoral Steering Committee (SSDSC).

The council shall adopt its own Rules of Procedure. It shall be able to draw on the expertise necessary to perform its functions. Attendance of the Council meetings shall be open to other stakeholders not represented and they shall act as observers. The Council reserves the right of admission of observers.

The term of service shall be for two years, renewable. The Council shall meet no less than 4 times a year.

The Council will act as per the mandate given to the SSDS-Sec with respect to approval, endorsement and financing of projects.

11.3 THE GOVERNANCE LEVEL

The second-tier shall consist of two bodies:

1. The National Coordinator for Sustainable Development shall have usual administrative and executive oversight responsibilities. The National Coordinator shall be an ex-officio member of the Council. The National Coordinator will have executive powers with respect to the proper functioning of operational level of the SSDS-Sec in matters of human resources management, outsourcing and financial management. The National Coordinator shall submit an annual report of activities to the Council and the SSDSC. The National Coordinator may consult the SSDS-Sec on stakeholder coordination and technical matters.

Partners who are not satisfied with the performance of the National Coordinator may submit an appropriate report for consideration by the Council, which shall act as final arbitrator in any such dispute.

2. The work of the Secretariat shall be guided and monitored by the Seychelles Sustainable Development Inter-sectoral Steering Committee (SSDSC) which shall meet not less than four times a year to review the work and progress of the Secretariat. This forum shall encompass ALL stakeholders involved or interested in the implementation of the SSDS. The SSDSC shall remain informed of all the proceedings of the Council through a periodic bulletin/communication and shall have the power to convene an emergency forum provided the appropriate amount of consensus is achieved. The work of the Council shall be subject to independent audits commissioned every two years and shall report to SSDSC, which will in turn make recommendations to the Council. The SSDSC will have powers to establish task forces and working committees to undertake specific tasks and assignments. The SSDSC shall be chaired by an elected representative from the non-governmental sector and a vice-chair nominated by government. The Chair of the SSDSC shall be a member of the Council.

11.4 THE OPERATIONAL LEVEL

The third Tier shall comprise of the operational aspects of the Secretariat namely:

- The Project Management Unit which shall be responsible for all project implementation matters and coordination of implementation of projects within the mandate of the SSDS. Organisations operating outside the framework but requiring the support of the Project Management Unit shall do so in the form of a MoU signed by the National Coordinator and endorsed by the Council.
- The Fund Mobilisation Unit shall be responsible for fund mobilisation, including support for project development and grant writing. It shall also be responsible for marketing the SSDS and ensuring stakeholders are aware of its role. It shall also be the international liaison office with donors.

- The Knowledge Base Unit shall be responsible for ensuring there is knowledge development and capture in the implementation of the SSDS. It shall maintain information systems to support the work of the Secretariat as well as develop a knowledge base accessible to all stakeholders. It shall be a repository of project reports and relevant outputs. It shall not be a repository of primary data unless specifically mandated by the specific project implementers. It shall not have the power to mandatorily acquire data or informationunless it is done through an appropriate information/data sharing agreement.
- The Monitoring and Evaluation Unit shall be responsible for ensuring transparency and appropriate implementation of the SSDS. It shall generate yearly monitoring and evaluation reports and shall be responsible for the development and maintenance of a quality system in the Secretariat.

11.5 ESTABLISHMENT OF THE SSDS-SEC

The SSDS-Sec shall be established in phases as proposed below. An interim committee shall be established under the office of the Principal Secretary of Environment until the existing structures shall fulfill the role of the SSDS-Sec. It is envisaged that the SSDS-Sec will be fully operational by the end of 2013.

The powers of the Secretariat shall be limited to the mandate described in the preceding sections. It shall not have the power to interfere in the implementation of projects in other independent organizations unless given a specific mandate to do so. Its powers shall be limited to the coordination and implementation of the SSDS. Although this will be two years into the implementation of the SSDS, a planned and phased approach is highly recommended to enable the right capacity to be recruited and developed.

12 STAKEHOLDER INVOLVEMENT STRATEGY

12.1 THE RATIONALE AND PROCESS

Stakeholder involvement is central to the implementation of a sustainable development strategy as it creates the appropriate platform for stakeholders to voice their views and concerns, and takes part in decision-making and participates. There is sufficient empirical evidence to show that appropriate consultations and stakeholder involvement have led to better designed, more effective and conflict-minimal action plans. Overall stakeholder identification and involvement needs careful planning and execution to ensure that the Government (national or local) is on board, and other stakeholders feel that their involvement is recognized. Stakeholders can also damage the prospects for successful outcomes if there are strong opposing political forces at work, conflicts among stakeholders themselves, or stakeholders feel there are other priorities.

Principle 10 of the Rio Declaration on Environment and Development emphasizes the importance and relevance of stakeholder consultation in projects that affect the environment and the community at large. Indeed many countries have this principle explicitly embedded in national policies and legislation, in particular, environment impact assessment legislation.

The stakeholder identification process was initiated at the outset of the preparation of the SSDS. Stakeholders were identified at thematic sector levels and prioritized in order of

relevance to the thematic area. The stakeholder involvement strategy involves the continuation of the Inter-sectoral steering committee – a platform which brings together stakeholders involved in the implementation and coordination of the SSDS. The strategic focus shall be on (i) ensuring effective governance of the SSDS, (ii) adequate coordination of initiatives, and (iii) access to information.

Strategic Focus of Partnership

12.2 THE SEYCHELLES SUSTAINABLE DEVELOPMENT INTER-SECTORAL STEERING COMMITTEE

The Seychelles Sustainable Development Inter-Sectoral Steering Committee (SSDSC) shall be established as a vehicle for wider consultations and exchange of information and views on sustainable development and implementation of the plan. The SSDSC shall be open to all stakeholders, irrespective of whether they are a project implementer, an organizational representative or an independent expert. The SSDSC shall also include representation from national committees, umbrella NGO, regional/international organizations represented in Seychelles, as well as private bodies or associations. The SSDSC shall be given a budget and access to facilities under the responsibility of the division in order to implement its work programme.

It's role and proposed implementation mechanism is summarized in the table below.

Role	Implementation Mechanism
Engage and manage stakeholders at all levels.	Establish a clearing house for sharing of information and exchange. Recruit a full-time 'Stakeholder Involvement Coordinator.'
Act as a platform for dialogue and cooperation in the implementation of the SSDS.	Maintain an online discussion forum and social network platform. Organize an annual conference and other meetings to discuss and analyse specific aspects.
Advise main project on issues of stakeholder consultation and issues. Discuss and provide recommendations on resolving potential conflicts and any resulting tradeoffs.	Provide input via discussion boards and other forums. Organize independent hearings, discussion sessions where views can be aired and recommendations framed.
Ensure that project components being implemented have had the benefit of adequate stakeholder consultation and involvement. Ensure implementation of the stakeholder involvement plan.	Access to project database and related documents. National SSDS Secretariat through the Stakeholder involvement Coordinator.

13 RESOURCE MOBILISATION STRATEGY

Part of the overall SSDS is the need to essentially define an appropriate resource mobilization strategy which takes into consideration the specific conditions of Seychelles and the global economic and financial environment. Seychelles, with a growing economy, despite challenges and vulnerability, has the potential to mobilize in-country resources for sustainable development. Indeed many companies have come forward to make donations for environment projects. Government contributes annually through a budget allocation. Despite these efforts, there is scope for more formal arrangements. Internationally, the major donors for initiatives aimed at sustainable development are the Global Environment Facility and the European Union. A number of bilateral country donors also offer support to Seychelles.

The table below presents the Seychelles resource mobilization strategy, which will be subject to appropriate revisions over the lifetime of the SSDS. It is important to note that resource mobilization needs to be coupled with effective systems of financial management as well as an adequate human capacity to deliver.

13.1 LESSONS LEARNT FROM ANALYZING CURRENT AND PAST RESOURCE MOBILIZATION

There are significant opportunities, but also the uncertain nature of resource mobilization for sustainable development, if the financing goal is to be realised. Resource mobilization in the previous EMPS was reviewed and lessons learnt are summarised here.

The EMPS 2000-2010 had a budget forecast of 173 USD million, with over 43% sourced as the government budget contribution. Without a revision of forecast or updates on how much was actually raised, it was difficult to evaluate resource mobilisation effectiveness. The Report on the Review of the EMPS 2000-2010 does not present a comprehensive review of the extent of resource mobilisation, although it does state that (i) lack of finance was a barrier to implementation in certain sectors; (ii) need to further involve the department of finance, and the (iii) need for proper documentation and accountability.

Furthermore, in order to take advantage of opportunities which lie outside traditional funding cycles and programmes, a continuous resource mobilisation strategy focused on a number of key targets – the private sector, individual donors, foundations and trusts, is more appropriate. However, such a strategy needs to go hand-in-hand with concerted marketing efforts and an economic climate that promotes contributions through tax incentives and other initiatives.

13.2 THE RESOURCE MOBILISATION STRATEGY

	Vision
Resource mobilization is a strategic issue.	Innovative-driven resource mobilisation strategy that supports the implementation of the SSDS.
Effective resource mobilization underpins implementation of the SSDS.	A fully resourced SSDS that meets the overall vision of the SSDS.
Resource mobilization requires a appropriate institutional support.	Establish a Resource Mobilisation Service (RMS) in the SSDS Secretariat with responsibility for fund raising, brand building, information and training.
Need for a detailed resource mobilization strategy and plan.	Develop and implement a resource mobilization framework after stakeholder and donor consultations.

Strategic options	Implementation Mechanism	Expected Result

Raising financing through regional and global projects & mechanisms.	Substantive representation of Seychelles in those organizations.	Large projects that implement key themes or components.
'Plug-in' to opportunistic sources of financing, such as grants & competitive bids.	Syndicated service on grant opportunities and training in project/ grant submissions.	Financing of small to medium-sized project/research components.
Specific core Government budget for implementing sustainable development.	Through government procurement services.	Ongoing support for long-term projects and retention of human capacity.
Tax Rebates and other financial incentives.	Revised tax structure which allows donors to enjoy tax benefits.	Enhanced financing for long-term projects. Implement actions which are not financed by other donors.
Environment Trust Funds & other national trust funds.	Project-based with a strong counterpart contribution component.	Implement actions which are not financed by other donors.
Formalise and strengthen local sources of financing.	Develop and integrate cause-based, corporate social responsibility programmes.	Implement actions which can bring about changes and also project visibility.
Overseas Development Aid	Multilateral and bilateral negotiations combined with calls for proposals.	Large projects as budget support and for civil society

Resource Mobilisation Strategy

13.3 ESTIMATED FINANCIAL RESOURCE NEEDS TO IMPLEMENT THE SSDS

An estimation of the resource implications for the SSDS is provided here. The figures are based upon estimates and do not take into consideration inflation, nor changes in economic growth which

may impact on government revenue, and global economic trends over the 2012-2020 period. It is envisaged as suggested in the strategy that the resource forecasts are revised every two years to take into consideration these factors and also other considerations.

Programmes	Estimated Resources Needed	
	SCR Million	USD million
Social and Human Development	50.5	4.2
Land Use, Coastal Zones and Urbanisation	294.3	24.5
Biodiversity and Forestry	275	22.9
Agriculture and Food Security	161	13.4
Fisheries and Marine Resources	1374	114.5
Water, Sanitation and Waste Management	2154	179.5
Tourism and Aesthetics	13	1.083
Economics of Sustainability	25.8	2.1
Sustainable Consumption and Production	407.5	33.9
Energy and Transport	1154	95.7
Climate Change	2486	207,2

Education for Sustainability	45.4	3.7
Policy, Institutional & Regulatory	13.3	1.1
Operationalisation of the SSDS	8	0.7
TOTAL	8463	704

Approx total per year = 75.8 million US Dollars or 10 % of the Seychelles GDP or 860 USD per Capita.

14 KNOWLEDGE MANAGEMENT

14.1 INTRODUCTION

Sustainable development is often seen as an end result rather than a process of learning. Agenda 21 makes several key references to sharing and management of knowledge for sustainable development.

Chapter 3 – Combating Poverty 3.7 (c)	Promoting or establishing grass-roots mechanisms to allow for the sharing of experience and knowledge between communities.
Chapter 5 Demographic Dynamics & sustainability 5.1 (a)	Developing and disseminating knowledge concerning the links between demographic trends and factors and sustainable development.
Chapter 35 Science for sustainable development 36.6(b)	Environmental and developmental policy formulation, building upon the best scientific knowledge and assessments, and taking into account the need to enhance international cooperation and the relative uncertainties of the various processes and options involved.
Chapter 40 Information for Decision-making 40.11	Countries, with the cooperation of international organizations, should establish supporting mechanisms to provide local communities and resource users with the information and know-how they need to manage their environment and resources sustainably, applying traditional and indigenous knowledge and approaches when appropriate. This is particularly relevant for rural and urban populations and indigenous women's and youth groups.

The need for mechanisms to manage knowledge is critical to sustainable development in Seychelles. Indeed, the goal of knowledge management (KM) is one that can be achieved in practice, such as improvements in capabilities through knowledge resources such as skills, experience and technologies. The management of knowledge is vital in supporting decision and policy-making as well as innovation in sustainability. To enable a shift in mindset and interest in sustainability

14.2 FACTORS DRIVING KNOWLEDGE MANAGEMENT

Knowledge management for sustainability is driven by the following factors, which are deemed important in the context of Seychelles.

Forces driving Knowledge Management:

• Knowledge is becoming central to environmental, economic and social decision-making in Seychelles;

• Seychelles, having a small human resource capacity, would benefit from improved management of knowledge;

• The complexity in managing the Seychelles environment and development requires a knowledge management system;

• Integrating new science & technology into sustainable development requires specific considerations in Seychelles;

- Maximizing impact and return on investments implemented from the SSDS;
- Take full advantage of the Information Technology development in Seychelles
- Institutional effectiveness through better communication and a move towards open

integrated and more effective networks. By creating KM programmes, each of these pillars can be implemented across the SSDS.

The KM Cycle

Knowledge Management

Relevance of Knowledge Management to SSDS

Pillar	Context in SSDS	KM Programmes
Leadership	Use of knowledge in Decision-making	• Establish information protocol for better decision-making. • Develop collaborative plat form for involving stakeholders in decision-making. • Implement feedback system which measures and documents effectiveness of decisions taken.
Organisation	Knowledge drives organizational change and effectiveness	• Identify critical knowledge gaps, opportunities, and risks. • Develop model and processes for collection, sharing and use of information. • Institutional strengthening and capacity building for knowledge management. • Maximise human resources through more effective use of knowledge systems.
Technology	Development of knowledge centres and use of better information collection technologies	• Investment in appropriate infrastructure for knowledge collection and access. • Capacity building programme of KM platforms and centres. • Develop links with international KM centres. • Support University infrastructure to consoli date availability of scientific knowledge.

Learning	Change in mindset and introduce approaches to adaptive learning	• Encourage access to better information and case studies for influencing change. • Promote the benefits of collaboration and sharing of information. • Training programme to encourage adaptative learning at all levels.

SEYCHELLS OFFSHORE SECTOR - STRATEGIC AND LEGAL INFORMATION

BASIC INFORMATION

BUSINESS ENVIRONMENT

The Seychelles is politically stable, with good air and sea transport links and modern telecommunications. The Government has been consistently business-friendly over a long period, and has actively supported the development of the offshore sector. Inevitably, in a country this small, professional services do not have the breadth available in a larger jurisdiction, but there are adequate banking and legal facilities.

There is no discrimination against foreigners with a serious business purpose, except that they need official approval to own land. There are licensing regimes for financial institutions and trust managers. There is an adequate level of secrecy in professional transactions, but the Court can order disclosure under a number of international agreements. The Anti-Money Laundering Act 1996 allows the Central Bank to overturn suspect transactions.

IMPORT OF FOREIGN CAPITAL

In 2001 the government amended exchange control and money and trade taxation laws to tackle the problem of growing black market activity. The amendments closed loopholes in laws such as the Exchange Control Act. Individuals who possess any foreign currency must show evidence that it is obtained from a registered dealer and the rules prohibit the buying and selling foreign currency by authorised dealers at rates above the maximum rate or below the minimum rate determined by the Central Bank as well as prohibiting the export and import of Seychelles currency notes and coins in excess of R2,000.

President Michael's 2005 budget speech included measures to lead to a more market-driven economy and reduce domestic costs with the purpose of improving the investment climate in the Seychelles: a series of incentives for the tourism industry; assistance to farmers and fishermen by reducing business tax on their activities and facilitating their access to vital equipment and resources; small businesses to be given better access to foreign exchange and an "open permit" system; everyone has the possibility of opening foreign exchange accounts locally; removal of the requirement for an import permit for most items, with the exception of a list of restricted items and items for resale; customs procedures at the ports to be streamlined and made more efficient and user-friendly; and reductions in the 'trades tax'.

FOREIGN INVESTMENT REGIME

The Seychelles government is keen to create a suitable environment for foreign investment. The Investment Promotion Act 1994 legislates inward investment Incentives are granted to approved projects in the domestic and export sectors, including tourism, agriculture, manufacturing and the service industries. Procedures for approval have been streamlined and the incentives include the following:

- Following the issue of a Certificate of Approval, subsequent tax changes cannot be to the detriment of the investor;
- Exemption from import duties on primary and intermediate inputs;

- Entitlement to employ 50% of foreign staff (first 25% at special rate of SR 500 per month; next 25% at the standard rate of SR 1,500 per month);
- Accelerated depreciation up to 150% for certain asset classes;
- Concessionary business tax rates of 15% (usually 40%) plus credits giving an effective rate of 9%.

For substantial investments, further incentives can be obtained from the Government on a negotiated basis.
The International Corporate Service Providers Act, 2003, substantially improved and simplify the regime for incoming investment. Previously, the Seychelles International Business Authority (SIBA) had power to issue a licence to offshore businesses, but entitlement to fiscal concessions depended on obtaining a certificate from the Ministry of Finance under the Investment Promotion Act.
The new Act streamlined the procedure for establishing an offshore business, avoiding the need for a separate IPA application to the Finance Ministry. See Offshore Legal and Tax Regimes for further details of the new legislation.
In June, 2004, the creation of the Seychelles Investment Bureau (SIB) brought the country's promotion and facilitation of investments under one umbrella, offering a focal point of contact for all matters relating to investment in Seychelles. SIB has been mandated to coordinate the development of the Investment Code, an instrument that will allow a more transparent and stable investment environment.

BACK TO TOPSEYCHELLES INTERNATIONAL TRADE ZONE

The International Trade Zone Act 1995 and the International Trade Zone Regulations 1995 provide for the establishment of free trade zones, which are delimited by a declaration of the Finance and Communications Minister, and can be for one company or many. The existing International Trade Zone (SITZ) on Mahe is established under the Act. Activities within the Zone are governed by the Seychelles International Business Authority (SIBA), which issues licenses to incoming companies. See Law of Offshore for details of the licensing process and requirements. The concessions available to licence holders in SITZ include:

- Exemption from customs duties on capital equipment to be used in SITZ;
- Exemption from social security contributions;
- Exemption from fees in respect of 'gainful occupation permits' (work permits);
- Entitlement to employ 100% foreign labour;
- A licence holder can apply for permission to sell within the domestic sector.

FORMS OF COMPANY

The vast majority of companies formed in the Seychelles for offshore purposes are incorporated under the International Business Companies Act 1994 (see below). However this law did not supersede the existing Companies Law 1972, which is based on English law and is used to form various types of company used by businesses trading in the Seychelles, and also for offshore businesses which are not permitted to use the IBC form, such as banks, insurance companies and mutual funds.

Companies formed under the Companies Act 1972 can be private companies limited by shares, by guarantee, or hybrid; or they can be unlimited, but that is rare. Public companies can also be formed under the Act. For all these types of company, Memorandum and Articles of Association must be filed at the Companies Registry, along with the registration fee.

Foreign companies can re-establish themselves in the Seychelles by way of continuation without the necessity for reciprocal arrangements in the original country of incorporation. An IBC wishing to leave the Seychelles may do so.

In 2003, the government legislated for additional types of company: Special Licence Companies, Protected Cell Companies and Limited Partnerships.

INTERNATIONAL BUSINESS COMPANY

The International Business Company is the most widely used vehicle for offshore operations in the Seychelles; it normally takes the form of a private company limited by shares, but can also be a Limited Life Company. The governing legislation is the International Business Companies Act 1994. Statutory requirements are minimal, and flexible:

- Only one director and one shareholder are required;
- Shareholders, directors and officers need not be resident in the Seychelles and there is no stipulation as to their nationality;
- There is no minimum capital requirement; shares may be either registered or bearer and may be issued in any currency;
- Accounts need not be kept; however, if they are kept there is no requirement for an audit.
- No returns are needed of shareholders, directors or officers;
- Shareholders and directors meetings need not be held in the Seychelles and can be held by telephone;
- The Memorandum and Articles of Association are the only documents to be held on the public record.

IBC status is granted subject to certain conditions:

- No business may be transacted with residents of the Seychelles;
- No ownership interest in real property in the Seychelles is permitted; property may be leased for office use only;
- Banking or trust business may be carried on only if an appropriate license is issued;
- Likewise, a licence is required to carry on insurance or re-insurance business;
- Engaging in the business of company management or providing registered facilities for Seychelles-incorporated companies is not permitted.

IBCs are permitted various activities within the Seychelles without compromising their offshore status under the Act; these include:

- professional contacts with lawyers, accountants etc;
- preparation and maintenance of books and records;
- the holding of directors' or shareholders' meetings;
- ownership of shares in other Seychelles companies, whether under the Act or the 1942 Companies Law;
- ownership of Government or Central Bank securities;
- ownership of a vessel registered in Seychelles.

It is usual to use a registered agent in the Seychelles to incorporate an IBC (eventually it is obligatory to appoint one anyway). Fees for incorporation of an IBC are based on the company's authorised share capital. Normally, the incorporation process takes no more than one day;

however, for banks, trust companies and insurers the process is lengthier (see Offshore Business Sectors).

Statutory incorporation fees are $100 for capital up to $5,000, $300 for capital up to $50,000, and $1,000 thereafter. The annual license fees are identical. These fee levels are fixed for the life of the company, whatever changes may be made for new companies.

BACK TO TOP

SPECIAL LICENCE COMPANY

Special Licence Companies (CSL) are formed under the Companies (Special Licence) Act, 2003 (the Act). Unlike the IBC, a CSL may carry on permitted business inside as well as outside of Seychelles. The CSL entity is a Seychelles domestic company (under the Companies Act 1972), which is granted a special licence under the Act. A CSL has substantial statutory tax advantages (see Offshore Legal and Tax Regime) including access to the Seychelles Double Tax Agreements, of which that with China is of particular current interest.

Key features of the CSL are as follows:

- A CSL may carry on any business as permitted under the Schedule to the Act - including as an international holding company, a headquarters company, a franchise company, a marketing company, a company holding intellectual property, an investment company, etc.
- Bearer shares are not permitted;
- Nominee shares are permitted, but the name and address of beneficial owner is required to be disclosed to the Registrar of Companies. This information is not made publicly available by the Registrar.
- Foreign shareholders are permitted;
- There is a minimum of 2 Directors, who may be located outside of the Seychelles;
- A Seychelles-resident Company Secretary is required;
- Directors' or shareholders' meetings can be hekd anywhere, including by telephone or video-link;
- An annual company return and audited accounts must be filed;
- There is provision for "redomiciliation" - a foreign or Seychelles IBC may be continued as a CSL - and an CSL may redomicile to another jurisdiction.

BACK TO TOP

LIMITED PARTNERSHIP

Limited Partnerships (LP) are formed under the Limited Partnership Act, 2003 (the Act). An LP has substantial statutory tax advantages (see Offshore Legal and Tax Regime) including the ability to receive income from sources outside of the Seychelles and distribute such income to foreign partners without incurring a Seychelles tax liability. A Seychelles LP is highly-suitable for international joint venture activities.

Key features of the LP are as follows:

- The LP is required to have one or more general partners who are liable for the debts of the LP, and one or more limited partners who are not so liable in most circumstances.
- At least one general partner must be a Seychelles person (either a resident individual or an IBC or domestic company or CSL or an LP);
- A Seychelles registered office is required;
- An LP shall not carry on business in Seychelles, except to the extent necessary for the carrying on of the LP's business outside of Seychelles;
- An annual certificate must be filed verifying compliance by the LP with the provisions of the Act.

PROTECTED CELL COMPANY

Protected Cell Companies (PCC) are formed under the Protected Cell Companies Act, 2003 (the Act). A PCC is a Seychelles domestic company that has the right to create one or more identifiable cells so as to segregate and protect cellular assets as permitted under the Act. While each cell created by a PCC is separately identifiable and may have its own cellular assets, no cell will constitute a legal entity separate from the company (ie. only the PCC is a separate legal entity).

The Directors of a PCC have a duty to keep cellular assets separate from non-cellular assets, and to keep the assets attributable to each cell separate from the assets attributable to other cells. Liabilities attributable to a particular cell of a PCC cannot attach the assets of other cells. As in other jurisdictions, the PCC has particular use and appeal for captive insurance and collective investment scheme applications. It is likely that approval will be limited to these areas and for non-domestic business only.

TRUSTS

The International Trusts Act 1994 established, for the first time, a regime for international trusts in the Seychelles; it does not provide for domestic trusts. The Act was drafted after a thorough study of current practice in a number of leading offshore jurisdictions. Under the Act, the Seychelles International Business Authority (SIBA) is appointed as the regulatory body for trusts, alongside the Court.

The following are some of the key features of the Seychelles Trust regime (see Law of Offshore for further details):

- An international trust may be created in writing, by will or by oral declaration; deemed trusts are admitted, as are those resulting from a decision of the Court;
- Purpose trusts are permitted;
- The settlor must reside outside the Seychelles for the duration of the trust; at least one trustee must reside in the jurisdiction, but this trustee may be an IBC, which shall not thus be deemed as resident; an IBC may therefore be a settlor;
- The trust property may not include any Seychelles movable or immovable property.
- The names of settlors and beneficiaries are confidential under the Act, unless a Court orders disclosure under the Anti-money Laundering Act;
- The standard perpetuity period is 100 years; but it does not apply to purpose trusts;
- The accumulation of income is permitted;
- Forced heirship judgements are specifically excluded.

An international trust is exempt from tax in the Seychelles; a registration fee of $100 is payable to SIBA. Registration of trusts must be carried out by one of the two licensed trustees currently operating in the Seychelles.

OFFSHORE BUSINESS SECTORS

Offshore business in Seychelles began its development in 1994 when the Government launched a series of legislative initiatives aimed at establishing the country as a thoroughly modern, world-class international offshore financial centre. Much of the legislation was based on that of successful jurisdictions such as the British Virgin Islands and the Bahamas.

In 1994 legislation was enacted covering the registration of offshore companies, offshore trusts and the licensing of international trade zone companies. Additional legislation was introduced covering the licensing of offshore banks, offshore insurance companies and the establishment of a securities industry; and in 2003, the government legislated for additional types of company: Special Licence Companies, Protected Cell Companies and Limited Partnerships.

The Seychelles International Business Authority (SIBA) was set up by the Seychelles International Business Authority Act 1994 to administer the offshore sector and deals with the registration of offshore companies as well as supervision of the Seychelles International Trade Zone (SITZ).

In May, 2003, the government said it wanted the offshore sector to become a 'third pillar' of the economy, saying that SIBA's efforts had led to a 40% increase in offshore incorporations: as of the end of 2004 there are now more than 17,000 International Business Companies in the Seychelles. An Interactive Gambling Bill was also passed in 2003, which incorporates this aspect of the gaming industry into existing law.

The International Corporate Service Providers Act, 2003, substantially improved and simplify the regime for incoming investment. Previously, the Seychelles International Business Authority (SIBA) had power to issue a licence to offshore businesses, but entitlement to fiscal concessions depended on obtaining a certificate from the Ministry of Finance under the Investment Promotion Act.

The new Act streamlined the procedure for establishing an offshore business, avoiding the need for a separate IPA application to the Finance Ministry. See Offshore Legal and Tax Regimes for further details of the new legislation.

In July, 2004, it was announced that the promotion of the Seychelles investment sector is to become the responsibility of a new body, the Seychelles Investment Bureau (SIB), which will take on the task from a number of other government offices. Chief executive officer of the SIB, Joseph Nourrice, explained that the bureau will act as a one stop shop for the investment community and will coordinate all promotion activities. “The amount of procedures will be reduced tremendously,” he observed.

Previously, the Investment Desk at the Ministry of Finance had played a large part in the jurisdiction’s promotional activities, and the SIB will also assume the promotional role previously taken on by the Seychelles International Business Authority, which is to concentrate on regulation.

An immediate priority for the SIB will be the drafting of an investment code for the Seychelles which according to Mr Nourrice “will act as the backbone for our marketing tools”.

This section of the site describes the most important types of offshore business activity carried out from the Seychelles.

BANKING

Banking in the Seychelles is governed by the Financial Institutions Act 1984 as amended in 1995. Licences are issued by the Offshore Banking Department of the Central Bank and are granted only to companies incorporated under the Companies Act 1972 or foreign companies which have registered under the Companies Act. Licenses are issued for domestic banking, offshore banking, or both. When both are conducted, it must be through separate offices. Offshore banks are permitted to operate numbered accounts for their clients.

Applicants must supply extensive information to the Central Bank, including copies of the last three balance sheets and a business plan. The Bank imposes various prudential requirements and requires monthly balance sheet submissions. See Law of Offshore for further details of the licensing and supervisory regimes.

The annual licence fee is US$15,000, payable to the Central Bank in any convertible currency. Currently there are five licensed foreign banks in the Seychelles, and two domestic banks.

All licensed offshore (non-domestic) banks are exempted from Seychelles taxes and duties for a 20 year period from the date the licence was granted, although a non-domestic bank may elect to pay business tax in Seychelles on its taxable income as agreed with the Commissioner of Taxes.

In December, 2004, the National Assembly passed the Central Bank of Seychelles Act 2004. The Act makes provision for the Central Bank to operate more as an independent institution. The government said that the enactment of the Bill would allow the Central Bank to operate without government interference and will be more efficient in ensuring accountability and transparency in the supervision of the monetary system and its quest to safeguard price stability through measures of control and fiscal policies.

In April, 2005, the Managing Director for Barclays Africa, Mr. Malcom Hewitt, announced the company's plan to start an Offshore Banking service in Seychelles as of 2005. Mr. Hewitt said that the unit will present a colossal opportunity for both Barclays and the Seychelles as a whole.

INSURANCE

See Offshore Business Review – Insurance for a more general treatment of captive insurance companies.

The Insurance Act 1994 is modelled on the Insurance Act of Singapore; 1995 amendments provide for the licensing of offshore insurance companies, insurance managers and principal insurance representatives; captives are also covered by the Insurance (Non-Domestic Insurance Business) Regulations 1996. In 2003 the Protected Cell Companies Act, 2003 was passed. A PCC is a Seychelles domestic company that has the right to create one or more identifiable cells so as to segregate and protect cellular assets as permitted under the Act.

Licensing of domestic and non-domestic (offshore) insurance companies is in the hands of the Insurance Authority under the Minister of Finance and Communications. Licenses are granted only to companies incorporated under the Companies Act 1972 or foreign companies which have registered under the Companies Act.

Applications for licences include at least the following information:

- A business plan detailing the extent of the commercial operations intended;
- Memorandum and Articles of Association, and enabling Board Minute;
- Certificate of incorporation or registration;
- List of shareholders, directors and managers including their addresses, nationalities and detauls of their relevant insurance expertise;
- Three references, one being from a reputable international financial institution.

The minimum paid up capital for general or life insurance companies is US$125,000, for reinsurance companies, US$1million, and for captive insurance companies, US$70,000. These

sums must be deposited at a bank licensed by the Seychelles Central Bank (see above). Domestic insurance companies need minimum capital of SR 2m, of which 30% must be invested in prescribed Government securities, and must have adequate reinsurance arrangements. See Offshore Legal and Tax Regimes for details of processing fees and annual licensing fees payable. The Insurance Authority imposes a number of continuing prudential and supervisory requirements on insurance companies.
All licensed offshore (non-domestic) insurance companies are exempted from Seychelles taxes and duties for a 20 year period from the date the licence was granted, although a non-domestic insurer may elect to pay business tax in Seychelles on its taxable income as agreed with the Commissioner of Taxes.

INVESTMENT FUND MANAGEMENT

The Government intends to foster the creation of a Mutual Funds sector in the Seychelles, and enabling legislation was put in place in 1997. The regulations made under the Act provide for a modern regulatory system aimed at attracting international mutual funds promoters from around the world.

Funds may be established either as investment companies or unit trusts. In the case of investment companies, a wide choice of vehicles are available. All funds must have a registered office and a licensed administrator in Seychelles.
The Act provides for a licensing regime for mutual funds and mutual fund administrators under the Central Bank. Licensed banks, insurance companies and International Business Companies are excluded from the operation of the Act. Applicants for licenses would need to be companies incorporated under the Companies Act 1972 or foreign companies which have registered under the Companies Act, or unit trusts.
An overseas mutual fund needs to have a local managing agent, or in the case of a unit trust, a resident trustee. The Act imposes prudential responsibilities on the Bank, and lays down some general principles for offering documents. A private mutual fund must have minimum paid-up capital of US$5m held by not more than 50 investors; a public fund needs authorised share capital of at least US$2m of which at least US$1m is paid-up (or issued and fully-paid in the case of a unit trust), or it can be listed on a recognised exchange.
Licensed mutual funds and fund administrators are exempt from taxes, including social security taxes.

SHIP MANAGEMENT AND MARITIME OPERATIONS

The Merchant Shipping Act 1992 governs the shipping industry in the Seychelles. Ships and yachts may be registered in the Seychelles under the terms of the Act. Consular and diplomatic representatives of Seychelles abroad are also empowered to issue provisional certificates of registration to vessels satisfying the ownership and registration criteria. The shipping law also provides for parallel registration of bareboat charters in the Seychelles registry; likewise, a Seychelles vessel may be parallel-registered abroad during chartering.
An International Business Company is the most effective vehicle for offshore ownership of a Seychelles-registered vessel or ship management operation. Such a company will be exempt from Seychelles taxation on profits and dividends. Sale and transfer of Seychelles-registered vessels or the companies owning them are also free of tax, as are the salaries of officers and crew of Seychelles-registered vessels operating internationally.
A normal range of documentation is required for Seychelles registration of a vessel. The age limit for registration is 15 years. The Government recognises most leading classification societies; for surveying and certification purposes the Government has appointed American bureau of Shipping, Bureau Veritas, Nippon kaiji Kyokai and Det Norske Veritas.

The Civil Aviation Act (amended in 1996) provides the framework for the registration of aircraft mortgages. As with ship registration, consular and diplomatic representatives of Seychelles abroad can issue provisional certification of registration.
The Seychelles is an increasingly popular centre for the leasing and insurance of ships and aircraft.

OFFSHORE LEGAL AND TAX REGIME

The main forms useful for offshore operations in the Seychelles are the International Business Company, the various types of Companies Act company, the Trust, and two new forms introduced in 2003: Special Licence Companies and Limited Partnerships. The International Corporate Service Providers Act, 2003, provides for the licensing of trust management and company formation agents.

FORMS OF OFFSHORE OPERATION

Offshore operations may take place within the following forms:

- Limited or Unlimited Companies Act Company
- International Business Company
- Limited Life Company
- Trust
- Special Licence Company (formed under the Companies Act)
- Limited Partnership

TAX TREATMENT OF OFFSHORE OPERATIONS

Offshore Seychelles entities are subject to the following fee and tax structures:
International Business Companies pay registration fees as follows:

- $100 for a company with authorised capital up to $5,000;
- $300 for a company with authorised capital over $5,000 and up to $50,000;
- $1,000 for a company whose authorised capital is over $50,000.

The continuing annual renewal fee for IBC status is the same amount. There is a scale of fees in the International Business Companies Act covering inspection of documents in the Registry, copies of entries, increase of capital etc. etc. The fee levels are fixed for the life of an IBC, whatever subsequent changes may take place to fee levels.
IBCs are exempt from the Business Tax, from withholding taxes and from Stamp Duty; however they pay social security contributions (see Personal Taxation) on the salaries of employees unless the IBC is in the International Trade Zone (see below) or the employees are crew members of a ship in international waters.

Offshore (Non-Domestic) Banks pay a license application processing fee of $2,000 and an annual license fee of $15,000. See Offshore Business Sectors for details of the licensing regime. Banks are exempt from the Business Tax and withholding taxes, from customs duties and from Stamp Duty. They can if they wish elect to pay Business Tax at a rate which is agreed with the Commissioner of Taxes. Banks pay social security contributions in respect of their employees (see Personal Taxation).
Offshore (Non-Domestic) Insurance Companies pay license application processing fees and annual license fees as follows:

- License application processing fee $500 for an offshore license;
- Annual license fee $1,500 for either offshore general insurance or offshore life insurance;
- Annual license fee $3,000 for both offshore life and general business;
- Annual license fee $1,000 for a single-parent captive insurer.

See Offshore Business Sectors for details of the licensing regime.
Offshore insurance companies are exempt from the Business Tax, from withholding taxes, from customs duties and from Stamp Duty. They can if they wish elect to pay Business Tax at a rate which is agreed with the Commissioner of Taxes. There is a guarantee of exemption from future taxes for 20 years from the time of registration. Insurance companies pay social security contributions in respect of their employees (see Personal Taxation).
International Free Zone (SITZ) Companies pay annual license fees and application processing fees as follows:

- Redistribution license: $550;
- Light Assembly License: $550;
- Manufacturing License: $2,700 plus $1,300 initial processing fee;
- Processing License: $2,700 plus $1,300 initial processing fee;
- Export Services License: $1,500 plus $500 initial processing fee.

These license fees are fixed for the life of a licensed company. See Law of Offshore for details of the regulatory regime and licensing process for SITZ companies.
SITZ companies are exempt from the Business Tax, from withholding taxes, from customs duties and from Stamp Duty. SITZ employers are also exempt from the need to pay social security contributions in respect of directors or employees.
International (Offshore) Trusts pay an initial registration fee of $100. Offshore Trusts are exempt from the Business Tax, from withholding taxes and from Stamp Duty. See Law of Offshore for a details of Seychelles Trust legislation.
Limited Partnerships pay a registration fee of US$200. They may receive income from sources outside of Seychelles and distribute such income to foreign partners without incurring a Seychelles tax liability. In addition:

- An LP is exempt from all Seychelles tax or duty on income or profits of the LP;
- An LP is exempt from stamp duty on property transfers, share transfers and other business transactions;
- An LP is exempt from trades tax on all furniture and equipment imported into Seychelles for office use;
- An LP has exemptions under the Social Security Act.

These exemptions granted under the LP Act are guaranteed for twenty years and continue in force thereafter unless otherwise provided for by written law.
Special Licence Companies (CSL) pay a US$200 application fee, an annual licence fee of US$1,000, and a US$200 annual filing fee. They may carry on permitted business inside as well as outside of Seychelles. The CSL entity is a Seychelles domestic company (under the Companies Act 1972), which is granted a special licence under the Companies (Special Licence) Act and has access to Seychelles' steadily expanding network of double taxation avoidance treaties - of particular interest is its DTA with China. In addition:

- A CSL is liable to Seychelles business tax at the rate of 1.5% on its world-wide income (as an exception to the Seychelles territorial tax system, any foreign income derived by a CSL will be deemed to be Seychelles-sourced income);

- A CSL is exempt from from withholding taxes on dividends, interest and royalties.
- A CSL is exempt from stamp duty on property transfers, share transfers and other business transactions.
- A CSL is exempt from trades tax on all furniture and equipment imported into Seychelles for office use.
- A CSL has exemptions under the Social Security Ac and from work permit fees for expatriate workers.

These exemptions granted under the CSL Act are guaranteed for ten years and continue in force thereafter unless otherwise provided for by written law.

TAXATION OF FOREIGN EMPLOYEES OF OFFSHORE OPERATIONS

There are no special rules applying to the foreign or Seychelles employees of offshore operations, other than the exemption from social security contributions applying to the crew of ships and aircraft. The various exemptions from Business Tax and social security contributions described above do not apply to employees. See Domestic Personal Taxes for the general principles of individual taxation in the Seychelles, which also apply to the resident employees of nonresident entities. Taxation of employees through low social security contributions is in fact very light.

Employers however do not only have to pay relatively high social security contributions in respect of employees (it amounts to an income tax in all but name), but for foreign employees they also have to pay the 'Gainful Occupation Permit' fee of $1,800 per employee per year unless they are a SITZ company.

EXCHANGE CONTROL

In the Seychelles there is no restriction placed on payment of imports or invisibles, although import permits are required for certain products. Under the Exchange Control (Exemption) (Amendment) Order, 1995, it is illegal to deal in foreign currency other than through an authorised dealer. Since the government maintains a highly over-priced currency rate against the US dollar for the Seychelles rupee, the currency is far from free and 'official' rupees are hard to come by. There is a thriving black market.

OFFSHORE ACTIVITIES

International Business Companies are permitted various activities within the Seychelles without compromising their offshore status under the Act; these include:

- professional contacts with lawyers, accountants etc.;
- preparation and maintenance of books and records;
- the holding of directors' or shareholders' meetings;
- ownership of shares in other Seychelles companies, whether under the Act or the 1942 Companies Law;
- ownership of Government or Central Bank securities;
- ownership of a vessel registered in Seychelles.

Companies operating within the Seychelles International Trade Zone may apply to the Seychelles International Business Authority, which governs its operations, to conduct trade with Seychelles partners or customers outside the Zone. Income from such activity must be accounted for separately, and will be subject to the Business Tax.

Banks and insurance companies operating offshore under license are prohibited from domestic trading, for which a separate license would be required; however they can undertake local activities broadly similar to those sketched out above for IBCs.

EMPLOYMENT AND RESIDENCE

In order to work in the Seychelles, a 'Gainful Occupation Permit' is needed, which must be applied for by the employer, and costs $360 per person per year. In addition there are restrictions on the percentage of foreign employees permitted in a company. Only in the SITZ can 100% of the workforce be foreign, and Permits are not required; normally the percentage is quite low, although there are exceptions for some types of offshore entity, and reduced rates of $120 per year apply to permits issued to approved investors under the Investment Promotion Act, who can employ up to 25% foreign staff on that basis, and another 25% at normal rates.
Foreigners cannot own land in the Seychelles without Government approval.

DOMESTIC CORPORATE TAXATION

The Seychelles has a territorial basis of taxation; that is, profits are taxed only if they are derived or deemed to be derived from a source in the Seychelles. There is no capital gains tax; interest, dividends and other payments received from abroad are likewise not taxed. There is no taxation of individual income, but social security contributions are payable which amount to an income tax - see Personal Taxation.

SCOPE OF BUSINESS TAX

The Business Tax Act 1987 as amended governs company taxation in the Seychelles. The Act states that resident, non-resident corporate and non-corporate businesses are liable to pay business tax on their income derived from the Seychelles. A company is considered resident if it is incorporated in Seychelles. A company not incorporated in the Seychelles that conducts business there is resident if its central management is located in the Seychelles or if its voting power is controlled by shareholders who reside there.

Income is defined as all income received by a sole trader, partnership, trust estate or company, less a number of types of exempted income of which the following are some of the main headings:

- the proceeds of rental properties other than dwellings;
- profits from dealing in or selling property;
- royalties;
- fees and commissions in respect of the sale of property or the processing of money loans;
- lease premiums;
- income on which a final withholding tax has been levied (see Withholding Tax below - the 10% and 40% rates are considered to be 'final').

BACK TO TOP

Rates of Business Tax
Tax rates are the same for corporate and non-corporate businesses. The following rates apply:

Taxable Income, SR		Tax on lower bands, SR	Rate on Excess, %
Exceeding	Not Exceeding		
	24,000		0
24,000	48,000		25

48,000	96,000	6,000	30
96,000		20,400	40

Note that an entity with a Certificate of Approval under the Investment Promotion Act 1994 may be exempt from part or all of the Business Tax, or may have special deductions or tax credits. Companies in the International Trade Zone also have tax privileges.

BACK TO TOP

Calculation of Taxable Base

Allowable expenditure is that incurred 'in the course of carrying on business activities', excluding capital, private and domestic expenses. A normal range of expenses are deductible. The following list gives some of the main additional deductions that are permitted:

- Pension scheme contributions;
- Professional fees incurred in preparation of the tax return;
- Net salaries and wages, but only if social security contributions have been deducted; owners and partners are not permitted a deduction of their salaries;
- Royalties and other payments made to non-residents from which withholding tax has been deducted (see below);
- Previous years' losses, which can be carried forward only for five years; losses cannot be carried back; capital losses are not deductible;
- Non-capital expenditure on repairs to premises, plant and machinery;
- Losses incurred in property dealing;
- Specific bad debt write-offs; provisions for this or other purposes are not deductible;
- Office buildings are depreciated at a rate of 50% for the first year and 25% for the second and third years; hotels are depreciated at a rate of 20% for the first year and 10% for the following eight years; other buildings are depreciated at a straight-line rate of 4%; other assets are depreciated at conventional straight-line rates;
- Interest on borrowings made for the purpose of producing assessable income; the rate of interest chargeable is limited by reference to Central Bank rates.

FILING REQUIREMENTS AND PAYMENT OF TAX

The tax year is normally the calendar year, ending 31st December. A tax return must be submitted by March 31st following the end of the tax year, along with the signed-off accounts.

BACK TO TOP

Withholding Tax

There are the following withholding taxes in the Seychelles:

- 15% on dividends paid to non-residents (this is a final tax);
- 10% on interest paid to non-residents other than financial institutions (for whom a nil rate applies); this is a final tax;
- 40% on interest payments by a Seychelles financial institution at maturity of a bearer security issued by that institution; this is a final tax;
- 15% on royalties paid to residents;
- 15% on royalties paid to non-residents on certain types of royalty (copyrights, patent, design and trademark royalties are exempt).

PERSONAL TAXATION

The only significant tax bearing on individuals is the social security tax; there is no income tax as such, no capital gains, gift, property or estate taxes. Foreign-source income is untaxed. There are import duties on many items and a VAT was introduced in 2003.

RESIDENCE AND LIABILITY FOR TAXATION

There are no statutory residence rules as such, but an individual is considered resident if he is present in the Seychelles for more than 180 days in any one tax year. The distinction between residence and non-residence is material only in respect of Seychelles-source dividends, interest and royalties, which mostly bear withholding tax if paid to non-residents (some types of royalty do not).

As regards taxation, there is no distinction between foreign and Seychellois individuals. There is no individual income tax as such, but all employees and their employers pay social security contributions, which at least as far as the employer is concerned amount to an income tax.

If an individual has Seychelles-source business income, whether from self-employment or as the sole proprietor of a business or as a partner in a business, then he will pay Business Tax on the net income - see Direct Corporate Taxation for the details. Foreign-source income is not taxable; neither is Seychelles-source income on which 'final' withholding tax has been levied; again, see Direct Corporate Taxation - Withholding Tax for the details. Payments on which social security charges have been levied are also exempt from Business Tax.

SOCIAL SECURITY TAX

Employers and employees make social security contributions in the Seychelles; these also apply to directors' fees, payments in kind and royalties paid for services performed.

The employee pays 5% of salary; the employer pays according to the following scale:

Monthly remuneration, SR		Employer's Contribution, %
Exceeding	Not Exceeding	
	1,000	10
1,000	2,000	20
2,000	10,000	35
10,000		40

The employer withholds both his and the employee's contributions and remits them monthly to the tax authorities.

LABOUR REGULATION

REGULATORY ENVIRONMENT

The main concern of employment legislation in the Seychelles is to improve the skill levels and employment prospects of the local work-force: the increasingly sophisticated requirements of the international businesses that the Government has succeeded in attracting to the country tend to suck in foreign workers to the detriment of local employment. This is also true of the more entrepreneurial Seychellois themselves, who start companies and then need to employ foreigners when the skills they need cannot be found locally. It is obviously a difficult thing for a population of 75,000 that was until quite recently predominantly agrarian to supply the range of skills needed by modern business.

WORK PERMITS

The employment market is quite closely regulated in the Seychelles, as explained above. There are quite low limits set on the percentage of foreign workers allowed in most businesses, and work permits, called 'Gainful Occupation Permits' cost RS 18,000 per annum per foreign employee. These rules are relaxed for businesses licensed under the Investment Promotion Act, and for businesses in the International Trade Zone.

IMPORTANT BUSINESS CONTACTS

LAW FIRMS

Côte d'Azur-Mahe Registered Agent Ltd

Trinity House, 1st Floor, P O Box 1402, Victoria,Mahe, Seychelles	Telephone +248 510024	Fax +248 610216

COMPANY FORMATION AND SHIP REGISTRATION

A.C.T. Registered Agents (Pty) Ltd

The Company Shop, 1st Floor Alied Building, P O Box 381, Victoria, Seychelles	Telephone +248 224899	Fax +248 244601

Côte d'Azur-Mahe Registered Agent Ltd

Trinity House, 1st Floor, P O Box 1402, Victoria,Mahe, Seychelles	Telephone +248 510024	Fax +248 610216

FIFCO (Offshore) Services Ltd

Suite 102, Premier Building, P O Box 308 Victoria, Mahe, Seychelles	Telephone +248 323332	Fax +248 324009

International Business Agency (Pty) Ltd

313 Victoria House, P O Box
673 Victoria,
Mahe, Seychelles

Telephone +248 225562 | Fax +248 225626

International Business Registration Agents (Pty) Ltd

Revolution Avenue, P O Box 18
Victoria, Mahe,
Seychelles

Telephone +248 322577 | Fax +248 324069

International Corporate Agents Limited

102 Aarti Chambers, Mont
Fleuri, P O Box 870
Victoria, Mahe, Seychelles

Telephone + 248 225755 | Fax +248 225991

Mayfair Trust Group Limited

Suites 25 & 27, Second Floor,
Oliaji Trade Centre
Francis Rachel Street, PO Box
1312
Victoria, Seychelles

Telephone + 248 226099 | Fax +248 226043

Victoria Corporate Agents

2nd Floor, Jivan's Complex,
P.O.Box 931
Mont Fleuri, Mahe, Seychelles

Telephone +248 610780 | Fax +248 610781

TRUST MANAGEMENT

Côte d'Azur-Mahe Registered Agent Ltd

Trinity House, 1st Floor,
P O Box 1402, Victoria,Mahe,
Seychelles

Telephone +248 376896 | Fax +248 376006

International Corporate Agents Limited

102 Aarti Chambers, Mont
Fleuri, P O Box 870
Victoria, Mahe, Seychelles

Telephone +248 225755 | Fax +248 225991

Mayfair Trust Group Limited

Suites 25 & 27, Second Floor, Oliaji Trade Centre
Francis Rachel Street, PO Box 1312

Telephone + 248 226099 | Fax +248 226043

Victoria, Seychelles

ISP HOSTING AND E-COMMERCE SERVICE PROVIDERS

WEB Seychelles		
Premier Building, Bureau 316, Victoria, Mahe, Seychelles	Telephone +248 32 12 82	Fax +248 32 12 82

BANKING SERVICES AND ASSET MANAGEMENT

FIFCO (Offshore) Services Ltd		
Suite 102, Premier Building, P O Box 308 Victoria, Mahe, Seychelles	Telephone +248 323332	Fax +248 324009

CAPTIVE INSURANCE MANAGEMENT

FIFCO (Offshore) Services Ltd		
Suite 102, Premier Building, P O Box 308 Victoria, Mahe, Seychelles	Telephone +248 323332	Fax +248 324009

INTERNATIONAL TRADE ZONE

SEYCHELLES INTERNATIONAL BUSINESS AUTHORITY
P.O. Box 991
Seychelles International Trade Zone
Roche Caiman
Mahé
Seychelles
Tel: +248 380800
Fax: +248 380888
Website: www.siba.net
Email: siba@seychelles.net

GENERAL BRIEF

The International Trade Zone (ITZ) is a zone created by an Act of Parliament to allow for international trading in and through Seychelles. The ITZ is managed by the Seychelles International Business Authority (SIBA). This Authority, known as the ITZ Authority is mandated by law to regulate and control the activities that take place inside any declared International Trade Zone in Seychelles.

All such zones, designated by the Minister of Industry & International Business, are effectively considered as ex-territorial and as such some specific laws do not apply. These laws are specified in the SITZ Act, 1995 and regulations to that same act and these same laws are the applicable laws. The laws that govern the operations and financial freedom of SITZ operators are designed to give an international competitive edge to the SITZ operator. This is not to say that no laws apply to operators inside a given zone. A copy of the law that governs SITZ operators is attached herewith.

All operators must abide strictly to the Act and its regulations. The ITZ Authority (SIBA) will be responsible for the total administration of the zone and will hence be the sole Authority which all ITZ operators are answerable to.

The ITZ itself is designed to cater for the needs of re-distributors, and exporters and re-exporters of goods and services. Seychelles is strategically placed in the Indian Ocean to serve the region and elsewhere. The SITZ licence application form, therefore allows the Authority to evaluate projects submitted by investors in order to assess their relative merits and qualification as potential ITZ operators. Information given therein will be treated in absolute confidence. Likewise it is expected that all information given is a true statement and not merely supplied to satisfy known and expected requirements of the ITZ Authority. Please note that the concessions granted to International Trade Zone licence holders are subject to the International Trade Zone Act as may be amended from time to time. Please read these Acts carefully. Should you be unsure of any item or details contained therein please consult SIBA or your attorney as you deem appropriate.

Finally, you will be reassured to note that all information provided to this office is kept in strict confidence. We hope you will be successful in your application and thank you for your interest in investing in Seychelles.

SETTING UP IN THE SEYCHELLES INTERNATIONAL TRADE ZONE (SITZ)

Incentives offered by the Seychelles International Trade Zone

The Seychelles International Trade Zone (SITZ) is an environment created by an Act of Parliament, through the SITZ Act 1994, to promote export oriented companies setting-up shop in Seychelles. The incentives provided are numerous and they include:

- 0% tax on business profits and dividends
- 0% import duty and GST for capital equipment*, raw materials, office furniture and equipment
- 0% trades tax and GST on intermediate and final products
- Employers are exempt form Social Security
- Exempt from Work Permit for foreign workers
- 100% foreign ownership permissible
- 0% withholding tax
- Able to open a foreign exchange bank account with a local bank and having 100% access to funds in that bank account
- Ability to import foreign workers for skills absent in Seychelles
- Confidentiality guaranteed under provisions of the SITZ Act
- Ready-made warehouses and offices available for rent in the zone that reduces set-up period

* 'Capital Equipment' does not, however, include motor vehicles used by owners/operators or their employees. Only under special circumstances may the minister grant exemption for trades tax payable and GST on the importation of motor vehicles.

TYPES OF LICENSED ACTIVITIES

The types of activities that are permissible are numerous, as long as the main focus of business operation is exporting. The following table outlines the fees associated with each type of licensed activity.

Activity	Annual fee (US$)	Processing fee (US$)*
Redistribution license	550	NIL

Light-Assembly License	550	NIL
Manufacturing License	2700	1300
Processing License	2700	1300
Management Export Services License	1500	500

* The processing fee is a one-time payment at the initial stage of the project being licensed

SALE TO THE DOMESTIC MARKET

However, the company is also allowed to sell a percentage to the local market, upon an application to the Ministry of Finance, through SIBA. The usual maximum percentage of total output that is permissible to be sold to the domestic market is approximately 20%.

Requirements when making an application for SITZ status
- **SITZ Application Form** and **Personal Questionnaire Form** have to be filled out.
- **Copy of passport, Curriculum Vitae** and **Bank Reference** must be submitted.
- A **detailed business** plan must accompany the above forms. The level of detail required is explained in a checklist that can be found on page 5 of the SITZ application form. Not all items will be of relevance to your proposed activity. However, we demand that an accurate representation of the proposed activities be given. Additionally, detail that has not been covered by the checklist should be included.
- **Cash-flow forecasts and Profit and Loss accounts forecasts** for three years must be submitted.
- If the proposed activity is an on-going activity, in the form of a branch or subsidiary, then we would require **Audited Accounts** of the past three years from the parent company to be submitted to SIBA. The information that you provide will be treated confidentially.
- The company will need to be **Incorporated with the Seychelles Registrar of Companies**. However, we recommend that you only incorporate the company after SIBA has given provisional approval of the project.
- A **Booking and Administrative Fee** will have to be paid once management approves the project upon submission of all documents required. These fees will guarantee that the warehouse unit or office requested will be available for a period of one month prior to setting-up of the operations. The period of one month is extendable (possibly at no extra cost) depending on the situation.

The administrative fee will cover any administrative costs that SIBA incurs during the processing of the application for SITZ status and preparing the handing-over of the warehouse or office.

The booking fee will amount to 50% of the requested unit's monthly rent. ***This fee is refundable*** once you physically set-up in the warehouse or office.

RATES OF WAREHOUSE AND OFFICES

Warehouse spaces (US$)

Warehouse Size (m^2)	Rate per m^2 per year	Monthly Rate	2 months deposit	Booking Fee	Administrative Fee
35	80	233.33	466.67	116.67	100
200	65	1083.33	2166.67	541.67	200
400	60	2000.00	4000.00	1000.00	400

500	60	2500.00	5000.00	1250.00	500
1000	55	4583.33	9166.67	2291.67	700
1500	55	6875.00	13750.00	3437.50	700

* The booking fee is refundable once the promoter has set-up his operations in the zone.

Warehouse-Offices (US$)

Office Size (m^2)	Rate per m^2 per year	Monthly Rate	2 months deposit	Booking Fee	Administrative Fee	Air-Condition maintenance fee per month
12	200	200.00	400.00	200.00	100	30
22	200	366.67	733.33	200.00	100	30
28	200	466.67	933.33	230.00	100	30
35	200	583.33	1166.67	230.00	100	30

* The booking fee is refundable once the promoter has set-up his operations in the zone.

FREQUENTLY ASKED QUESTIONS

1. What projects are allowed?

1.1 Any Project that:
- involves redistribution of goods from Seychelles
- involves the light assembly of goods in Seychelles
- involves manufacturing or processing of goods in Seychelles
- involves management services for export markets including:
- regional headquarters
- Professionals Services Companies such as Software Development Companies, Consultancy etc....
- e-commerce services from Seychelles

1.2 All projects must be geared predominantly at an export market

1.3 The projects must not pose a threat to the environment

2. Who do I see first?

- The Seychelles International Business Authority (SIBA) is the authority that will issue an ITZ licence.
- SIBA will firstly need to have an idea of what your project is about
- This can be done by arranging a meeting between yourself and SIBA
- Otherwise, you can contact one of our locally licensed agents, "International Corporate Service Providers", who can guide you through the application process. A list of these agents can be downloaded from our website, www.siba.net .

3. What and Where is SIBA?

- SIBA is autonomous corporate body established by an Act and is a one stop shop for all licensing, imports etc., into the zone
- SIBA's offices are found on the International Trade Zone at Roche Caiman
- Call in at the SIBA Headquarters at International Trade Zone Roche Caiman and you will be guided to the appropriate offices.
- Contact address:

P.O. Box 991
Victoria, Mahé
Seychelles
Tel: +248 380800
Fax: +248 380888

E-mail: siba@seychelles.net
Website: http://www.siba.net

4. What documents do I need to submit for application?

- Application Form
- Personal Questionnaire Forms
- Copy of Passport
- Curriculum Vitae
- Bank Reference
- Detailed Business Plan
- 3 year Cashflow or Profit and Loss Account
- Audited Accounts for the past 3 years (if applicable)

5. What is the next step once approval is given?

- You will need to register a company through the Registrar of local companies
- Once this is done, SIBA will require a copy of your certificate of incorporation and the Memorandum and Articles of Association
- An ITZ Licence will then be issued to you

6. What concessions am I entitled to?

Essentially no taxes are applicable to you in the ITZ. Hence you are exempted from:

- Business Tax
- Trades Tax and GST on intermediate and final products
- Trades Tax and GST on imports of capital equipment*
- Employer's contribution to Social Security
- Withholding Tax
- Payment of Gainful Occupation Permit fees for allowed expatriate workers

* 'Capital Equipment' does not, however, include motor vehicles used by owners/operators or their employees. Only under special circumstances may the minister grant exemption for trades tax and GST payable on the importation of motor vehicles.

Once licensed, your company will be able to maintain its own foreign exchange bank accounts

7. What else does SIBA provide?

- SIBA owns offices, large warehouses or shell factory facilities in secure zones
- These will be leased to you at competitive rates
- A guarantee that concessions granted to you will last for the duration of the licence, even if new regulations are issued subsequent to the granting of your licence. Should more favourable regulations be issued, you will, however, benefit.

8. What must I undertake?

- You must ensure that your output is geared for an export market as the ITZ is predominantly export oriented.
- You must ensure that you provide insurance cover for all your workers within the zone.
- You must ensure that all transactions are carried out in conformity with the laws of the zone.
- You must ensure that books and records are properly kept and regular reporting must be done to SIBA.
- You must ensure that your project does not pose a threat to the environment.

9. What are the licence Fees

The annual fees are as follows:

- Redistribution Licence: US$550
- Light-Assembly Licence: US$550
- Manufacturing Licence: US$2,700 plus US$1,300 one off processing fee
- Processing Licence: US$2,700 plus US$1,300 one off processing fee
- Export Services Licence including headquarters operations: US$1,500 plus US$500 one off processing fee

SEYCHELLES LAW OF OFFSHORE AND ECONOMIC DEVELOPMENT STRATEGY

INDIAN OCEAN TAX HAVEN

The Seychelles are a string of 92 small islands that lie about 1,000 miles off the east coast of Africa in the middle of the Indian Ocean. The Seychelles islands have historically been a tourist destination. Devoid of human inhabitants until the early part of the 17th Century, when it was ruled by France, the Seychelles' multi-lingual population today is made up of Indian, African, Chinese and Europeans, with English the official language. The Seychelles population numbers about 73,000, with most living on the Seychelles economy 73,000, with most living on the main island of Malle. While the mainstay of the Seychelles economy in tourism, according to a recent article in The National Enquirer (March, 12 – 1996), recently the Seychelles government has taken measures to attract a less affable element – wealthy drug kingpins from around the world!

According to Philip Smith of the National Enquirer, (largest circulation of any paper in America) mobsters and drug kingpins from the U.S. and other countries now have a safe haven where the long arm of the law can't touch them.

The Seychelles Islands government – which gets $3 million a year in U.S. tax payers' money is offering citizenship and immunity from prosecution . . . to any thug who'll fork over $10 million! "We're deeply concerned by this," said Jonathan M. Winer, deputy assistant secretary of state for law enforcement at the U.S. State Department.

"It's a very popular tourist spot for Europeans because of its beauty and climate," said Sheri Sprigg of the U.S. State Department. "It's very safe. There's very little crime."

Last November, in an attempt to boost the country's economy, President Erance Rene announced that for $10 million, the Seychelles would grant "immunity from prosecution for all criminal proceedings whatsoever." That means well-heeled criminals won't be extradited from the Seychelles to any foreign country for trial.

So far, four men suspected of extensive criminal activities in Europe are believed to have obtained citizenship there. The U.S., along with Britain and France, has lodged strong protests.

"It's outrageous that the Seychelles governments is doing this – and to think that American taxpayers are helping them!" said Mort Feldman, executive vice president of the Nation al Association of Chiefs of Police. "Our government should stop sending them money. "Unless we do something about this, every major drug dealer and organized crime figure is going to hightail it over there and bask in the sun – happy in the knowledge they can thumb their noses at the rest of the world!"

HEADING IN A NEW DIRECTION

Seychelles gained its independence in 1976. Since then a number of major economic, social and political developments have taken place. In the early 1990s a major shift in policy was announced. In 1993, a new constitution was drafted and approved by national referendum based on multi-party democracy.

Following the new constitution, the new Government undertook a total reform of the economy and material policy decisions were announced with a number of steps taken to promote inward bound investment by the private sector. In 1994, the Seychelles announced its intention to turn the country into a full-fledged international business center (a.k.a. a tax haven), following a study, which had been commissioned and implemented by foreign consultants.

NEW LAWS AND REGULATIONS

The corner stones of the jurisdictions' new economic expansion was the setting up of a collection of modern business legislations modeled after other successful havens, including the British Virgin Islands, the Bahamas, the Cook Islands, Panama, and the Caymans. The new legislation include:

1 – The International Business Companies Act, 1994;

2 – The International Trusts Act, 1994;

3 – The Seychelles International Business Authority Act;

4 – The Seychelles International Trade Zone Act.

Aside from these legislations there was a necessity for a regulatory body. In early 1995, the Seychelles International Business Authority (SIBA) was set up to act as regulator for the new of business legislation being introduced. Made up of both private sector members and Government Statutory members, the SIBA's main role is to advance the jurisdiction as a center for International business activity, safeguard that international business transactions are conducted in a proper fashion, and carry out the function of an Authority or Registrar under the law.

BUILDING THE INTERNATIONAL BUSINESS CENTER

Another pillar in the establishing of the nation as an offshore center has been the development within four main areas of the international Business Center. These include: The incorporation of international businesses in the jurisdiction: The development of Seychelles as an International businesses; the promotion of the registration and licensing of certain activities in the jurisdiction including those under the Merchant Shipping Act and the Air Navigation Act.

LOW AND NO TAXES A PROMISES

If new legislation, and the creation of International trade center, were to be the keys to converting the jurisdiction into a successful tax haven like the Cook Islands or BVI, then the need for a steady tax regime has been another. Recognizing this need, the Government has recently enacted the Investment Promotion Act 1994, which enables businesses to operate under a guaranteed taxation climate with special incentives laid.

Employers receive an automatic entitlement to employ up to 25% of employees from overseas, at a confessional fee of SR. 500 per month per employee out in the legislation. In order to assist investors a 'one stop shop' IDEAS (Investment Development Advisory Service) has been up in the Ministry of Finance and Communications.

INVESTMENT PROMOTION ACT 1994

Applications for Certificate of Approval under the legislation have to be filed, and when approved will give the investor access to all the incentives for the category of investment. The legislation applies to both existing and potential investments, and both local and foreign owned businesses are eligible.

Investments are classified as Agricultural and Marine Resources, Industrial and Manufacturing, Professional Services, Small Scale Industrial Investments and Tourism Development Investments.

COMMON LAW TRUST LEGISLATION?

The jurisdiction's legal system has been influenced by the principles of the Napoleonic civil code and common law. As such the trust concept, which is familiar to all English speaking jurisdictions, is not recognized by the Seychelles civil code. Nevertheless, in order to provide a strong legislative environment for international trust, the International Trusts Act 1994 has been introduced recently by the Government.

INTERNATIONAL TRUST ACT 1994

For the most part, there are few restrictions as to what a trust can and cannot do in Seychelles. Revocable and irrevocable Trusts are permitted. Trusts cannot involve any land in Seychelles, but trusts may own and trade-in other shares, open bank accounts or even deal in Government securities in the country.

Neither the trust, nor the transfer or disposition by a person creating an international trust can be nullified by any foreign rule or forced heir ship. An international trust may be charitable or non-charitable. **An international trust may be created by an oral declaration or by an instrument in writing, a will or codicil.** There are no limitations on the accumulation of income.

No requirement to specify the name of the grantor or the name of the beneficiary, unless the latter is a Seychelles national or a body corporate resident in Seychelles. Confidentiality is maintained, and it is illegal to divulge or produce any information or certificate relating to an international trust, except under an injunction of the Seychelles. An international trust is valid and executable in Seychelles.

An international trust may be set up to trade (commercial trust), to deal with life insurance (life insurance trust), to manage provident and pension funds or cash deposits etc. The grantors (i.e. trust creator or settlor) or the trustees can be named as beneficiaries under the trust. The grantor does not at any time during the duration of the trust have to be a resident of Seychelles, but at least one trustee must be so resident. The law governing an international trust is the law chosen by the grantor to be the proper law, expressed or implied, in the terms of the trust.

SETTING-UP AN INTERNATIONAL TRUST

How can you form an International Trust in Seychelles, and what about taxation? It is required that you apply through a licensed trustee incorporated in the jurisdiction. The licensed trustee would prepare the necessary documentation on your behalf and submit it to the SIBA, which would then register the cost. The standard fee for government registration is US$100. There are no taxes on international trusts and there is no demand for stamp duty or capital gains tax.

THE IBC ACT 1994

The IBC Act 1994 states that no fee will affect an IBC incorporated under the Act, before the coming into force of the fee increase. Accordingly, the fees paid by an IBC are fixed for life.

INTERNATIONAL TRADE ZONE

The current legislation proposes that most of the earnings of a Seychelles International Trade Zone (SITZ) company would have to originate from the re-export of goods through the jurisdiction. All companies who operate within the SITZ will enjoy the following: Exemption from all trades tax and duties on imports and exports Exemption from Business Tax and all

1 – Income and Corporate Taxes

2 – Exemption from the payment of Social Security Contribution and Pension scheme

3 – Exemption from payment of work permits for expatriate workers.

The success of the International Business Center revolves around maximizing the use or the strategic location of the Seychelles, and in particular the development of an International Trade Zone. A number of elements favor the jurisdiction in this regard, not least its geographical location, centrally placed and surrounded by Africa, India and Australia in an area with perfect climate conditions. A modern airport and port are operational, prime area land is available for development, and there are 6 licensed banks, in addition to 8 licensed management companies, operating in the country.

The Seychelles is a signatory to the Lome TV convention benefiting form the provisions of the convention, a member state of the African Caribbean Pacific countries, and a signatory to the Multilateral Investment Guarantee Agency, which protects all investors from expropriation. With extensive co-operation of neighboring countries, the region is coming to be known as the 'Indian Pacific Rim.'

STATUTES

Central Bank of Seychelles Act 2004
Civil Aviation Act 1996
Companies Law 1972
Companies (Special Licence) Act, 2003
Financial Institutions Act 1984
Insurance Act 1994
Insurance (Non-Domestic Insurance Business) Regulations 1996
International Business Companies Act 1994
Interactive Gambling Act 2003
International Corporate Service Providers Act 2003
International Trade Zone Regulations 1995
International Trusts Act 1994
Investment Promotion Act 1994
Limited Partnership Act, 2003
Merchant Shipping Act 1992
Mutual Assistance in Criminal Matters Act 1995
Mutual Funds Act 1997
Protected Cell Companies Act, 2003
Seychelles International Business Authority Act 1994
Companies (Special Licence) Act, 2003
Anti Money Laundering Act, 1996
Companies Ordinance, 1972
Electronic Transactions Act, 2001
Financial Institutions Act,1984
Insurance Act,1994
Interactive Gambling Act, 2003
International Business Companies Act, 1994
International Corporate Services Providers Act, 2003)
Limited Partnerships Act, 2003
Mutual Fund Act, 1997
Protected Cell Companies Act, 2003
Seychelles International Business Authority Act, 1994

DOUBLE TAXATION AGREEMENTS

Double Taxation Agreement with China
Double Taxation Agreement with Oman
Double Taxation Agreement with South Africa
Double Taxation Agreement with Indonesia
Double Taxation Agreement with Zimbabwe
Double Taxation Agreement with Malaysia
Double Taxation Agreement with Botswana

Double Taxation Agreement with Thailand
Double Taxation Agreement with Mauritius

In May 2001 it was announced that several amendments to the current exchange control and money and trade taxation laws would be considered by the National Assembly in order to tackle the country's growing black market. The Seychelles aimed to close loopholes that existed in laws such as the Foreign Earnings Act, Exchange Control Act, Central Bank of Seychelles Act and the Trades Tax Act.

An amendment to the Foreign Earnings Act ensured that foreign exchange earners are obligated to use the country's banking system. A new definition of 'non-resident' enlarged on the term to include 'any person in or resident in Seychelles who engages in a trade, business or activity with another such person for or on behalf of or for the benefit or purpose of any person not resident in Seychelles.'

Amendments to the Trades Tax Act strengthened price controls and enable dthe authorities to put a 'true' value on imported goods. Changes to the Exchange Control Act required individuals who possess any foreign currency to show evidence that it was obtained from a registered dealer and prohibit the buying and selling foreign currency by authorised dealers at rates above the maximum rate or below the minimum rate determined by the Central Bank as well as prohibiting the export and import of Seychelles currency notes and coins in excess of R2,000. Amendments to the Central Bank Act led to the appointment of an Exchange Controller.

The Central Bank of Seychelles Act 2004 makes provision for the Central Bank to operate more as an independent institution.

Incoming President James Michel announced in his 2005 budget that he would oversee a programme of partial liberalisation of the foreign exchange regime, which has a restricting effect on investment.

BANKING LAW

Banking in the Seychelles is governed by the Financial Institutions Act 1984 as amended in 1995. Licences are issued by the Offshore Banking Department of the Central Bank and are granted only to companies incorporated under the Companies Act 1942 or foreign companies which have registered under the Companies Act. Licenses are issued for domestic banking, offshore banking, or both. When both are conducted, it must be through separate offices. Offshore banks are permitted to operate numbered accounts for their clients.

Applicants must supply extensive information to the Central Bank, including at least the following:

- the Memorandum and Articles of Association or Statutes;
- Head Office address and a list of shareholders (members);
- names of chief officers;
- the last three sets of financial accounts;

- a full business plan;
- an undertaking that funds will be provided to cover all obligations and liabilities incurred in the local office.

The Central Bank has 90 days to respond to an application, and does not have to give a reason for refusal. The refused applicant may appeal to the Minister and to the Court.
The Bank imposes various prudential requirements including the following:

- maintenance of unimpaired capital at a level agreed between the applicant and the Bank and in proportion to assets;
- maintenance of a reserve fund to which at least 10% of annual profits must be transferred until the fund equals the amount of paid-up or assigned capital;
- the average level of liquid assets must be maintained at the currently prescribed percentage of total liabilities.

The Bank requires monthly balance sheet submissions; accounts must be prepared and audited each year, and then published.
The Act contains extensive confidentiality provisions. For non-domestic banking business, disclosure is only permitted on order of the Court in response to an application by the Attorney-General.
The Bank has considerable powers of inspection and control over what it considers to be unsafe, unsound or unlawful practices.

TRUST LAW

The International Trusts Act 1994 established, for the first time, a regime for international trusts in the Seychelles; it does not provide for domestic trusts. The Act was drafted after a thorough study of current practice in a number of leading offshore jurisdictions. Under the Act, the Seychelles International Business Authority (SIBA) is appointed as the regulatory body for trusts, alongside the Court.
The Seychelles is mostly a civil law jurisdiction to which the concept of the trust was unknown; thus the Trusts Act has to be sufficient unto itself, and indeed it contains some basic definitions which include the admittance of charitable, trust, purpose trusts, constructive trusts, and trusts resulting from action by the Court. The following are some of the key features of the Seychelles Trust regime:

- An international trust may be created in writing, by will or by oral declaration;
- The settlor must reside outside the Seychelles for the duration of the trust; at least one trustee must reside in the jurisdiction, but this trustee may be an International Business Company (IBC), which shall not thus be deemed as resident; an IBC may therefore be a settlor;
- A financial institution licensed under the Financial Institutions Act 1994 may also be a settlor;
- The trust property may not include any Seychelles movable or immovable property or interests or rights to them in a Seychelles company owning such property;
- The local trustee may with permission own local property for the trustees' accommodation, and, again with permission, may invest in local securities;
- The settlor may choose the proper law of the trust; in the absence of a choice, the Act provides guidelines for establishing the proper law; in any event, the Seychelles Court has exclusive jurisdiction, and will apply the proper law itself (this allows the Act's forced heirship provisions to be effective);

- The names of settlors and beneficiaries and the trust accounts are confidential under the Act, unless a Court orders disclosure under the Anti-money Laundering Act;
- The standard perpetuity period is 100 years; but it does not apply to charitable or purpose trusts; a settlor cannot revoke a trust, but the beneficiaries can; the Court may revoke a fraudulent trust;
- The accumulation of income is permitted;
- A settlor can also be a trustee, and a beneficiary but not the sole beneficiary;
- Forced heirship judgements are specifically excluded.

The Act contains extensive wording dealing with all aspects of the setting-up of trusts, the rights and responsibilities of trustees, and the powers of the Court. The above brief details are given for purposes of general information, but reference should be made to the Act itself and to professional advisers before any action is taken.

ELECTRONIC GAMBLING LAW

The Interactive Gambling Act, 2003 provides for the licencing and regulation of any internet gambling business carried on in or from Seychelles. The Act conforms to strict international regulatory norms and draws heavily from solid Australian legislation.
"Interactive gaming" under the new Act extends to where:

- a prize of money or something else is offered, or can be won, under the rules of the game;
- a player enters, or takes a step in, the game by means of a telecommunication device (including interaction via a computer) and pays or undertakes to pay money or other valuable consideration to enter the game; and
- the winner is decided wholly or partly by chance; or by a competition or other activity in which the outcome is wholly or partly dependent on the player's skill.

The Act provides for the creation of special "players' accounts" whereby the operator can hold funds of a player on trust for them and with the operator having the right to debit the amount of a wager in an authorised game. Winnings may also be paid directly into these players' accounts. This option ensures that the player does not have to produce credit card and personal information for every wager, only when "recharging" his or her account. Player protection is afforded through these trust accounts, as well as operator and player security. An operator cannot provide credit to a player.
The regulatory authority will only grant licences to fit and proper persons and retains the right of approval of the gaming software and control system. The Act requires the annual auditing of an operator's accounts and financial statements; and submission of a copy of the audit report to the regulatory authority. The Act also provides for inspectors who will have powers of entry and search in the course of monitoring or enforcing compliance with the Act.

SEYCHELLES INTERNATIONAL TRADE ZONE

The International Trade Zone Act 1995 and the International Trade Zone Regulations 1995 provide for the establishment of free trade zones, which are delimited by a declaration of the Finance and Communications Minister, and can be for one company or many. The existing International Trade Zone (SITZ) on Mahe is established under the Act. Activities within the Zone are governed by the Seychelles International Business Authority (SIBA), which issues licenses to incoming companies.
Licenses are available for manufacturing, assembling, redistribution or service activities; retailing is not normally permitted within the Zone or from it, but SIBA has authority to give consent for it.

SIBA can request information at its discretion from an applicant for a license. See Offshore Legal and Tax Regimes for details of fees and taxes payable in the SITZ.
The Authority is responsible for the physical security of the Zone, and controls access to it. Officials of SIBA or of the Zone or police officers can search vehicles and shipments moving in and out of the Zone, and have power to seize goods they suspect are illegitimate. A license issued by SIBA can be revoked if the holder does not begin, or ceases the activity covered by the license. There is an appeal process, eventually to the Supreme Court. License holders must keep records of their activities, and these can be inspected by SITZ on demand, as can premises occupied by licence-holders. Information obtained by SITZ may not be divulged except on a Court order.The concessions available to licence holders in SITZ include:

- Exemption from customs duties on capital equipment to be used in SITZ;
- Exemption from social security contributions;
- Exemption from fees in respect of 'gainful occupation permits' (work permits);
- Entitlement to employ 100% foreign labour;
- Permission to acquire interests in immovable property or a company owning such an interest, for the purpose of carrying on activities in SITZ.

These concessions are given by way of disapplying the relevant other Acts or parts of them.

DOUBLE TAX TREATIES

The Seychelles has Double Tax Agreements in force with China, South Africa, Indonesia, Thailand, Oman, Malaysia, Namibia and Zimbabwe. Negotiations are said to have been concluded with Russia, Botswana, Vietnam, Malaysia, and Egypt. Discussions are underway with Tunisia, Cyprus, Malta, Indian and the Czech Republic.

The Government sees such treaties as being an important part of its scheme to develop as a key financial hub in the Indian Ocean, and is actively negotiating more treaties with a number of its trading partners. An Agreement on Double Taxation Avoidance and Prevention of Fiscal Evasion with respect to taxes on income between the Government of the Republic of Mauritius and the Government of the Republic of Seychelles was signed on 11 March 2005 by the Prime Minister of Mauritius, Paul Raymond Bérenger and the President of Seychelles, James Alix Michel.

OTHER INTERNATIONAL AGREEMENTS

Mutual Assistance Treaties: The Seychelles has no international treaties bearing on exchange of information, but the double tax treaties it is negotiating will include such clauses based on the OECD model. However there are a number of pieces of domestic legislation, including the Mutual Assistance in Criminal Matters Act 1995, the Anti-Money Laundering Act 1996, and most of the sectoral 'offshore' Acts which accept the need to provide information internationally when criminal behaviour is suspected. Usually the Court has to be involved, sometimes at the behest of the Attorney-General. In some cases, the legislation admits the possibility of 'fiscal' crime, which is not always the case among the country's competitors.

In its endeavour to participate in the fight against terrorism, Seychelles ratified in 2003 the following conventions: Convention Against the Taking of Hostages; Convention for the Suppression of Terrorist Bombings; Convention for the Suppression of the Financing of Terrorism; Convention Against Trans-National Organized Crime; Statute Establishing the International Criminal Court; Convention on the Physical Protection of Nuclear Material; and the Convention on the Marking of Plastic Explosives for the Purposes of Detection.

TRAVEL TO SEYCHELLES

US STATE DEPARTMENT SUGGESTIONS

PASSPORTS, VISAS & CUSTOMS

Passports
Everyone traveling to Seychelles must have a passport valid for at least 6 months beyond the end of travel.

Visas
Visas are not required. A Visitor's Permit, good for 4 weeks, is issued upon arrival at the airport. Travelers must have a return (or onward) air ticket, prebooked accommodations and sufficient money for their stay. If not, visitors may be required to post a security bond. The Permit may be renewed for 3 months at no cost and for 3 additional 3 month periods at a fee of 200 Seychelles rupees (US$40).

Gold Card
Not required.

In 1998 there was an initiative to require the purchase of a Gold Card by all visitors to Seychelles. This requirement was never made into law and is not in effect. Incorrect information on many websites states that the Gold Card is required.

Customs
Arriving passengers may import 200 cigarettes, 50 cigars or 250g tobacco; 1 liter of spirits or wine; 125 ml perfume or 250 ml toilet water; and other normally dutiable goods worth up to 1000 Seychelles rupees (US$200).

Firearms (including air powered devices), spear fishing equipment and non-prescription drugs are prohibited. The entry animals or food is subject to licensing. Pets may only be imported with written permission of the Chief Veterinary Officer of the country.

Currency Exchange
Banks are available for all arriving flights in the airport for currency exchange.

Departure Tax
Everyone over 12 years old must pay a US$40 departure tax when leaving the country. The tax may be purchased at any bank and can be purchased before arrival at the airport or at a bank in the airport.

Embassies
Telephone numbers for embassies (E), consulates (C) and honorary consuls (HC) of other countries in Seychelles:

USA*
UK (E)
China (E)
Cuba (E)
Cyprus (C)

Denmark (C)
Finland (C)
France (C)
Germany (HC)
India (E)
Madagascar (HC)
Mauritius (C)
Monaco (C)
Netherlands (C)
Norway (C)
Russia (E)
Sweden (C)
Switzerland (C)
(230) 208-2347*
(248) 225225
(248) 266808
(248) 224094
(248) 376215
(248) 224710
(248) 224710
(248) 224523
(248) 261222
(248) 224489
(248) 344030
(248) 376441
(248) 233316
(248) 261200
(248) 380300
(248) 266590
(248) 224710
(248) 371050

*US Embassy in Mauritius.

State Department Information
You are encouraged to read the following government information before your departure:

PUBLIC HOLIDAYS

Sunday	Dimanche
1st and **2nd January**	Le **1er** et le **2 janvier**
Good Friday	Vendredi Saint
Easter Saturday	Samedi Saint
1st May	Le **1er mai**
(Labour Day)	(Fête du Travail)
Corpus Christi	Fête Dieu
5th June	Le **5 juin**
(Liberation Day)	(Fête de Libération)
18th June (National Day)	Le **18 juin** (Fête Nationale)

29th June (Independence Day)	Le **29 juin** (Fête de l'Indépendence)
15th August (Assumption)	Le **15 Août** (l'Assomption)
1st November (All Saints Day)	Le **1er novembre** (La Toussaint)
8th December (Immaculate Conception)	Le **8 décembre** (l'Immaculée Conception)
25th December (Christmas Day)	Le **25 décembre** (Noël)

SUPPLEMENTS

BANKS

The Mauritius Commercial Bank (Seychelles) Limited
Caravelle House
P.O. Box 122
Victoria, Mahé
SEYCHELLES
Contact: Mr. Jocelyn Ah-Yue, Managing Director
Phone: (+248) 284555
Fax: (+248) 322676
Website: http://www.mcbseychelles.com

Barclays Bank Seychelles Ltd
P.O. Box 167
Victoria, Mahé
SEYCHELLES
Contact: Mr. Loganaden Sidambaram, Managing Director or Mr. Philip Bailey, Director Offshore Unit
Phone: (+248) 383838
Fax: (+248) 225062

Bank of Baroda
Trinity House
Albert Street
P.O. Box 124
Victoria, Mahé
SEYCHELLES
Contact: Mr. M. Phogat, Chief Executive
Phone: (+248) 323038
Fax: (+248) 324057

Habib Bank Limited
Sound & Vision House
Francis Rachel Street
P.O. Box 702
Victoria, Mahé
SEYCHELLES
Contact: Mr. Bilal Qureshi, Country Manager
Phone: (+248) 224371
Fax: (+248) 225614

Seychelles Savings Bank
Orion Mall
P.O. Box 531
Victoria, Mahé
SEYCHELLES
Contact: Mrs. Mathilda Bibi, Administration Officer
Phone: (+248) 294000
Fax: (+248) 224713

NOUVOBANQ
P.O. Box 241
Victoria, Mahé
SEYCHELLES
Contact: Mr. Ahmed Saeed, Managing Director
Phone: (+248) 293000
Fax: (+248) 224670

BMI Offshore Bank (Seychelles) Limited
P.O. Box 672, Office 12, Marina House, Eden Island
Victoria, Mahé
SEYCHELLES
Contact: Mr. Frank Hoareau, Managing Director
Phone: (+248) 345660
Fax: (+248) 344590
Website: http://www.bmi.com.sc/

ATTORNEYS & NOTARIES

Mr. Ramnikal Valabhji
Attorney at Law & Notary Public
State House Avenue
P.O. Box 297
Victoria, Mahé
SEYCHELLES
Phone: (+248) 322608 / 232608
Fax: (+248) 324176

Mr. Jacques Hodoul
Attorney at Law & Notary Public
Mont Fleuri, Mahé
SEYCHELLES
Phone: (+248) 224322
Fax: (+248) 224460

Mr. Pesi Pardiwalla, Mr. Conrad Lablache, Mr. Melchior Vidot
Pardiwalla Twomey Lablache
Attorneys at Law & Notary Public

Room 109
Premier Building
Victoria, Mahé
SEYCHELLES
Phone: (+248) 321071
Fax: (+248) 324100

Mr. Kieran Shah
Attorney at Law & Notary Public
State House Avenue
P.O. Box 297
Victoria, Mahé
SEYCHELLES
Phone: (+248) 322608 / 232608
Fax: (+248) 324176

Mr. Francis Mac Gregor
Attorney at Law & Notary Public
Law Centre
Oceangate House
P.O. Box 337
Victoria, Mahé
SEYCHELLES
Phone: (+248) 224564
Fax: (+248) 224599

Mr. Francis Chang Sam, Mr. Frank Ally
Attorneys at Law & Notary Public
Chambers of Francis Chang Sam
Room 16 – Kingsgate House
P.O. Box 1355
Victoria, Mahé
SEYCHELLES
Phone: (+248) 322912
Fax: (+248) 324221

Mr. Phillipe Boulle
Attorney at Law & Notary Public
Victoria Chambers
307 Victoria House
Victoria, Mahé
SEYCHELLES
Phone: (+248) 289200
Fax: (+248) 289210

Mr. Bernard Georges, Mrs Annette Georges
Attorneys at Law & Notary Public
Georges & Georges
Trinity House
SEYCHELLES
Phone: (+248) 224280
Fax: (+248) 224043

Mr. John Renaud
Attorney at Law & Notary Public
Allied Building
Victoria, Mahé
SEYCHELLES
Phone: (+248) 224881
Fax: (+248) 225044

Mr. Somasundaram Rajasundaram
Attorney at Law
Michel Building
Victoria, Mahé
SEYCHELLES
Phone: (+248) 226281
Fax:(+248) 225931

Mr. Serge Rouillon
Attorney at Law & Notary Public
Suite 102 – Aarti Chambers
P.O. Box 870
Victoria, Mont Fleuri, Mahé
SEYCHELLES
Phone: (+248) 225276
Mobile: (+248) 515276
Fax: (+248) 225991

Mr. Anthony Derjacques, Mr. Frank Elizabeth
Attorneys at Law & Notaries Public
Derjacques & Elizabeth Chambers
Victoria Law Firm
Trinity House
Victoria, Mahé
SEYCHELLES
Phone: (+248) 321900 / 324044
Fax: (+248) 225185
Mobile: (+248) 512171 / 515565

Mr. Danny Lucas
Attorney at Law & Notary Public
Victoria House
P.O. Box 59
Victoria, Mahé
SEYCHELLES
Phone: (+248) 225224
Fax: (+248) 224791

Mr. Charles Lucas
Attorney at Law & Notary Public
Room 206, Premier Building
P.O. Box 484
Victoria, Mahé

SEYCHELLES
Phone: (+248) 324685
Fax: (+248) 321722

Mr. France Bonte
Attorney at Law & Notary Public
Salamat House
Francis Rachel Street, Mahé
SEYCHELLES
Phone: (+248) 225855 / 225616
Fax: (+248) 225521
Mobile: (+248) 510012

Mr. Wilby Lucas
Attorney at Law
Law Chamber of Wilby Lucas
Kingsgate House
Victoria, Mahé
SEYCHELLES
Phone: (+248) 224564 / 361562
Fax: (+248) 224599
Mobile: (+248) 764559

Ms. Karen Domingue
Attorney at Law
Trinity House, 2nd Floor
Victoria, Mahé
SEYCHELLES
Phone: (+248) 226243
Fax: (+248) 225260

Mr. Sammy Freminot
Attorney at Law
Salamat House
Francis Rachel Street
Victoria, Mahé
SEYCHELLES
Phone: (+248) 225855 / 225616
Fax: (+248) 225521

Mr. Anthony Juliette
Attorney at Law & Public Notary
3rd Floor, Ebrahim Building
Victoria, Mahé
SEYCHELLES
Phone: (+248) 224517
Fax: (+248) 224517 / 225403

Mr. Daniel Belle
Attorney at Law & Public Notary
Room 109, Premier Building
Victoria, Mahé
SEYCHELLES
Phone: (+248) 322955
Fax: (+248) 322960
Mobile: (+248) 511211

Mr. Gerard Maurel
Attorney at Law & Notary Public
Kingsgate House Room 41
P.O. Box 443
Victoria, Mahé
SEYCHELLES
Phone: (+248) 224270
Fax: (+248) 224730

Mr. Simon Mitchell
Attorney at Law
Second Floor, Capital City
Independence Avenue
P.O. Box 784
Victoria, Mahé
SEYCHELLES
Phone: (+248) 438877
Fax: (+248) 438800
Email: info@seychelleslawyers.com

Mrs. Alexia G. Antao
Barrister & Attorney at Law
Antao & Antao Law Practice
104 Premier Building
Victoria, Mahé
SEYCHELLES
Phone: (+248) 322400 / 241964
Fax: (+248) 321152

Ms. Dora Zatte
Attorney & Barrister at Law
Victoria Chambers
Upper Floor
Ex Bestway Plumbing Building
Francis Rachel Street
Victoria, Mahé
SEYCHELLES
Phone: (+248) 289200
Fax: (+248) 289210

Ms. Lucy Pool
Attorney & Barrister at Law
Premier Building Room 209
Victoria, Mahé
SEYCHELLES
Phone: (+248) 225038
Fax: (+248) 375794

Ms. Caroline Houareau
Attorney at Law & Notary
Trinity House
Victoria, Mahé
SEYCHELLES
Phone: (+248) 226243
Fax: (+248) 225260

Ms. Priscille Chetty
Barrister, Attorney at Law & Notary
Chetty & Hoareau Chambers
2nd Floor, MS Complex
P.O. Box 930
Victoria, Mahé
SEYCHELLES
Phone: (+248) 611140
Fax: (+248) 611144
Email: chchambers@seychelles.sc

Mr. Basil Hoareau
Barrister, Attorney at Law & Notary
Chetty & Hoareau Chambers
2nd Floor, MS Complex
P.O. Box 930
Victoria, Mahé
SEYCHELLES
Phone: (+248) 611140
Fax: (+248) 611144
Email: chchambers@seychelles.sc

Mr. Elvis Chetty
Barrister, Attorney at Law & Notary
Chetty & Hoareau Chambers
2nd Floor, MS Complex
P.O. Box 930
Victoria, Mahé
SEYCHELLES
Phone: (+248) 611140
Fax: (+248) 611144
Email: chchambers@seychelles.sc

Mr. Jude M. Bonte
Attorney at Law
Salamat House
Francis Rachel Street
P.O. Box 908
Victoria, Mahé
SEYCHELLES
Phone: (+248) 225855
Fax: (+248) 225521

ACCOUNTANTS

Mr. T. S. K. Nair
Nair & Co
Auditors & Management Consultant
Room 204, Premier Building
P.O. Box 239
Victoria, Mahé
SEYCHELLES
Phone: (+248) 322725 / 321705
Fax: (+248) 225456

Mr. Frederic Savy
S & N Associates
P.O. Box 618
Victoria, Mahé
SEYCHELLES
Phone (+248) 224906
Fax: (+248) 225289

Mr. Egbert Moustache
Moustache Associates & Consultant
Rue Des Freres Maristes
Victoria, Mahé
SEYCHELLES
Phone: (+248) 324293
Fax: (+248) 323330

Mr. Eddy Mancienne
Director
Advanced Business Solutions
2nd Floor Trinity House
P.O. Box 1018
Victoria, Mahé
SEYCHELLES
Phone: (+248) 321166
Fax: (+248) 224650

Mr. Wilfred Jackson, FCCA
24 Kingsgate House
P.O. Box 455
Victoria, Mahé
SEYCHELLES
Phone: (+248) 715105
Fax: (+248) 224437 / 225746

Mr. N. Ramani
Ramani & Co
Chartered Accountants
Sound & Vision Building
P.O. Box 847
Victoria, Mahé
SEYCHELLES

Phone: (+248) 323767 / 323561
Fax: (+248) 323087

Mr. Bernard Pool, Mr. Suketu Patel
KPMG Pool & Patel
Maison La Rosiere
P.O. Box 117
Victoria, Mahé
SEYCHELLES
Phone: (+248) 323201 / 323365
Fax: (+248) 323518

Mr. A J Shah, Mr. Sunil Shah
A J Shah & Associates
Chartered Accountants
Revolution Avenue
P.O. Box 18
Victoria, Mahé
SEYCHELLES
Phone: (+248) 322577
FAX: (+248) 324069

Mr J. Richardson
Partner
Halpern & Woolf
Allied Building
P.O. Box 381
Victoria, Mahé
SEYCHELLES
Phone: (+248) 224245
Fax: (+248) 224601

INTERNATIONAL CORPORATE SERVICE PROVIDERS

A.C.T.- OFFSHORE LIMITED
Oliaji Trade Centre – 1st floor
P.O. Box 1377, Victoria, Mahé,
SEYCHELLES
Contacts: Mr. Peter J Ward or Mr. Karl Pragassen
Phone: (+248) 224899
Mobile :(+248) 521333
Fax: (+248) 324777
Email: email@actseychelles.com
Website: http://www.offshorecompanies.net

AAA INTERNATIONAL SERVICES LTD
Global Gateway 8, Rue de la Perle,
Providence
P.O. Box 440, Victoria, Mahé,
SEYCHELLES
Contacts: Ms. Selma Francis
Phone: (+248) 374000
Mobile: (+248) 529888
Fax: (+248) 374300
Email: info@aaainternationalservices.sc

AAMIL (Seychelles) Limited
Suite 213, 2nd Floor, Premier Building
P.O. Box 850, Victoria, Mahé,
SEYCHELLES
Contact: Mr. Frank Ally
Phone: (+248) 610940
Fax: (+248) 610941
Email: seychelles@aamil.com
Website: http://www.aamil.com

ABACUS (Seychelles) Limited
Mont Fleuri
Mahé, SEYCHELLES
Contact: Ms. Malika Jivan
Phone: (+248) 610780
Mobile: (+248) 719606
Fax: (+248) 611769
Email: services@abacus-offshore.com
Website: http://www.abacus-offshore.com

ABC INTERNATIONAL SERVICES (SEYCHELLES) LIMITED
Dekk House, Rue de Zippora, Providence Industrial Estate
P.O. Box 1345, Mahé, SEYCHELLES
Contact: Mr. Vicky Sowumber
Phone: (+248) 374088
Fax: (+248) 374188
Mobile: (+248) 523710
Email:
v.sowumber@abcmanagementservices.sc
Website:
http://www.abcmanagementservices.com

ACM CORPORATE SERVICES LIMITED
1st Floor Allied Plaza, Francis Rachel St
P.O. Box 1289, Victoria, Mahé,
SEYCHELLES
Contact: Mr. Jean-Marie Moutia
Phone: (+248) 224220
Fax: (+248) 226246
Email: acm@acmfinancials.com
Website: http://www.acmfinancials.com

ACTIVE SERVICE PROVIDERS (PROPRIETARY) LIMITED
MS Complex
2nd Floor, Room 4,
Victoria, Mahe
Seychelles
Contact: Ms. Priscille Chetty
Phone: (+248) 611147
Fax: (+248) 611148
Email: pchetty@seychelles.sc

All About Offshore (Seychelles) Limited
Suite 15, Oliaji Trade Centre, Francis Rachel Street
P.O. Box 1004, Victoria, Mahé, SEYCHELLES
Contacts: Mr. Peter VanderValk or Mr. Patrick Bonnelame
Phone: (+248) 322622
Mobile: (+248) 522330
Fax: (+248) 322667
Email: info@aabol.sc
Website: http://www.aabol.sc

Alpha Consulting Ltd
Suite 1, Second Floor, Sound & Vision House, Francis Rachel Street
P.O. Box 513, Victoria, Mahé, SEYCHELLES
Contacts: Mrs. Victoria Valkovskaya
Phone: (+248) 321370
Mobile: (+248) 596878
Fax: (+248) 324285
Email: info@alpha-offshore.com
Email: victoria@intelvision.net

APEX CORPORATE SERVICES (SEYCHELLES) LIMITED
2nd Floor, Capital City, Independence Avenue
P.O. Box 309, Victoria, Mahé, SEYCHELLES
Contacts: Ms. Daniella Hoareau
Phone: (+248) 438893
Fax: (+248) 438800
Email: apexseychelles@alcogal.com

APOLLO BUSINESS SOLUTIONS (PTY) LTD
103 Sham Peng Tong Plaza
Victoria, Mahé, SEYCHELLES
Contact: Mr. Andrei Balabanov
Phone: (+248) 323464
Mobile: (+248) 713664
Fax: (+248) 324328
Email: info@apollo.sc
Website: http://www.apollo.sc

APPLEBY CORPORATE SERVICES (SEYCHELLES) LIMITED
Level 2B, Caravelle House, Manglier Street
Victoria, Mahé, SEYCHELLES
Contact: Mr. Conrad Benoiton
Phone: (+248) 225281
Fax: (+248) 225282
Email: sc-info@applebyglobal.com

CHAPLIN, BÉNÉDICTE & CO LTD
105 Sham Peng Tong Plaza
Victoria, Mahé, SEYCHELLES
Contact: Ms. Cinthia Alcindor
Phone: (+248) 321540
Fax: (+248) 321542
Email: offshore@cbc-legal.com

Cititrust (Seychelles) International Limited
Mont Fleuri, Mahé, SEYCHELLES
Contact: Ms. Malika Jivan
Phone: (+248) 610785
Fax: (+248) 611769
Email: seychelles@cititrust.biz

CKLB FIDUCIARY (SEYCHELLES) LIMITED
Suite 8, 3rd Floor, Capital City Building, Independence Avenue
P.O. Box 355, Victoria, Mahé, SEYCHELLES
Contact: Mrs. Audrey Nanon
Phone: (+248) 430050
Fax: (+248) 430060
Email: infoseychelles@cklb.com
Website: http://www.cklb.com

CLIFTON SC LIMITED
Suite 202, Sham Peng Tong Plaza
Victoria, Mahé, SEYCHELLES
Contact: Mrs. Janette Powell
Phone: (+248) 322090
Fax: (+248) 322094
Email: admin@cliftonsc.com

Cote D'azur- Mahe Registered Agent Ltd
1st Floor, Trinity House
P.O. Box 1402, Victoria, Mahé,

SEYCHELLES
Contact: Mr. Dominique Guichard
Phone: (+248) 610215
Mobile: (+248) 510024
Fax: (+248) 610216
Email: info@societe-internationale.com
Website: http://www.societe-internationale.com

Crystal (Seychelles) Limited
Oliaji Trade Centre
P.O. Box 1101, Victoria, Mahé, SEYCHELLES
Contact: Mrs. Anne Lesperance
Phone: (+248) 224109
Fax: (+248) 225977
Email: anne@crwwgroup.net
Website: http://www.crwwgroup.net

EQUATOR TRUSTEES LIMITED
Suite 106, First Floor, Sham Peng Tong Plaza
P.O. Box 1028, Victoria, Mahé, SEYCHELLES
Contact: Mrs. Jenny Gontier
Phone: (+248) 226105
Fax: (+248) 224578
Mobile: (+248) 521585
Email: info@equatortrustees.com
Website: http://www.equatortrustees.com

Fidelity Corporate Services (Seychelles) Ltd
Suite 9, Ansuya Estate
Revolution Avenue, Victoria, Mahé, SEYCHELLES
Contact: Mrs. Stella Constance
Phone: (+248) 610770
Fax :(+248) 610771
Email: fidelity@seychellesoffshore.com
Website: http://www.seychellesoffshore.com

FIFCO (Offshore) Services Ltd
Suite 103, Premier Building
P.O. Box 308, Victoria, Mahé, SEYCHELLES
Contact: Mr. Paul B Chow
Phone: (+248) 323332
Fax: (+248) 324009
Email: offshore@fifcogroup.com

FIRST ISLAND TRUST (SEYCHELLES) LTD
Suite 309, Capital City Building
Victoria, Mahé, SEYCHELLES
Contacts: Mr. Denis SekSum or Mrs. Marie Claire Tze or Ms. Yvette Kwami
Phone: (+248) 430800
Fax: (+248) 430789
Email: fitseyc@intelvision.net

GenPro Consulting (Seychelles) Limited
1st Floor, #5 DEKK House, De Zippora Street, Providence Industrial Estate
P.O. Box 456, Mahé, SEYCHELLES
Contacts: Ms. Kalyanee Bheegoo or Mr. Tommy Lo
Phone: (+248) 373789
Fax: (+248) 373900
Email: genpro@email.sc
Website: http://www.genpro.com.tw

GLOBAL CORPORATE SERVICES LIMITED
304 Aarti Chambers, Mont Fleuri
P.O. Box 983, Victoria, Mahé, SEYCHELLES
Contact: Ms. Natalie Rath
Phone: (+248) 322338
Fax: (+248) 321888
Email: mail@globalcorporateservices.net
Website: http://www.globalcorporateservices.net

GOLD–In Co., Ltd
Dekk House, Rue de Zippora, Providence Industrial Estate
Mahé, SEYCHELLES
Contact: Ms. Marie–Therese Francoise
Phone: (+248) 374388
Fax: (+248) 374118
Website: http://www.atctw.com
Email: seychelles@atctw.com

ICAZA, GONZALEZ-RUIZ & ALEMAN (SEYCHELLES) LIMITED
Suite 205, 2nd Floor, Capital City Building, Independence Avenue, P.O. Box 903, Victoria, Mahé, SEYCHELLES
Contact: Ms. Bernadette Julie
Phone: (+248) 438862
Fax: (+248) 438800
Email: seychelles@icazalaw.com

INTERCONSULT (SEYCHELLES) LIMITED
Suite 103, Aarti Chambers, Mont Fleuri
P.O. Box 662, Victoria, Mahé,
SEYCHELLES
Contact: Ms. Nahil Francois
Phone: (+248) 323442
Fax: (+248) 324264
Email: interconsult@seychelles.net

INTERCONTINENTAL TRUST (SEYCHELLES) LIMITED
1st Floor, #5 DEKK House, De Zippora Street, Providence Industrial Estate
P.O. Box 456, Mahé, SEYCHELLES
Contacts: Mr. Neil A.J. Puresh or Mr. Tommy Lo or Mr. Ben Lim
Phone: (+248) 373689
Fax: (+248) 373299
Email: seychelles@intercontinentaltrust.sc
Website: http://www.intercontinentaltrust.sc

International Business Registration Agents (Pty) Ltd
The Creole Spirit, Ground Floor, East Wing, Quincy Street
P.O. Box 18, Victoria, Mahé, SEYCHELLES
Contact: Mr. Anant J Shah
Phone: (+248) 612612
Fax: (+248) 612300
Email: aj@ajshah.sc

International Corporate Agents Ltd
Suite 102, Aarti Chambers
P.O. Box 870, Victoria, Mahé,
SEYCHELLES
Contact: Ms. Nahil Francois
Phone: (+248) 225755
Fax: (+248) 225991
Email: ical@seychelles.net
Email: ical@ibcagent.com
Website: http://www.ibcagent.com

International Investment Services Ltd
Suite No.2, Sound & Vision House
P.O. Box 847, Victoria, Mahé,
SEYCHELLES
Contact: Mr. Narasimhan Ramani
Phone: (+248) 289555
Fax: (+248) 321389
Email: rramani@seychelles.net
Website: http://www.iis.sc

International Law & Corporate Services (Pty) Ltd
2nd Floor Allied Building Annex, Francis Rachel Street
P.O. Box 1137, Victoria, Mahé,
SEYCHELLES
Contact: Dr. Shelton Jolicoeur
Phone: (+248) 323850
Fax: (+248) 225432
Email: ibc@ilcssez.com
Email: info@ilcssez.com
Website: http://www.ilcssez.com

INTERNATIONAL OFFSHORE CORPORATE & CONSULTANCY SERVICES (PTY) LTD
Trinity House, Suite 5 & 6 Huteau Lane
P.O. Box 332, Mahé, Seychelles
Contacts: Mr. Anthony Derjacques / Mr. Brian Julie
Phone: (+248) 321900
Fax: (+248) 225185
Email: ioccs@seychelles.net
Website: http://www.ioccs.sc

Intershore Consult (Pty) Ltd
Room 306 Victoria House
P.O. Box 673, Victoria, Mahé,
SEYCHELLES
Contact: Mr. Philippe Boullé
Phone: (+248) 289206 / 289209
Fax: (+248) 289211
Email: info@intershore.com
Website: http://www.intershore.com

Jordans (Seychelles) Limited
Suite 3, Trinity House
Victoria, Mahé, SEYCHELLES
Contact: Mr. Bernard Domingue, Mrs. Karishma Lablache-Nekitsing
Phone: (+248) 225558
Mobile: (+248) 511533
Fax: (+248) 225307
Email: bernard_domingue@jordans-sey.com
Email: karishma_lablache@jordans-sey.com
Website: http://www.jordans-international.com

LA POUDRIERE LAW & CONSULTANCY CHAMBERS (PTY) LIMITED
Salamat House, La Poudriere Lane
P.O. Box 534, Victoria, Mahé,

SEYCHELLES
Contact: Mr. France G. Bonté
Phone: (+248) 225855
Fax: (+248) 225521
Email: law@lapoudrierelaw.sc

La Rosiere (Registered Agents & Trustees) Ltd
Maison La Rosiere, Palm Street
P.O. Box 117, Victoria, Mahé,
SEYCHELLES
Contact: Mr. Bernard Pool
Phone: (+248) 323201
Fax: (+248) 323518
Email: bpool@pnp.sc

LAVECO LTD
Suite No 2, Olivier Maradan Building, Olivier Maradan Street
Victoria, Mahé, SEYCHELLES
Contact: Ms. Lynn Esparon
Phone: (+248) 322261
Fax: (+248) 324932
Email: seychelles@laveco.com

LEVERNAM MANAGEMENT LIMITED
Orion Complex, Room 107
P.O. Box 1288, Victoria, Mahé,
SEYCHELLES
Contact: Mr. Arnaud Revel
Phone: (+248) 321054
Fax: (+248) 324511
Email: info@levernam.com
Website: http://www.levernam.com

MAYFAIR TRUST GROUP LIMITED
Second Floor, Capital City, Independence Avenue
P.O. Box 1312, Victoria, Mahé,
SEYCHELLES
Contact: Mr. Peter Burian
Phone: (+248) 438888
Fax: (+248) 438800
Email: info@mayfair-offshore.com
Website: http://www.mayfair-offshore.com

MITCO Limited
1st Floor, Oliaji Trade Centre
P.O. Box 1377, Victoria, Mahé,
SEYCHELLES
Contact: Ms. Vanessa Pillay
Phone: (+248) 325045
Fax: (+248) 325047
Email: mitco@email.sc

Mossack Fonseca & Co (Seychelles) Ltd
Suite 13, Oliaji Building, Francis Rachel Street
Victoria, Mahé, SEYCHELLES
Contact: Mrs. Helen Ernesta
Phone: (+248) 324866
Fax: (+248) 324867
Email: seychelles@mossfon.com
Website: http://www.mossfon.com

Nobel Capital Group Limited
Room 3, Dekk House, Rue De Zippora, Providence
P.O Box 2009, Mahé, SEYCHELLES
Contact: Mr. Nichol Gabriel, Ms Pauline Morel, Ms Samantha Port Louis
Phone: (+248) 374470
Mobile: (+248) 527345 or (+248) 511982
Fax: (+248) 373671
Email: info@nobelcapitaloffshore.com

NovaSage Incorporations (Seychelles) Limited
Second Floor, Capital City
Independence Avenue
P.O. Box 1008, Victoria, Mahé,
SEYCHELLES
Contact: Ms. Tania Benoiton
Phone: (+248) 438861
Fax: (+248) 438800
Email: info@nova-sage.com
Website: http://www.nova-sage.com

OCRA (Seychelles) Limited
303 Aarti Building
P.O. Box 983, Victoria, Mahé,
SEYCHELLES
Contact: Ms. Natalie Rath
Phone: (+248) 225555
Fax: (+248) 225999
Email: ocra@ocra-seychelles.com
Website: http://www.ocra.com

OFFSHORE INCORPORATION (SEYCHELLES) LTD
P.O.Box 1239, Victoria, Mahé,
SEYCHELLES
Contact: Ms. Anne Pool
Phone: (+248) 324668

Fax: (+248) 322114
Email: sales@offshore-inc.com
Website: http://www.offshore-inc.com

Omega International Agents Ltd
Room 1, Salamat House, La Pourdriere Lane
Victoria, Mahé, SEYCHELLES
Contact: Mr. Ivor Omson
Phone: (+248) 225356
Fax : (+248) 224394
Email: omega@email.sc
Website: http://www.omega.com.sc

Portcullis TrustNet (Seychelles) Ltd
Second Floor, Capital City, Independence Avenue
P.O. Box 716, Victoria, Mahé, SEYCHELLES
Contact: Ms. Gemma Mein
Phone: (+248) 438892
Fax: (+248) 438800
Email: info.singapore@portcullis-trustnet.com
Website: http://www.portcullis-trustnet.com

Power Point Management (Seychelles) Limited
No.24, Lesperance, Providence Industrial Estate
Mahé, SEYCHELLES
Contact: Ms. Isabel Lee
Phone: (+248) 373202
Fax: (+248) 373578
Email: seychelles@powerpoint-group.com
Website: http://www.powerpoint-group.com

Premier Offshore Limited
Suite 206, Premier Building
P.O. Box 484, Victoria, Mahé, SEYCHELLES
Contact: Mr. Charles Lucas
Phone: (+248) 321385
Mobile: (+248) 716456
Fax: (+248) 322515
Email: premierlaw@seychelles.net
Website: http://www.premier-offshore.biz

Professional Offshore Limited
Suites 204 & 205 Victoria House
P.O. Box 1356, Victoria, Mahé, SEYCHELLES
Contact: Mr. Patrick Flynn, LLB
Phone: (+248) 610960 / 713903
Fax: (+248) 610996 / 247765
Email: info@prooc.com
Website: http://www.prooc.com

Rhodes Corporate Services Ltd
Caravelle House, Manglier Street
P.O. Box 882, Victoria, Mahé, SEYCHELLES
Contact: Mrs. Gentry Jordan
Phone: (+248) 601188
Mobile: (+248) 715848
Fax: (+248) 601189
Email: enquiry@rhodes-offshore.com
Website: http://rhodes-offshore.com

SAST OFFSHORE SERVICES LIMITED
Office 14, First Floor, Trinity House
P.O. Box 998, Victoria, Mahé, SEYCHELLES
Contact: Mr. David J. Lowseck
Phone: (+248) 226111
Fax: (+248) 226111
Email: sast@seychelles.net
Email: offshore@seychelles.net

SFM LTD
Unit 117, Orion Mall, Palm Street
P.O. Box 828, Victoria, Mahé, SEYCHELLES
Contact: Ms. Lindy marcel
Phone: (+248) 225908
Fax: (+248) 225397
Email: seychelles@sfm-offshore.com
Website: http://www.sfm-offshore.com

Sovereign Trust (Seychelles) Limited
1st Floor, #4 DEKK House, De Zippora Street, Providence Industrial Estate
P.O. Box 505, Mahé, SEYCHELLES
Contacts: Mr. Neil Puresh
Phone: (+248) 321000
Fax: (+248) 321822
Email: sc@sovereigngroup.com
Website: http://www.sovereigngroup.com

STERLING OFFSHORE LIMITED
Suites 303-305, Capital City Building
Victoria, Mahé, SEYCHELLES
Contacts: Mr. Bobby L. Brantley Jr., MBA or Mrs. Laura Alcindor Valabhji, LLB

Phone: (+248) 410940
Fax: (+248) 410941
Email: info@sterlingoffshore.com
Website: http://www.sterlingoffshore.com

Trident Trust Company (Seychelles) Limited
Trident Chambers
P.O. Box 1388
Victoria, Mahé, SEYCHELLES
Contact: Mr. Jimmy Ernesta
Phone: (+248) 422000
Fax: (+248) 422010
Email: seychelles@tridenttrust.com
Website: http://www.tridenttrust.com

Trust & Fiduciary Services Ltd
Suites No. 3-11, 3rd Floor, Capital City Building, Independence Avenue
Victoria, Mahé, SEYCHELLES
Contact: Mr. Joseph Athanasius
Phone: (+248) 430000
Fax: (+248) 430010
Email: info@trustsey.com
Website: http://www.trustsey.com

Turnstone Corporate (Seychelles) Limited
Suite 108, Premier Building
P.O. Box 1389, Victoria, Mahé, SEYCHELLES
Contact: Mr. Jean-Marc Lablache
Phone: (+248) 224074
Fax: (+248) 225732
Email: seychelles@turnstone-group.com
Website: http://www.turnstone-group.com

VERTEX MANAGEMENT LIMITED
Office 406, Premier Building
P.O. Box 1189, Victoria, Mahé, SEYCHELLES
Contact: Mr. Vadim Zaslonov
Phone: (+248) 610551
Mobile: (+248) 718471
Fax: (+248) 610552
Email: vertex@seychelles.sc

VICTORIA CORPORATE AGENTS
Suite 108, Premier Building
P.O. Box 343, Victoria, Mahé, SEYCHELLES
Contact: Ms. Anne Pool
Phone: (+248) 323844
Fax: (+248) 324100
Email: vca@seychelles.net

Zen Offshore Services (PTY) Ltd
Jivan's Complex
Mont Fleuri, Mahé, SEYCHELLES
Contact: Ms. Deepa Jivan
Phone: (+248) 611777
Fax: (+248) 610707
Email: deepa@zenoffshore.sc

Zetland Corporate Services (Seychelles) Limited
Suite 03-07, Capital City Building, Independence Avenue
P.O. Box 255, Victoria, Mahé, SEYCHELLES
Contact: Mr. John Powell
Phone: (+248) 410911 / 410912
Fax: (+248) 410913
Email: seychelles@zetland.biz
Website: http://www.zetland.biz

INTERNATIONAL TRUSTEE SERVICE PROVIDERS

A.C.T.- OFFSHORE LIMITED
Oliaji Trade Centre – 1st floor
P.O. Box 1377.Victoria, Mahé, SEYCHELLES
Contacts: Mr. Peter J Ward or Mr. Karl Pragassen
Phone: (+248) 224899 / 321 377
Fax: (+248) 324777
Email: email@actseychelles.com
Website: http://www.offshorecompanies.net

ABACUS (Seychelles) Limited
Mont Fleuri
Mahé, SEYCHELLES
Contact: Ms. Malika Jivan
Phone: (+248) 610780
Mobile: (+248) 719606
Fax: (+248) 610781
Email: services@abacus-offshore.com
Website: http://www.abacus-offshore.com

Access Financial Solutions Ltd
1st Floor Allied Plaza, Francis Rachel Street
P.O.Box 1289, Victoria, Mahé, SEYCHELLES
Contact: Mr. Jean-Marie Moutia

Phone: (+248) 224220
Fax: (+248) 226246
Email: acm@acmfinancials.com
Website: http://www.acmfinancials.com

APOLLO TRUSTS (PTY) LTD
First floor, Room 103, Sham-Peng-Tong Plaza
Victoria, Mahé, SEYCHELLES
Contact: Ms. Karen Domingue or Mrs. Tatiana Balabanova
Phone: (+248) 226243
Fax: (+248) 324328
Email: info@apollo-trusts.com

APPLEBY CORPORATE SERVICES (SEYCHELLES) LIMITED
Level 2B, Caravelle House, Manglier Street
Victoria, Mahé, SEYCHELLES
Contact: Mr. Conrad Benoiton
Phone: (+248) 225281
Fax: (+248) 225282
Email: sc-info@applebyglobal.com

CLIFTON TRUST LIMITED
Suite 202, Sham Peng Tong Plaza
Victoria, Mahé, SEYCHELLES
Contact: Mrs. Janette Powell
Phone: (+248) 322090
Fax: (+248) 322094
Email: admin@cliftonsc.com

EQUATOR TRUSTEES LIMITED
Suite 106, First Floor, Sham Peng Tong Plaza
P.O. Box 1028, Victoria, Mahé, SEYCHELLES
Contact: Mrs. Jenny Gontier
Phone: (+248) 226105
Mobile: (+248) 521585
Fax: (+248) 224578
Email: info@equatortrustees.com
Website: http://www.equatortrustees.com

GLOBAL CORPORATE SERVICES LIMITED
304 Aarti Chambers, Mont Fleuri
Victoria, Mahé, SEYCHELLES
Contact: Ms. Natalie Rath
Phone: (+248) 322338
Fax: (+248) 321888
Email: mail@globalcorporateservices.net
Website:
http://www.globalcorporateservices.net

INTERCONTINENTAL TRUST (SEYCHELLES) LIMITED
1st Floor, #5 DEKK House, De Zippora Street, Providence Industrial Estate
P.O. Box 456, Mahé, SEYCHELLES
Contacts: Mr. Neil A.J. Puresh or Mr. Tommy Lo or Mr. Ben Lim
Phone: (+248) 373689
Fax: (+248) 373299
Email: seychelles@intercontinentaltrust.sc
Website: http://www.intercontinentaltrust.sc

International Corporate Agents Limited
Suite 102, Aarti Chambers
Mont Fleuri, Mahé, SEYCHELLES
Contact: Ms.Nahil Francois
Phone: (+248) 225755
Fax: (+248) 225991
Email: ical@seychelles.net
Email: ical@ibcagent.com
Website: http://www.ibcagent.com

International Law & Corporate Services (Pty) Ltd
2nd Floor Allied Building Annex, Francis Rachel Street
P.O. Box 1137, Victoria, Mahé, SEYCHELLES
Contact: Dr. Shelton Jolicoeur
Phone: (+248) 323850
Fax: (+248) 225432
Email: ibc@ilcssez.com
Email: info@ilcssez.com
Website: http://www.ilcssez.com

INTERSHORE TRUST LTD
Room 314 Victoria House
P.O. Box 673, Victoria, Mahé, SEYCHELLES
Contact: Mr. Philippe Boullé
Phone: (+248) 289206 / 289208
Fax: (+248) 289211
Email: info@intershore.com

LA POUDRIERE LAW & CONSULTANCY CHAMBERS (PTY) LIMITED
P.O. Box 534, Salamat House
La Poudriere, Mahé, SEYCHELLES
Contact: Mr. France G. Bonté

Phone: (+248) 225855
Fax: (+248) 225521
Email: law@lapoudrierelaw.sc

La Rosiere (Registered Agents & Trustees) Ltd
Maison La Rosiere
P.O. Box 117, Victoria, Mahé,
SEYCHELLES
Contact: Mr.Bernard Pool
Phone: (+248) 323201
Fax: (+248) 323518
Email: bpool@pnp.sc

MAYFAIR TRUST GROUP LIMITED
Second Floor, Capital City
Independence Avenue
P.O. Box 1312, Victoria, Mahé,
SEYCHELLES
Contact: Mr. Peter Burian
Phone: (+248) 438888
Fax: (+248) 438800
Email: info@mayfair-offshore.com
Website: http://www.mayfair-offshore.com

OCRA TRUSTEES (SEYCHELLES) LIMITED
303 Aarti Building,
P.O. Box 983, Victoria, Mahé,
SEYCHELLES
Contact: Ms. Natalie Rath
Phone: (+248) 225555
Fax: (+248) 225999
Email: ocra@ocra-seychelles.com
Website: http://www.ocra.com

Omega International Agents Ltd
Room 1, Salamat House, La Pourdriere Lane
Victoria, Mahé, SEYCHELLES
Contact: Mr. Ivor Omson
Phone: (+248) 225 356
Fax: (+248) 224 394
Email: omega@email.sc
Website: http://www.omega.com.sc

Rhodes Trustees Ltd
Caravelle House
Manglier Street
P.O. Box 882, Victoria, Mahé,
SEYCHELLES
Contact: Mr. Alessandro Pagano
Phone: (+248) 601188
Mobile: (+248) 715848
Fax: (+248) 601189
Email: enquiry@rhodes-offshore.com
Website: http://rhodes-offshore.com

Trust & Fiduciary Services Ltd
2nd Floor Allied Building Annex, Francis Rachel Street
P.O. Box 1137, Victoria, Mahé,
SEYCHELLES
Contact: Dr. Shelton Jolicoeur
Phone: (+248) 323850
Fax: (+248) 225432
Email: info@trustsey.com
Website: http://www.tafs.com.sg

VERTEX MANAGEMENT LIMITED
Office 406, Premier Building
P.O. Box 1189, Victoria, Mahé,
SEYCHELLES
Contact: Mr. Vadim Zaslonov
Phone: (+248) 610551
Mobile: (+248) 718471
Fax: (+248) 610552
Email: vertex@seychelles.sc

VICTORIA CORPORATE AGENTS
Suite 108, Premier Building
P.O. Box 343, Victoria, Mahé,
SEYCHELLES
Contact: Ms. Anne Pool
Phone: (+248) 323844
Fax: (+248) 324100

OFFSHORE COMPANY MANAGERS

AAA International Services Ltd
Address: Tel: (+248) 374000
Global Gateway 8 Fax: (+248) 374300
Rue de la Perle, Providence Email: info@aaainternationalservices.sc
Mahe, Seychelles Website: www.aaainternationalservices.com

Abacus (Seychelles) Limited
Address: Tel: (+248) 610780, (+248) 610784
P.O.Box 931 Fax: (+248) 610781
Mont Fleuri, Mahe Email: malika@abacus-offshore.com

Seychelles Website: www.abacus-offshore.com

ABC International Services (Seychelles) Limited
Address: Tel: (+248) 374 088
P.O. Box 1345 Fax: (+248) 374 188
1st Floor, Dekk House Email: v.sowumber@abcmanagements...
Zippora Street Website: www.abcmanagementservices.com
Providence Industrial Estate
Mahe, Seychelles

ACM Corporate Services
Address: Tel: (+248) 224 220
P.O. Box 1289 Fax: (+248) 226 246
1st Floor, Allied Plaza Email: acm@acmfinancials.com
Francis Rachel Street Website: www.abcmanagementservices.com
Victoria, Mahe
Seychelles

A.C.T. – Offshore (Pty) Limited
Address: Tel: (+248) 321377
Oliaji Trade Centre – 1st Floor Fax: (+248) 324777
Victoria, Mahe Email: email@actoffshore.com
Seychelles Website: www.actoffshore.com

Alpha Consulting
Address: Tel: (+248) 321370
Suite 1, Second Floor Fax: (+248) 324285
Sound & Vision House Email: info@alpha-offshore.com
Francis Rachel Str. , Victoria Website: www.alpha-offshore.com

Mahe, Seychelles
CKLB Fiduciary (Seychelles) Limited
Address: Tel: (+248) 430050
P.O. Box 355 Fax: (+248) 430060
Suite 8, 3rd Floor Email: audreynanon@cklb.com
Capital City Building Website:
Independence Avenue
Victoria, Mahe, Seychelles
Clifton Sc Limited
Address: Tel: (+248) 322090
Suite 202 Fax: (+248) 322094
Sham Peng Tong Plaza Email: clifton@euroci.com
Victoria Website:
Mahe, Seychelles

COTE D'AZUR-MAHE Registered Agent Ltd
Address: Tel: (+248) 510024
P.O. Box 1402 Fax: (+248) 610216
Trinity House 1st & 2nd Floor Email: info@societe-internationale.com
Albert Street, Victoria Website: www.societe-internationale.com
Mahe, Seychelles

Crystal (Seychelles) Limited
Address: Tel: (+248) 224109
P.O Box 1101 Fax: (+248) 225977
Oliaji Trade Centre Email: anne@crwwgroup.net
Victoria Website: www.crwwgroup.net
Mahe, Seychelles

Fidelity Corporate Services (Seychelles) Ltd
Address: Tel: (+248) 610770
P.O.Box 940 Fax: (+248) 610771
Suite 9, Ansuya Estate Email: fidelity@seychellesoffshore.com
Revolution Avenue Website: www.seychellesoffshore.com
Victoria, Mahe, Seychelles

FIFCO (Offshore) Services Ltd
Address: Tel: (+248) 323332
P.O. Box 308 Fax: (+248) 324009
Suite 103 Email: fifco@seychelles.sc
Premier Building Website:
Victoria, Mahe, Seychelles

Intercontinental Trust (Seychelles) Limited
Address: Tel: (+248) 373 689
P.O.Box 456 Fax: (+248) 373 299
1st Floor, # 5 DEKK House Email: seychelles@intercontinentalt...
De Zippora Street Website: www.intercontinentaltrust.sc
Providence Industrial Estate
Mahe, Seychelles

International Corporate Agents Limited
Address: Tel: (+248) 225755, (+248) 226256,
P.O.Box 870 (+248) 510749

Suite 102, Aarti Chambers Fax: (+248) 225991
Mont Fleuri, Victoria Email: ical@seychelles.net
Mahe, Seychelles ical@ibcagent.com
Website: www.ibcagent.com

International Investment Services Ltd
Address: Tel: (+248) 323767
P.O Box 847 Fax: (+248) 323087
Suite No: 2 Email: rramani@seychelles.net
Sound & Vision House Website: www.iis.sc
Victoria, Mahe, Seychelles

International Law & Corporate Services
Address: Tel: (+248) 323850, (+248) 321217
P.O. Box 1137 Fax: (+248) 225432
2nd Floor Email: info@ilcssez.com
Allied Building Annex Website: www.ilcssez.com
Francis Rachel Street
Victoria, Mahe, Seychelles

Intershore Consult (PTY) LTD
Address: Tel: (+248) 289200
306 Victoria House Fax: (+248) 289211
Victoria, Mahe Email: info@intershore.com
Seychelles Website: www.intershore.com

Jordans (Seychelles) Limited
Address: Tel: (+248) 225558, (+248) 511533
Suite 3, Trinity House Fax: (+248) 225307
Mahe, Victoria Email:
Seychelles Website: www.jordans-international.com

La Poudriere Law & Consultancy Chambers (PTY) Limited
Address: Tel: (+248) 225855
P.O. Box 534 Fax: (+248) 225521
Salamat House Email: law@lapoudrierelaw.sc
La Poudriere Lane Website:
Victoria, Mahe, Seychelles

La Rosiere (Registered Agents & Trustees) Ltd
Address: Tel: (+248) 323201
P.O Box 117 Fax: (+248) 323518
Maison La Rosiere Email: bpool@pnp.sc
Mahe, Victoria pnp@seychelles.net
Seychelles Website:

Levernam Management Limited
Address: Tel: (+248) 321054
P.O. Box 1288 Fax: (+248) 324511
Room 107, Orion Complex Email: info@levernam.com
Victoria, Mahe Website:
Seychelles

Lotus Holding Company Limited
Address: Tel: (+248) 323105
Suite 310 Fax: (+248) 324798
Premier Building Email: lotus79@seychelles.net
Mahe, Victoria lotus69@seychelles.net
Seychelles Website:

Mayfair Trust Group Limited
Address: Tel: (+248) 438888
P.O.Box 1312 Fax: (+248) 438800
Second Floor Email: info@mayfair-offshore.com
Capital City Building Website: www.mayfair-offshore.com
Independence Avenue
Victoria, Mahe, Seychelles

Mossack Fonseca & Co. (Seychelles) Limited
Address: Tel: (+248) 324866
Suite 13, First Floor Fax: (+248) 324867
Oliaji Trade Centre Email: seychelles@mossfon.com
Francis Rachel Street Website: www.mossfon.com
Victoria, Mahe, Seychelles

NovaSage Incorporations (Seychelles) Limited
Address: Tel: (+248) 438861
P.O. Box 1008 Fax: (+248) 438800
Second Floor, Capital City Email: info@nova-sage.com
Independence Avenue Website: www.nova-sage.com
Victoria, Mahe, Seychelles

OCRA (Seychelles) Limited
Address: Tel: (+248) 225 555
P.O.Box 983 Fax: (+248) 225 999
303 Aarti Chambers Email: ocra@ocra-seychelles.com

Mont Fleuri Website: www.ocra-seychelles.com
Victoria, Seychelles

Premier Corporate And Trust Services Limited
Address: Tel: (+248) 321385
P.O. Box 484 Fax: (+248) 322515
Suite 206, Premier Building Email: premierlaw@seychelles.sc
Victoria, Mahe Website: www.pcts.sc
Seychelles

Professional Offshore Limited
Address: Tel: (+248) 610992, (+248) 610993
Suites 204 & 205 (+248) 610994 (+248) 713903
Victoria House Fax: (+248) 610996
State House Avenue, Victoria Email: info@prooc.com
Mahe, Seychelles patrick.flynn@prooc.com
Website: www.prooc.com

Rhodes Corporate Services Ltd
Address: Tel: (+248) 601188
P.O. Box 882 Fax: (+248) 601189
The Wharf Hotel & Marina Email:
Providence Website: rhodes-offshore.com
Victoria, Mahe, Seychelles

SAST Offshore Services Limited
Address: Tel: (+248) 226111, 579348, 323944
P.O.Box 1046 Fax: (+248) 226111, 324226
Office 14, First Floor Email: sast@seychelles.net
Trinity House offshore@seychelles.net
Victoria, Mahe, Seychelles Website:

SFM LTD
Address: Tel: (+248) 225908
P.O. Box 828 Fax: (+248) 225397
Unit 117, Orion Mall Email: marcel@sfm-offshore.com
Palm Street, Victoria, Mahe Website: www.sfm-offshore.com
Seychelles

Sterling Offshore Limited
Address: Tel: (+248) 410940
Suite 303-306 Fax: (+248) 410941
Capital City Building, Email: info@sterlingoffshore.com
Independence Avenue Website: www.sterlingoffshore.com
Victoria, Mahe, Seychelles

Trust & Fiduciary Services Limited
Address: Tel: (+248) 410 271
Suite No. 3-11, 3rd Floor Fax: (+248) 410 267
Capital City Building, Email: info@trustsey.com
Independence Avenue, Website: www.trustsey.com
Victoria, Mahe, Seychelles

Victoria Corporate Agents (Pty) Limited
Address: Tel: (+248) 323844
Suite 108, Premier Building Fax: (+248) 324100
Victoria Email: vca@seychelles.net

Mahe, Seychelles Website:
Zen Offshore Services
Address: Tel: (+248) 611777, (+248) 716007
Jivan's Complex Fax: (+248) 610707
Mont Fleuri, Mahe Email: deepa@zenoffshore.sc
Seychelles Website:

Zetland Corporate Services (Seychelles) Limited
Address: Tel: (+248) 410911, (+248) 410912
P.O.Box 255 Fax: (+248) 410913
Suite 03-07, Email: seychelles@zetland.biz
Capital City Building, Website: www.zetland.biz
Independence Avenue
Victoria, Mahe, Seychelles

HONORARY COUNSELS

AUSTRIA, REPUBLIC OF

Consulate of the Republic of Austria,

P O Box 1181, Bodco (Plastics) Ltd, Bodco Building, Harbour Trading Estate, Victoria, Mahé, Seychelles

Telephone N°: [248] 22 46 66
Telefax N°: [248] 22 40 65

E-mail: pconsult@seychelles.net

Office Hours: Monday to Friday, 1300 to 1600

Honorary Consul
Mr. Otto BURIAN

Machabée, Mahé, Seychelles
Telephone N°: [248] 24 15 15

BELGIUM, KINGDOM OF

Consulate of the Kingdom of Belgium,
Bel Ombre, P O Box 232, Victoria, Mahé, Seychelles

Telephone N°: [248] 344551
Telefax N°: [248] 344754

E-mail: kreolor@seychelles.net

Office Hours: Monday to Friday, 0800 to 1200
and 1300 to 1600 (by appointment)

Honorary Consul
Mr. Marc SINGLET

Bel Ombre, Mahé, Seychelles
Telephone N°: [248] 24 78 38
Telefax N°: [248] 24 78 38

CYPRUS, REPUBLIC OF

Consulate of the Republic of Cyprus,
P O Box 450, Skychef Ltd, Seychelles International Airport, Mahé, Seychelles

Telephone N°: [248] 373050/373155
Telefax N°: [248] 373456

Telex: 2278 DOBBS

Honorary Consul
Mr Panos PAPAKOKINOS

Turtle Bay Estate , House # 47, Anse Aux Pins, Mahé, Seychelles
Telephone N°: [248] 376215

DENMARK, KINGDOM OF
Consulate of the Kingdom of Denmark
P O Box 231, BODCO Building 1st Floor, New Port, Victoria, Mahé, Seychelles

Telephone N°: **Telefax N°:**
[248] 224710/224666 [248] 224065

E-mail: soundy@seychelles.net

Telex: 2270 BODCO SZ

Office Hours: Monday to Saturday, 0915 to 1200

Honorary Consul
Mr Basil SOUNDY

Villa Caballero, Turtle Bay Estate, Anse Aux Pins, Mahé, Seychelles
Telephone N°: [248] 375675

FINLAND, REPUBLIC OF

Consulate of the Republic of Finland
P O Box 231, BODCO Building 1st Floor, New Port, Victoria, Mahé, Seychelles

Telephone N°: **Telefax N°:**
[248] 224710/224666 [248] 224065

E-mail: soundy@seychelles.net

Telex: 2270 BODCO SZ

Office Hours: Monday to Saturday, 0915 to 1200

Honorary Consul
Mr Basil SOUNDY

Villa Caballero, Turtle Bay Estate, Anse Aux Pins, Mahé, Seychelles
Telephone N°: [248] 375675

GERMANY, FEDERAL REPUBLIC OF

Consulate of the Federal Republic of Germany,
Northolme Hotel, Glacis, Mahé, Seychelles

Telephone N°: **Telefax N°:**
[248] 261222 [248] 261223

E-mail: northolm@seychelles.net

Telex: 2355 COSNOR SZ

Office Hours: Monday to Friday, 1000 to 1300

Honorary Consul
Mrs Maryse EICHLER

Pointe Au Sel, Mahé, Seychelles
Telephone N°: [248] 371413

GREECE (HELLENIC REPUBLIC)

Consulate of the Hellenic Republic,
P O Box 450, Skychef Ltd,
Seychelles International Airport, Mahé, Seychelles

Telephone N°:	**Telefax N°:**
[248] 373050/373155	[248] 373456

Telex: 2278 DOBBS

Office Hours: Monday to Friday, 0830 to 1630
Saturday, 0830 to 1230

Honorary Consul
Mr Panos PAPAKOKINOS

Turtle Bay Estate House # 47,
Anse Aux Pins, Mahé, Seychelles
Telephone N°: [248] 376215

HUNGARY, REPUBLIC OF

Consulate of the Republic of Hungary
C/o 7° South, Shipping House, P O Box 475, Revolution Avenue, Victoria, Mahé, Seychelles

Telephone N°:	**Telefax N°:**
[248] 32 26 82	[248] 32 13 22

E-mail: 7south@seychelles.net

Office Hours: Monday to Friday, 1300hrs to 1600hrs

Honorary Consul
Mrs Anna BUTLER-PAYETTE

Souvenir, La Misère, Mahé, Seychelles
Telephone N°: [248] 37 83 53

INDONESIA, REPUBLIC OF

Consulate of the Republic of Indonesia
P O Box 31, C/O Tirant Associates,
Room 4, 1st Floor, Oceangate House,

Victoria, Mahé, Seychelles

Telephone N°: **Telefax N°:**
[248] 22 48 35 [248] 22 51 56
[248] 22 50 77

E-mail: tass@seychelles.net

Honorary Consul
Mr Harry TIRANT

Anse Etoile, Mahé, Seychelles
Telephone N°: [248] 24 14 23

ITALIAN REPUBLIC

Consulate of the Italian Republic
P O Box 545, C/O Seyplant, New Port,
Victoria, Mahé, Seychelles

Telephone N°: **Telefax N°:**
[248] 61 01 16 [248] 61 01 21

E-mail: italcons@seychelles.net

Telex: 2313 SEYPLAN

Honorary Consul
Mr Franco ESPOSITO

Mare Anglaise, Mahé, Seychelles
Telephone N°: [248] 247044

KOREA, REPUBLIC OF

Consulate of the Republic of Korea
First International Financial Co. (Ltd), Premier Building, Victoria, Mahé, Seychelles

Telephone N°: **Telefax N°:**
[248] 323332 [248] 324009

E-mail address: fifco@seychelles.net

Office Hours: Monday to Friday, 0800 to 1600

Honorary Consul
Mr Paul CHOW

Mare Anglaise, Mahé, Seychelles
Telephone N°: [248] 261343

MADAGASCAR, REPUBLIQUE DE

Consulat de la République de Madagascar,
B.P. 68, Plaisance, Mahé, Seychelles

Numéro de téléphone: [248] 344030

Horaires de Travail: Lundi à Vendredi
08h00 à 12h00

Consul Honoraire
M. Guy LIONNET

MAURITIUS, REPUBLIC OF

Consulate of the Republic of Mauritius
Room 202, Aarti Chambers, P.O. Box 1310,
Mont Fleuri, Mahé, Seychelles

Telephone N°: [248] 22 50 97
Fax N°: [248] 22 51 21

E-mail: birdlife@seychelles.net

Office Hours: Monday to Friday
0800 to 1200 1300 to 1600

Honorary Consul
Mr. Nirmal Jivan SHAH

Sans Souci, Mahé, Seychelles
Home Telephone N°: [248] 22 53 21

NETHERLANDS, KINGDOM OF THE

Consulate of the Kingdom of the Netherlands
P O Box 372, Sunset Beach Hotel
Glacis, Mahé, Seychelles

Telephone N°: [248] 261111
Telefax N°: [248] 261221

E-mail: sunset@seychelles.net

Telex: 2344 SUNSET SZ

Office Hours: Monday to Friday, 0800 to 1600

Honorary Consul
Mr Albert GEERS

Beach House, Bel Ombre, Mahé, Seychelles
Telephone N°: [248] 247106

NORWAY, KINGDOM OF

Consulate of the Kingdom of Norway,
P O Box 14, C/O Hunt Deltel, Trinity House
Victoria, Mahé, Seychelles

Telephone N°: [248] 38 03 00
Telefax N°: [248] 22 53 67

E-mail: achetty@hundel.sc

Office Hours: Monday to Friday, 0800 to 1600

Honorary Consul
Mr Arnold CHETTY

Bel Ombre, Mahé, Seychelles
Telephone N°: [248] 24 72 92

PHILIPPINES, REPUBLIC OF THE

Consulate of the Republic of the Philippines,
c/o Norman's Car Hire & Travel Services Co. Ltd.,
P. O. Box 1227, Victoria House Building, Victoria, Mahé, Seychelles

Telephone N°: [248] 22 53 03
Telefax N°: [248] 22 51 93

E-mail: avis@seychelles.net

Office Hours: Monday to Friday, 0800 to 1600
(by appointment)

Honorary Consul
Mr. Julien Kaven PARCOU

Beau Vallon, Mahé, Seychelles
Cellular Telephone N°: [248] 71 04 40

SPAIN, KINGDOM OF

Consulate of the Kingdom of Spain
P O Box 14, C/O Hunt Deltel, Trinity House, Victoria, Mahé, Seychelles

Telephone N°: **Telefax N°:**

[248] 38 03 00 [248] 22 53 67

E-mail: hundel@seychelles.net

Telex: 2249 HUNDEL SZ

Office Hours: Monday to Friday, 0800 to 1600
Saturday, 0800 to 1200

Honorary Consul
Capt. Edmond HOAREAU

L'Ilot, Glacis, Mahé, Seychelles
Telephone N°: [248] 241475

SWEDEN, KINGDOM OF
Consulate of Sweden, P O Box 270, BODCO Building, New Port, Victoria, Mahé, Seychelles

Telephone N°: **Telefax N°:**
[248] 224710/224666 [248] 224065

E-mail: soundy@seychelles.net

Telex: 2270 SZ

Office Hours: Monday to Saturday, 0915 to 1200

Honorary Consul
Mr Basil SOUNDY

Villa Caballero, Turtle Bay Estate, Anse Aux Pins, Mahé, Seychelles
Telephone N°: [248] 375675

SWITZERLAND
Consulate of Switzerland, P O Box 935
Marketing PLUS Ltd, Kingsgate House, Suite 18,
Victoria, Mahé, Seychelles

Telephone N°: **Telefax N°:**
[248] 32 21 14 [248] 32 47 50

Cellular Telephone N°: [248] 51 11 04

E-mail: markplus@seychelles.net

Office Hours: Monday to Saturday, 1300 to 1600
(by appointment)

Honorary Consul:
Mrs Angelika MAUREL-MUEHLHEIM

Mare Anglaise, Mahé, Seychelles
Tel N°: [248] 26 11 04
Telefax N°: [248] 26 11 04

THAILAND, KINGDOM OF

Consulate of the Kingdom of Thailand,
P O Box 933, Michel Building, Revolution Avenue, Victoria, Mahé, Seychelles

Telephone N°:	**Telefax N°:**
[248] 22 45 47	[248] 32 38 88

E-mail: jmsa@seychelles.net

Office Hours: Monday to Friday (by appointment only)

Honorary Consul
Mr. Joe CHUNG-FAYE

Machabée, Mahé, Seychelles
Tel N°: [248] 24 13 48

YUGOSLAVIA, FEDERAL REPUBLIC OF

Consulate of the Federal Republic of Yugoslavia,
P O Box 1001, Victoria, Mahé, Seychelles

Telephone N°:	**Telefax N°:**
[248] 71 23 33	[248] 32 30 47

E-mail: miodrag@seychelles.net

Office Hours: Monday to Friday (by appointment only)

Honorary Consul
Dr. Miodrag TODOROVIC

Glacis, Mahé, Seychelles
Tel N°: [248] 26 11 75

FOREIGN MISSIONS

UNITED STATES OF AMERICA CONSULATE

Consular Agency of the United States of America
Room 112, 1st Floor, Victoria House,
Victoria, Mahé, Seychelles

Telephone N°: [248] 22 52 56
Telefax N°: [248] 22 51 89

E-mail: usoffice@seychelles.net

Office Hours: Monday to Friday
0800 to 1600

Consular Agent
Ms. Susan ROSE

Anse des Gênets
Cellular Telephone N°: [248] 51 44 11

ALGERIE REPUBLIQUE ALGERIENNE DEMOCRATIQUE ET POPULAIRE

Ambassade de la République Algérienne Démocratique et Populaire,
B.P.634, Ivandry, Antananarivo, Madagascar

Numéro de Téléphone: [+ 261 20] 22 42 864
Numéro de Téléfax [+ 261 20] 22 42 205

E-mail: ambalg.tnr@dts.mg

Horaires de Travail: Lundi à Jeudi
08h00 à 13h00 14h00 à 16h00
Vendredi 08h00 à 13h00

Ambassadeur
S.E. M. Abderrahmane BENMOHKTAR
désigné

VISA: Issued by Embassy in Madagascar

ARGENTINA ARGENTINE REPUBLIC

Embassy of the Argentine Republic,
P.O. Box 30283,
Posta Sacco Plaza, 6th Floor,
University Way/Uhuru Highway,
Nairobi, Kenya

Telephone N°:
[+ 254 2] 33 52 42
[+ 254 2] 33 99 49

Telefax N°:
[+ 254 2] 21 76 93

E-mail Address: ekeny@africaonline.co.ke

Telegraphic Address: EMBARGENT:NAIROBI

Office Hours:
Monday to Friday, 0900 to 1400

Ambassador
Vacant
Kitisuru Estate, Nairobi, Kenya

Telephone: [+ 254 2] 58 27 91
[+ 254 2] 58 01 61

Charge d'Affaires a.i.: Mr. Carlos A. PEZZONI

VISA: Issued by Embassy in Nairobi

AUSTRALIA,
COMMONWEALTH OF

High Commission of Australia,
P O Box 541, 2nd Floor, Rogers House,
President John Kennedy Street,
Port Louis, Mauritius

Telephone N°:	Telefax N°:
[+ 230] 20 81700	[+ 230] 20 88 878
[+ 230] 20 81701	
[+ 230] 20 81702	

E-mail address: austhc@intnet.mu

Telex: 4414 AUSTCOM IW

Office Hours: Monday to Friday 0830hrs to 1621hrs

High Commissioner:
H.E. Mr Christopher Simon MARCHANT
Deburgh Edward Street, Floréal, Mauritius

Telephone: [+ 230] 68 62 638
Mobile Phone: [+ 230] 256 1140

VISA: Issued by High Commission in Port-Louis. Forms obtainable from the Air Seychelles Head Office in Victoria.

AUSTRIA,
REPUBLIC OF

Austrian Embassy,

P O Box 30560, 2nd Floor, City House,
Wabera Street, Nairobi, Kenya

Telephone N°: [+ 254 2] 22 82 81
[+ 254 2] 22 82 82
[+ 254 2] 33 32 72

Telefax N°: [+ 254 2] 33 17 92

E-mail address: austria@africaonline.co.ke

Office Hours:
Monday to Friday 0800 to 1600

Ambassador
Vacant
Limuru Road, Nairobi, Kenya

Telephone: [+ 254 2] 749045

VISA: Schengen Visa issued by Embassy of France in Victoria

BANGLADESH,
PEOPLE'S REPUBLIC OF

High Commission of the People's Republic of Bangladesh,
P O Box 41645, Ole Odume Road, Off Argwings Kodhek Road, Kilimani, Nairobi, Kenya

Telephone N°: [+ 254 2] 562815
[+ 254 2] 562816

Telefax N°: [+ 254 2] 56 28 17

Office Hours: Monday to Thursday, 0800 to 1400
Friday 0800 to 1230

High Commissioner
(Vacant)
State House Avenue, Nairobi, Kenya

Telephone: [+ 254 2] 721627
[+ 254 2] 721727

NO VISA REQUIRED

BELGIQUE,
ROYAUME DE

Ambassade de Belgique,
BP 30461, Limuru Road, Nairobi, Kenya

Numéro de Téléphone:	**Numéro de Téléfax**
[+ 254 2] 52 20 11	[+ 254 2] 52 30 50
[+ 254 2] 52 21 66	
[+ 254 2] 52 21 81	
[+ 254 2] 52 30 93	

E-mail: belgianemb.ke@form-net.com

Télex: 22269 AMBEL KE NAIROBI

Horaires de Travail:
Lundi à Vendredi 08h30 à 16h30

Ambassadeur
S.E. M. Leo WILLEMS
Karura Avenue, Muthaiga, Nairobi, Kenya

Téléphone: [+ 254 2] 52 28 44

VISA: Schengen Visa issued by Embassy of France in Victoria

BRAZIL, FEDERATIVE REPUBLIC OF

Embassy of the Republic of Brazil,
1, Avenue Kenneth Kaunda, Nº 296
Caixa Postal 1167 Maputo, Mozambique

Telephone N°:	**Telefax N°:**
[+ 258 1] 42 93 87	[+ 258 1] 49 09 86
[+ 258 1] 42 93 88	[+ 258 1] 49 27 51
	[+ 258 1] 42 09 00

E-mail address: ebrasil@teledata.mz

Ambassador
H.E. Mr. Helder Martins de MORAES
E-mail address: tohelder@hotmail.com

VISA: Issued by Embassy in Maputo, Mozambique

BULGARIA, REPUBLIC OF

Embassy of the Republic of Bulgaria,
P O Box 44778, Nairobi, Kenya

Telephone N°: [+ 254 2] 567308

Office Hours: Monday to Friday
0830 hrs to 1430 hrs

Ambassador
(Vacant)

16 Kenyatta Drive, Nairobi, Kenya
Telephone: [+ 254 2] 67256

VISA: Issued by Embassy in Nairobi, Kenya

**CAMBODIA,
KINGDOM OF**

**Royal Embassy of Cambodia
N-14, Panchsheel Park
New Delhi – 110 017, India**

Telephone N°: [+ 91 11] 642 5368
Telefax N°: [+ 91 11] 647 5233

Office Hours: Monday to Friday
0900hrs to 1230hrs 1400hrs to 1700hrs

Ambassador
Vacant

N-14, Panchsheel Park, New Delhi – 110 017, India
Telephone: [+ 91 11] 693417
[+ 91 11] 623157

Charge d'Affaires a.i.
Mr. Hem HENG

VISA: Issued by Embassy in New Delhi, India

CANADA

**Canadian High Commission
P O Box 1022, 38, Mirambo at Garden Avenue,
Dar Es Salaam, Tanzania**

Telephone N°: [+ 255 22] 211 28 31
Telefax N°: [+ 255 22] 211 68 96

E-mail: dslam@dfait-maeci.gc.ca

Telex: 41015 DOMCAN TZ

Office Hours: Monday to Friday
0730hrs to 1530hrs

High Commissioner
H.E. Mr Wayne HAMMOND
286, Toure Drive, Dar Es Salaam, Tanzania

VISA: Issued by Canadian High Commission in Nairobi, Kenya. Forms obtainable from British High Commission in Victoria.

CHINA
PEOPLE'S REPUBLIC OF
Embassy of the People's Republic of China
P O Box 680, St Louis, Mahé, Seychelles

Telephone N°: **Telefax N°:**
[+ 248] 26 68 08 [+ 248] 26 68 66
[+ 248] 26 65 88

E-mail address: china@seychelles.net

Telex: 2398 CHINA EM SZ

Office Hours: Monday to Friday
0830 to 1200 1400 to 1630

Ambassador
H.E. Mr. HOU Guixin

ST LOUIS, MAHE, SEYCHELLES

Telephone:[+ 248] 26 65 88
Cellular Telelephone: [+ 248] 51 51 78

First Secretary: *Mr. XU Jingli*
St Louis, Mahé, Seychelles
Telelephone: [+ 248] 26 65 88
Cellular Telelephone: [+ 248] 51 58 88

First Secretary: *Mr. JU Chaoqing*
St Louis, Mahé, Seychelles
Telelephone: [+ 248] 26 68 08

Second Secretary: *Mr. Li LONG*
St Louis, Mahé, Seychelles
Telephone: [+ 248] 26 68 08

Third Secretary: *Mr. DONG Guangli*
St Louis, Mahé, Seychelles
Telephone: [+ 248] 26 63 69

Third Secretary: *Mr. ZHANG Shaowen*

St Louis, Mahé, Seychelles
Telephone: [+ 248] 26 65 88

Third Secretary: *Mr. ZHANG Zhe*
St Louis, Mahé, Seychelles
Telephone: [+ 248] 26 65 88

Staff Member: *Mrs ZHANG Xu*
St Louis, Mahé, Seychelles
Telephone: [+ 248] 26 65 88

VISA: Issued by Embassy in Victoria. Not required for Diplomatic Passport holders.

CONGO
REPUBLIQUE DEMOCRATIQUE DU

Ambassade de la République Démocratique du Congo.
B P 48106, 12ème Etage, Electricity House
Harambee Avenue, Nairobi, Kenya

Numéro de téléphone:
[+ 254 2] 22 97 71
[+ 254 2] 22 97 72

Numéro de téléfax:
[+ 254 2] 33 45 39

E-mail: ambcon@insightkenya.com

Horaires de Travail: Lundi à Vendredi
08h30 à 12h30 14h30 à 16h00

Ambassadeur
(Vacant)

Charge d'Affaires a.i.:
Prof. Gaspard MUGARUKA BIN-MUBIBI
Karura Avenue, Muthaiga
Téléphone portable:[+ 254] 72521853

VISA: Issued by Embassy in Nairobi, Kenya

CONGO
REPUBLIQUE DU

Ambassade de la République du Congo,
BP 5639, Addis Abéba, Ethiopie

Numéro de Téléphone:
[+ 251 1] 51 41 88

Numéro de Téléfax
[+ 251 1] 51 43 31

Télex: 21406 ARCE-ET

Horaires de Travail:

Ambassadeur
S.E. M. Victor NIMI
Désigné

VISA: Issued by Embassy in Nairobi, Kenya

CUBA
REPUBLIC OF

Embassy of the Republic of Cuba,
P.O. Box 730, Belle Eau, Mahé, Seychelles

Telephone N°: **Telefax N°:**
[+ 248] 22 40 94 [+ 248] 22 43 76

E-mail address: cuabasey@seychelles.net

Telex N°: 2354 M CUBA SZ

Office Hours: Monday to Friday
0800 to 1200 1400 to 1600

Ambassador:
H.E. Mr. Evangelo Nicolas Montero HERNANDEZ
designate

Chargé d'Affaires *a.i.*:
Mr. Orlando Pino Lobaina FOURNIER

Telephone: [+ 248] 22 40 94

VISA: Issued by Embassy in Victoria. Not required for Diplomatic Passport holders

CYPRUS,
REPUBLIC OF

High Commission of the Republic of Cyprus,
P O Box 30739, 5th Floor, Eagle House,
Kimathi Street, Nairobi, Kenya

Telephone N°: **Telefax N°:**
[+ 254 2] 220881 [+ 254 2] 331232

E-mail address: cyphc@net2000ke.com

Telex: 22436 CYPROHC

Office Hours: Monday to Friday

0900 to 1230 1400 to 1600

High Commissioner:
H.E. Mr Costas A. PAPADEMAS
Off Karabasiran Road, Lavington, Nairobi, Kenya

Telephone: [+ 254 2] 441954

NO VISA REQUIRED FOR STAY UP TO 3 MONTHS

CZECH REPUBLIC

Embassy of the Czech Republic,
P O Box 48785, Embassy House,
Harambee Avenue, Nairobi, Kenya

Telephone N°:	**Telefax N°:**
[+ 254 2] 21 04 94	[+ 254 2] 22 34 47
[+ 254 2] 22 34 48	

E-mail address: zamini.cz@net2000ke.com
nairobi@embassy.mzv.cz

Office Hours: Monday to Friday, 0830hrs to 1430hrs

Ambassador
(Vacant)
68 Muthaiga Road, Nairobi, Kenya

Telephone: [+ 254 2] 748224

Chargé d'Affaires a.i.: ***Mr. Zdeněk DOBIÁŠ***
Telephone: [+ 254 2] 74 89 93

VISA: Issued by Embassy in Nairobi, Kenya

DENMARK,
KINGDOM OF

The Royal Danish Embassy,
P O Box 40412, 11th Floor, HFCK Building,
Koinange Street, Nairobi, Kenya

Telephone N°:	**Telefax N°:**
[+ 254 2] 331088	[+ 254 2] 331492
[+ 254 2] 331089	
[+ 254 2] 331090	

E-mail: nboamb@nboamb.um.dk

Telex: 22216 AMBADANE

Office Hours: Monday to Friday, 0745 to 1500

Ambassador
H.E. Mr. Klaus DAHLGAARD
Corner Naivasha Avenue, Muthaiga Road, Nairobi, Kenya

Telephone: [+ 254 2] 761717

VISA: Issued by Danish Consulate in Victoria

EGYPT,
ARAB REPUBLIC OF

Embassy of the Arab Republic of Egypt,
P O Box 30285, Kingara Road, Lavington,
Nairobi, Kenya

Telephone N°:	**Telefax N°:**
[+ 254 2] 57 03 60	[+ 254 2] 57 03 83
[+ 254 2] 57 02 78	
[+ 254 2] 57 02 98	

E-mail address: egyembnb@net2000ke.com

Telex: 22335 BOUSTAN

Office Hours: Monday to Friday, 0900 to 1530

Ambassador
H.E. Mr. Refaat Alansary Aly Refaa ALANSARY
Riara Road, Off Ngong Road, Nairobi, Kenya

Telephone: [+ 254 2] 564646

VISA: Issued by Embassy in Nairobi, Kenya. Can be issued on arrival if it has not been possible to obtain visa prior to entering Cairo.

ETHIOPIA,
FEDERAL DEMOCRATIC REPUBLIC OF

Embassy of the Federal Democratic
Republic of Ethiopia,
P O Box 45198, State House Avenue, Nairobi, Kenya

Telephone N°: Telefax: [+ 254 2] 72 34 01
[+ 254 2] 72 30 35
[+ 254 2] 72 30 27
[+ 254 2] 72 30 53

Telex: 22864 ETHERMB KE

Office Hours: Monday to Friday
0800 to 1230 1400 to 1700

Ambassador
H.E. Mr Teshome Toga CHANAKA
Designate
State House Avenue, Nairobi, Kenya

Telephone: [+ 254 2] 723400

VISA: Issued by Embassy in Nairobi, Kenya

FINLAND,
REPUBLIC OF
Embassy of the Republic of Finland,
P O Box 30379, 2nd Floor, International House,
Mama Ngina Street, Nairobi, Kenya

Telephone N°:	Telefax N°:
[+ 254 2] 336717	[+ 254 2] 335986
[+ 254 2] 336740	[+ 254 2] 229379
[+ 254 2] 334408	
[+ 254 2] 334777	
[+ 254 2] 334778	

E-mail: embassy@finembkenya.org

Telex: 22010 FINAMB KE
Telegraphic Address: FINLANDIA NAIROBI

Office Hours: September to May
Monday to Thursday 0800 to 1200
1315 to 1615
Friday 0800 to 1230 1300 to 1445
June to August:
Monday to Friday, 0800 to 1230 1315 to 1515

Ambassador
H.E. Mr. Lauri KANGAS
Telephone: [+ 254 2] 521612
[+ 254 2] 521767

NO VISA REQUIRED

FRANCE
Ambassade de France,
B P 478, 4ème Etage, Victoria House,
Victoria, Mahé, Seychelles

Numéro de téléphone: Numéro de téléfax
[+ 248] 38 25 00 [+ 248] 38 25 10

E-mail: ambafran@seychelles.net
Télex: 2238 FRANCE SZ

Horaires de Travail:
Lundi à Vendredi 08h00 à 16h30
Pour Visa *08h00 à 12h00*

Ambassadeur
S.E. M. Marcel SURBIGUET (m)
La Misère, Mahé, Seychelles
Numéro de téléphone: [+ 248] 34 43 03 (domicile)

Premier Conseiller: *M. Gerard TOURNIER*
Bel Ombre, Mahé, Seychelles
Numéro de téléphone: [+ 248] 38 25 02 (bureau)

Vice Consul: *Mme Cathy EVERAERT* (m)
Forêt Noire, Mahé, Seychelles
Numéro de téléphone: [+ 248] 38 25 03 (bureau)
Numéro de téléphone: [+ 248] 32 44 79 (domicile)

Comptable à l'Ambassade de France:
M. Jean-Bernard MARIE (m)
Sans Souci, Mahé, Seychelles
Numéro de téléphone: [+ 248] 38 25 04 (bureau)
Numéro de téléphone: [+ 248] 22 55 44 (domicile)

Attaché de Défense: *Capitaine du Frégate Marc GUITTARD* Basé à la Réunion

Consultant Economique et Commerciale:
M. Henri FONTAINE Basé à Maurice

Service de Coopération et d'Action Culturelle
près de l'Ambassade de France,
B. P. 598, 4ème Etage, Victoria House,
Victoria, Mahé, Seychelles

Numéro de téléphone: Numéro de téléfax
[+ 248] 38 25 20 [+ 248] 38 25 30

E-mail: coopsey@seychelles.net

Chef du Service de Coopération et d'Action Culturelle: *M. Alain LE RAVALLEC*
"Carpe Diem", Glacis, Mahé, Seychelles
Numéro de téléphone: [+ 248] 38 25 21 (bureau)
Numéro de téléphone: [+ 248] 26 13 19 (domicile)

Conseiller du Service de Coopération et d'Action Culturelle: *M. Jean-Pierre MAZOCCHIN* (m)
Glacis, Mahé, Seychelles
Numéro de téléphone: [+ 248] 38 25 22 (bureau)
Numéro de téléphone: [+ 248] 26 12 17 (domicile)

VISA: Schengen Visa issued by Embassy of France in Victoria

GABON, REPUBLIQUE GABONAISE

Ministère des Affaires Etrangères et de la Coopération
Boite Postale 2245, Libreville
République Gabonaise

Numéro de Téléphone:	**Numéro de Téléfax:**
[+ 241] 72 95 21	[+ 241] 76 12 72
[+ 241] 73 94 67	

Ambassadeur
S.E. M. Paul ENEMBE OBAME

VISA: Issued by Embassy of France in Victoria

GERMANY, FEDERAL REPUBLIC OF

Embassy of the Federal Republic of Germany,
P.O. Box 30180, 8th/9th Floors, Williamson House,
4th Ngong Avenue, Nairobi, Kenya

Telephone N°:	**Telefax N°:**
[+ 254 2] 71 25 27	[+ 254 2] 71 48 86
[+ 254 2] 71 93 86	[+ 254 2] 71 54 99
[+ 254 2] 71 93 88	

E-mail: Ger-emb@form-net.com

Telex: 22221 / 22189

Office Hours: Monday to Friday, 0830 to 1230

Ambassador
H.E. Mr. Juergen WEERTH
Twiga Road, Muthaiga, Nairobi, Kenya
Telephone: [+ 254 2] 74 82 96

VISA: Schengen Visa issued by Embassy of France in Victoria

GHANA,
REPUBLIC OF

High Commission of the Republic of Ghana
P. O. Box 12537, Hatfield 0028, Pretoria,
Republic of South Africa

Telephone N°:	Telefax N°:
[+ 27 12] 342 58 47	[+ 27 12] 342 5863
[+ 27 12] 342 58 48	
[+ 27 12] 342 58 49	

E-mail: ghcom27@icon.co.za

Office Hours: Monday to Friday, mornings

Ambassador
H.E. Mr. Patrick Reginald HAYFORD
Designate
VISA: Issued by High Commission in Pretoria, South Africa

GREECE
(HELLENIC REPUBLIC)

Embassy of Greece,
P O Box 30543, 4th Floor, IPS Building,
Kimathi, Nairobi, Kenya

Telephone N°:	Telefax N°:
[+ 254 2] 340722	[+ 254 2] 216044
[+ 254 2] 340744	

Telex: 22008 EMBAGREECE

Office Hours: Monday to Friday, 0900 to 1400

Ambassador
H.E. Mr. Ioannis KORINTHIOS

Muthaiga Road # 12, Muthaiga, Nairobi, Kenya
Telephone: [+ 254 2] 762836

VISA: Schengen Visa issued by Embassy of France in Victoria

GUINEE,
REPUBLIQUE DE

Ambassade de la République de Guinée,
Debre Zeit Road, Higher 18, Kebele 41,
House # 058, Addis Abéba, Ethiopie

Numéro de téléphone: Numéro de téléfax
[+ 251 1] 65 13 08
[+ 251 1] 65 25 39

Télex: 21757

Horaires de Travail: Lundi à Vendredi
08h00 à 15h00

Ambassadeur
S.E. M. Mamadi DIAWARA
Désigné
Mesfin Harar Road, Higher 9, Kebele 10, House No. 398, Addis Abéba, Ethiopie

Numéro de téléphone: [+ 251 1] 55 23 11

VISA: Issued by Embassy in Addis Ababa, Ethiopia

HUNGARY,
REPUBLIC OF

Embassy of the Republic of Hungary,
P O Box 1213, Addis Ababa, Ethiopia

Telephone N°: **Telefax N°:**
[+ 251 1] 65 18 50
[+ 251 1] 65 17 51

Telex: 21176

Office Hours: Monday to Friday,

Ambassador
(Vacant)

NO VISA REQUIRED

INDIA,

REPUBLIC OF

High Commission of India,
P O Box 488, Francis Rachel Street, Mahé, Seychelles

Telephone N°: [+ 248] 22 44 89
Telefax N°: [+ 248] 22 48 10

E-mail: hicomind@seychelles.net

Telex: 2349 HICOM SZ

Office Hours: Monday to Friday
0800 to 1230 1300 to 1530

High Commissioner
H.E. Mr. River O'Nell WALLANG (m.)

Val Riche, Sans Souci, Mahé, Seychelles
Telephone N°: [+ 248] 22 41 50

First Secretary:
Mr. Rajendra V. GHUGE (m.)
Belle Eau, Mahé, Seychelles
Telephone N°: [+ 248] 22 52 67

Attaché : *Mr. Partha RAY (m.)*
English River, Mahé, Seychelles
Telephone N°: [+ 248] 32 35 75

Defence Adviser: *Captain Anandamoy GHOSAL*
Based in Nairobi

VISA: Issued by High Commission in Victoria

INDONESIA,
REPUBLIC OF

Embassy of the Republic of Indonesia,
P O Box 48868, Menengai Road, Upper Hill,
Nairobi, Kenya

Telephone N°:
[+ 254 2] 71 41 96
[+ 254 2] 71 41 97
[+ 254 2] 71 41 98

Telefax N°: [+ 254 2] 71 34 75

E-mail: indonbi@arcc.or.ke

Telex: 23171 INDO KE

Office Hours: Monday to Friday
0900 to 1700

Ambassador
H.E. Mr Isslamet POERNOMO
"Wisma Duta Indonesia"
Urafiki Lane, Limuru Road, Muthaiga, Nairobi, Kenya
Telephone N°: [+ 254 2] 740542

VISA: Issued by Indonesian Consulate in Victoria

IRAN,
REPUBLIQUE ISLAMIQUE DE

Ambassade de la République Islamique d'Iran,
B P 3920, Route Circulaire, Antananarivo, Madagascar

Numero de téléphone:	Numéro de téléfax
[+ 261 20] 22 28 639	[+ 261 20] 22 22 298
[+ 261 20] 22 28 527	

E-mail: amari@simicro.mg

Télex: 22510 IRANTA MG

Ambassadeur
S. E. Monsieur Faramarz LATIFI NAMIN

VISA: Issued by Embassy in Antananarivo, Madagascar

IRAQ,
REPUBLIC OF

Embassy of the Republic of Iraq,
P O Box 49213, Loresho Ridge, Nairobi, Kenya

Telephone N°:	Telefax N°:
[+ 254 2] 58 11 43	[+ 254 2] 58 02 67

Telex: 23020

Telegraphic Address: IRAQIYA

Office Hours: Monday to Friday, 0800 to 1300
1400 to 1700

Ambassador

(Vacant)

Chargé d'Affaires *a.i.*: Mr. Sabah Talat KADRET

VISA: Issued by Embassy in Nairobi, Kenya

ISRAEL,
STATE OF

Embassy of the State of Israel,
P O Box 30354, Bishops Road, Nairobi, Kenya

Telephone N°:	**Telefax N°:**
[+ 254 2] 722182	[+ 254 2] 715966
[+ 254 2] 722183	
[+ 254 2] 724021	
[+ 254 2] 724022	

E-mail address: israemb@africaonline.co.ke

Office Hours: Monday to Friday, 0830 to 1630

Ambassador
H.E. Mr. Yaacov AMITAI
55 Thigiri Gardens, Nairobi, Kenya

Telephone N°: [+ 254 2] 520821

VISA: Issued by Embassy in Nairobi, Kenya

ITALY
ITALIAN REPUBLIC

Italian Embassy,
P O Box 30107, 9th Floor, International House,
Mama Ngina Street, Nairobi, Kenya

Telephone N°:	**Telefax N°:**
[+ 254 2] 33 73 56	[+ 254 2] 33 70 56
[+ 254 2] 33 73 57	

E-mail: italdipl@ambnair.org

Website www.ceemail.com/italembassy.html

Telex: 22251 ITALDIPL

Office Hours: Monday to Tuesday
0800 to 1300 1400 to 1800
Wednesday to Friday, 0800 to 1400

Ambassador
H.E. Dr Alberto BALBONI
Karura Avenue, Muthaiga, Nairobi, Kenya

Telephone N°: [+ 254 2] 748856

VISA: Schengen Visa issued by Embassy of France in Victoria

JAPAN

Embassy of Japan,
P O Box 60202, 15th Floor, ICEA Building,
Kenyatta Avenue, Nairobi, Kenya

Telephone N°: [+ 254 2] 332955
Telefax N°: [+ 254 2] 216530

E-mail: jinfocul@japanembassy.or.ke

Telex: 22286 TAISI

Office Hours: Monday to Friday
0830 to 1230 1400 to 1630

Ambassador
H.E. Mr Morihisa AOKI
Riverside Drive, Nairobi,Kenya

Telephone N°: [+ 254 2] 47518

VISA: Issued by Embassy in Nairobi, Kenya

KOREA,
DEMOCRATIC PEOPLE'S REPUBLIC OF

Embassy of the Democratic People's Republic of Korea,
B. P. 4276, Antananarivo, Madagascar

Telephone N°: [+ 261 20] 22 44442
Telefax: [+ 261 20] 22 44795

Telex:

Office Hours: Monday to Friday
0800 to 1300 1400 to 1700

Ambassador
H.E. Mr Ri Yong HAK

VISA: Issued by Embassy in Dar Es Salaam, Tanzania

KOREA,
REPUBLIC OF
Embassy of the Republic of Korea,
15th Floor, Anniversary Towers, University Way,
P O Box 30455, Nairobi, Kenya

Telephone N°:	**Telefax N°:**
[+ 254 2] 33 35 81	[+ 254 2] 21 77 72
[+ 254 2] 33 35 82	
[+ 254 2] 33 28 39	

E-mail: emb-ke@mofat.go.kr

Telex: 22300

Office Hours:

Monday to Thursday	0730 to 1200
	1300 to 1530
Friday	0730 to 1300

Ambassador
H.E. Mr. Jong-rak KWON
Mzima Springs Lane, Off Riverside Drive, Nairobi, Kenya
Telephone N°: [+ 254 2] 49 129
[+ 254 2] 49 551

VISA: Issued by Embassy in Nairobi, Kenya

LIBYE

Bureau Populaire de la Jamahiriya Arabe Libyenne Populaire Socialiste La Grande,
BP 116, Antananarivo, Madagascar

Numéro de téléphone:	**Numéro de téléfax**
[+ 261 20] 22 21 892	[+ 261 20] 22 25 672
[+ 261 20] 22 21 885	
[+ 261 20] 22 25 672	

Télex: 22238 LIB TA MG

Horaires de Travail: Lundi à Vendredi
08h30 à 15h00

Secrétaire du Bureau Populaire
(Vacant)

BP 116, Antananarivo, Madagascar
Numéro de éléphone: [+ 261 20] 22 44 520

Charge d'Affaires *a.i.* du Bureau Populaire:
M. Mansur Milad ALKADUSHI

VISA: Issued by the Bureau in Antananarivo, Madagascar

MADAGASCAR,
RREPUBLIQUE DE

Ambassade de la République de Madagascar,
Rue Guiot Pasceau, Floréal, BP 03, Maurice

Numéro de Téléphone:	**Numéro de Téléfax:**
[+ 230] 686 5015	[+ 230] 686 7040
[+ 230] 686 5016	

E-mail: madmail@intnet.mu

Télex: 4340 IW

Ambassadeur
S.E. M. Paul André TSILANIZARA

VISA: Issued by Honorary Consul in Seychelles or upon arrival in Madagascar

MALAYSIA

High Commission of Malaysia
P. O. Box 5570, 40 Downie Avenue, Avondale
Harare, Zimbabwe

Telephone N°:	**Telefax N°:**
[+ 263 4] 33 44 13	[+ 263 4] 33 44 15
[+ 263 4] 33 44 14	

E-mail Address: mwharare@africaonline.co.zw

Telex: 22506

Office Hours: Monday to Friday
0830 to 1630

High Commissioner
H.E. Mr Ali bin ABDULLAH
24, Broadmead Lane, Colne Valley
Harare, Zimbabwe

Telephone N°: [+ 263 4] 49 01 53

NO VISA REQUIRED

ORDRE SOVERAIN MILITAIRE DE MALTE

Ambassade de l'Ordre Souverain Militaire de Malte,
68 Via Condotti, Palazzo Di Malta, 00187 Rome, Italy

Numéro de Téléphone	Numéro de Téléfax
[+ 39 6] 6758110	[+ 39 6] 6797202
[+ 39 6] 6758111	
[+ 39 6] 6758112	

Ambassadeur
S.E. le Chevalier Dr Antonio SPADA

MAROC,
ROYAUME DU

Ambassade du Royaume du Maroc
Jabavu Road, Hurlingham, P. O. Box 61098,
Nairobi, Kenya

Numéro de Téléphone	Numéro de Téléfax
[+ 254 2] 71 06 47	[+ 254 2] 71 98 40
[+ 254 2] 71 04 35	

E-mail: sifmanbi@africaonline.co.ke

Ambassadeur
S. E. M. Mohammed CHRAIBI
Muthaiga Grove, Nairobi, Kenya
Numéro de Téléphone: [+ 254 2] 76 55 74

VISA: Issued by Embassy in Nairobi, Kenya

MOZAMBIQUE,
REPUBLIC OF

High Commission of the Republic of Mozambique,
P O Box 9370, 25 Garden Avenue,
Dar Es Salaam, Tanzania

Telephone N°: **Telefax:**
[+ 255 222] 46973
[+ 255 222] 46974
[+ 255 222] 33063

Telex: 41214 EMBA MOC

Office Hours: Monday to Friday, 0830 to 1600

High Commissioner
H.E. Mr Pedro Gaivao ODALLAH
Msasani Peninsula, Plot # 1407, Dar Es Salaam, Tanzania

Telephone N°: [+ 255 222] 40062

VISA: Issued by Embassy in Nairobi, Kenya (P.O. Box 6692 Tel: 221979/21 41 91) Fax: 222 446, E-mail: mozhicom@swiftkenya.com

NETHERLANDS,
KINGDOM OF THE

Royal Netherlands Embassy,
Off Riverside Drive, Riverside Lane,
P. O. Box 41537, Nairobi, Kenya

Telephone N°: **Telefax N°:**
[+ 254 2] 44 74 12 [+ 254 2] 44 74 16
[+ 254 2] 44 74 13
[+ 254 2] 44 74 14
[+ 254 2] 44 74 15

E-mail: nlgovnai@nbnet.co.ke

Office Hours: Monday to Thursday 0745 to 1615
Friday 0745 to 1345

Ambassador
H.E. Mr. Gertjan STORM
Mutumdu Road, Muthaiga, Nairobi, Kenya

VISA: Schengen Visa issued by Embassy of France in Victoria

NIGERIA,
FEDERAL REPUBLIC OF

High Commission of the Federal Republic of Nigeria,
P O Box 30516
Lenana Road, Nairobi, Kenya

Telephone N°: [+ 254 2] 56 41 16, [+ 254 2] 56 41 18
Telefax N°: [+ 254 2] 56 27 76

Office Hours: Monday to Friday, 0800 to 1530

High Commissioner
Vacant

VISA: Issued by Embassy in Nairobi, Kenya

NORWAY, KINGDOM OF

Royal Norwegian Embassy,
P O Box 2646, Plot # 160, Mirambo Street,
Dar Es Salaam, Tanzania

Telephone N°: [+ 255 22] 211 33 66, [+ 255 22] 211 36 23
Telefax N°: [+ 255 22] 211 65 64

Outside Office Hours
Telephone N°: [+ 255 742] 76 98 11
[+ 255 742] 76 98 12

E-mail: ambassaden-dsm@raha.com
Website: www.norway.go.tz

Office Hours: Monday to Friday, 0800 to 1400

Ambassador
H.E. Mr Nils-Johan JØRGENSEN
Plot 1130 Msasani Road, Mzinga Way, Dar Es Salaam, Tanzania
Telephone N°: [+ 255 22] 26 83 60

NO VISA REQUIRED UNTIL 24TH MARCH 2001. As of 25th March 2001, Norway will be part of the Schengen cooperation of the EU and Seychellois will require to obtain a visa prior to entering into Norway.

OMAN, SULTANATE OF

Embassy of the Sultanate of Oman,
16 Olof Palmer Marg, Vasant Vihar,
New Delhi - 110 057, India

Telephone N°:	**Telefax N°:**
[+ 91 11] 670215	[+ 91 11] 61 46 478
[+ 91 11] 674798	[+ 91 11] 61 52 661
[+ 91 11] 671704	
[+ 91 11] 673980 *(Ambassador's Office)*	

E-mail address: omandelhi@vsnl.com

Telex: 3172342 OMAN IN

Office Hours: Monday to Friday, 0900 to 1530

Ambassador
H.E. Mr. Khalifa Bin Ali Bin Essa AL-HARTHY
A - 33 Vasant Marg, Vasant Vihar,
New Delhi - 110 057, India

Telephone N°: [+ 91 11] 672559
[+ 91 11] 672870

VISA: Issued by Embassy in New Delhi, India

**PAKISTAN,
ISLAMIC REPUBLIC OF**

**High Commission for Pakistan,
P O Box 42
9-A Queen Mary Avenue, Floreal, Mauritius**

Telephone N°:	**Telefax N°:**
[+ 230] 698 8501	[+ 230] 698 8405
[+ 230] 698 8502	

E-mail: pareppportlouis@intnet.mu

Telex: 4609 PAKEMB IW

Telegraphic Address: PAREP PORT LOUIS

Office Hours: Monday to Friday, 0900 to 1600

High Commissioner
Vacant
Avenue Rouillard, Floréal, Mauritius

Acting High Commissioner:
Mr. Ghulum Rasool BALUCH

VISA: Issued by High Commission in Mauritius

PALESTINE,
STATE OF

Embassy of the State of Palestine,
P O Box 20307, 612 United Nations Road, Upanga,
Dar Es Salaam, Tanzania

Telephone N°: [+ 255 222] 15 04 85
Telefax N°: [+ 255 222] 15 35 09

Telex: 41425 HADI TZ/41223 TANSA TZ

Office Hours: Monday to Thursday, 0900 to 1400
Friday 0900 to 1230

Ambassador
(Vacant)
Plot 74, Upanga Road, Dar Es Salaam, Tanzania

Telephone N°: [+ 255 812] 78 23 31
[+ 255 812] 78 23 32

PHILIPPINES,
REPUBLIC OF THE

Embassy of the Republic of the Philippines,
P O Box 47941, Nairobi, Kenya

Telephone N°: [+ 254 2] 72 17 91
Telefax N°: [+ 254 2] 72 58 97

Telex: 22925 PUBLICNRB

Office Hours: Monday to Friday
0800 to 1200 1300 to 1700

Ambassador
H.E. Mr. Rolando M. LIBAS
House # 6, Kileleshwa Ring Road Corner, Riverside Drive, Nairobi, Kenya

Telephone N°: [+ 254 2] 44 66 89

VISA: Tourist visa of up to 3 months issued upon arrival

PORTUGAL
PORTUGUESE REPUBLIC

Embassy of Portugal,
P O Box 34020, 10th Floor,
Reinsurance Plaza, Taifa Road, Nairobi, Kenya

Telephone N°:	**Telefax N°:**
[+ 254 2] 338990	[+ 254 2] 214711
[+ 254 2] 339853	

Telex: 22634 EMBPORT K

Office Hours: Monday to Friday, 0900 to 1600

Ambassador
Mr. José Manuel de Carvalho LAMEIRAS
House N° 622, Mutundu Road, Muthaiga, Nairobi, Kenya

Telephone N°: [+ 254 2] 76 16 17

VISA: Schengen Visa issued by Embassy of France in Victoria

RUSSIAN FEDERATION

Embassy of the Russian Federation,
P O Box 632, St Louis, Mahé, Seychelles

Telephone N°:	**Telefax N°:**
[+ 248] 26 65 90	[+ 248] 26 66 53
[+ 248] 71 16 53	

E-mail: rfembsey@seychelles.net

Telex: 2392 SOVEMB SZ

Office Hours:

Monday-Thursday	0800 to 1200	1330 to 1630
Friday	0800 to 1200	1330 to 1615

Ambassador
Mr. Vladimir Nikolaevitch KALININ (m)
Bel Ombre, Mahé, Seychelles
Telephone N°: [+ 248] 24 75 33

Counsellor.: *Mr. Igor Degtiarev*
St Louis, Mahé, Seychelles
Telephone N°: [+248] 26 61 22

Second Secretary/Head of Consular Department:
Mr. Youry Ivanov (m)

St Louis, Mahé, Seychelles
Telephone N°: [+248] 26 61 22
[+248] 71 17 21

Attaché: *Mr. Vladimir Stefankov (m)*
St Louis, Mahé, Seychelles
Telephone N°: [+ 248] 26 65 90

Attaché: *Mr. Vladimir Grishin (m)*
St Louis, Mahé, Seychelles
Telephone N°: [+ 248] 26 65 90

VISA: Issued by Embassy in Victoria

REPUBLIQUE ARABE SAHRAOUIE DEMOCRATIQUE

**Ambassade de la République Arabe Sahraouie Démocratique,
22, Rue Rév. Père Radley, Antanimena,
B P 805, 101 Antananarivo, Madagascar**

Numéro de téléphone: [+ 261 20] 22 64 379
Numéro de téléfax: [+ 261 20] 2266 743

E-mail: amb.rasd@dts.mg

Horaires de Travail: Lundi à Vendredi
08h30 à 12h00 14h00 à 16h30

Ambassadeur
S.E. M. BOUKHREIS Habib
Ambaranjana
Numéro de téléphone: [+ 261 20] 22 375 37

Premier Secrétaire: M. Andalla SIDATI
Antanimena
Numéro de téléphone: [+ 261 20] 22 63 883

**SENEGAL,
REPUBLIQUE DU**

Ministère des Affaires Etrangères et des Sénégalais de l'Extérieur, Dakar, République du Sénégal

Numéro de Téléphone:
Numéro de Téléfax:

Télex:

Horaires de Travail: Lundi à Vendredi

Ambassadeur
S.E. M. Mohamed Abdou Razack BENGELOUN
Désigné

VISA: Issued by Embassy of France in Victoria

SLOVAK REPUBLIC

Embassy of the Slovak Republic
P.O. Box 30204, Milimani Road, Nairobi, Kenya

Telephone N°:	**Telefax N°:**
[+ 254 2]72 18 96	[+ 254 2] 72 18 98
[+ 254 2] 72 18 97	

Telex N°: 25371 ZAMINI KE

Ambassador
H.E. Mr. Radomir BOHÁČ

VISA: Issued by Embassy in Nairobi, Kenya

SOUTH AFRICA,
REPUBLIC OF

High Commission of the Republic of South Africa,
4th Floor, BAI Building, Pope Hennessy Street,
Port Louis, Mauritius

Telephone N°:	**Telefax N°:**
[+ 230]212 69 25	[+ 230] 212 93 46
[+ 230] 212 69 26	[+ 230] 212 69 36
[+ 230] 212 69 28	
[+ 230] 212 69 90	
[+ 230] 212 69 30	

E-mail address: sahc@intnet.mu

High Commissioner
H. E. Mr. Lulu Louis Aaron MNGUNI

VISA: No visa required for a stay up to 30 days.

SPAIN,
KINGDOM OF

Embassy of Spain,
P O Box 45503, Bruce House,
Standard Street, Nairobi, Kenya

Telephone N°: **Telefax N°:**
[+ 254 2] 335711 [+ 254 2] 332858
[+ 254 2] 335712

E-mail address: embespke@mail.mae.es

Telex: 22157 EMBAES KE

Office Hours: Monday to Friday
0830 to 1300 1430 to 1630
Saturday, 0930 to 1230

Ambassador
H.E. Mr. Luis Francisco García CEREZO

VISA: Schengen Visa issued by Embassy of France in Victoria

SRI LANKA,
DEMOCRATIC SOCIALIST REPUBLIC OF

High Commission of the Democratic Socialist
Republic of Sri Lanka
410, Alexander Street, Brooklyn 0181
Pretoria, Republic of South Africa

Telephone N°: **Telefax N°:**
[+ 27 12] 46 76 79 [+ 27 12] 46 77 02
[+ 27 12] 46 76 90

E-mail address: srilanka@global.co.za

Website: http://www.srilanka.co.za/

Office Hours:
Monday to Friday: 0830 to 1630

High Commissioner
H.E. Mr. Gamini S. MUNASINGHE

VISA: Issued by High Commission in Pretoria

SWEDEN,
KINGDOM OF

Embassy of Sweden
P. O. Box 30600

10th Floor, International House,
Mama Ngina Street
Nairobi, Kenya

Telephone N°: [+ 254 2] 22 90 42 / [+ 254 2] 22 90 43 / [+ 254 2] 22 90 44 / [+ 254 2] 22 90 45

Telefax N°: [+ 254 2] 21 89 08

E-mail: embassy.nairobi@sida.se

Office Hours:
Monday to Friday: 0800 to 1600

Ambassador
H.E. Mrs Inga BJÖRK-KLEVBY

NO VISA REQUIRED

SUISSE
CONFEDERATION SUISSE

Ambassade de Suisse,
7ème Etage, International House,
Mama Ngina Street, BP 30752, Nairobi, Kenya

Numéro de téléphone: [+ 254 2] 22 87 35 / [+ 254 2] 22 87 36

Numéro de téléfax: [+ 254 2] 21 73 88 / [+ 254 2] 21 84 16

E-mail: swissemb@africaonline.co.ke

Télex: 22181

Horaires de Travail:
Lundi à Vendredi, 07h30 à 12h30

Ambassadeur
S.E. M. Josef BUCHER
Muthaiga Road, Limuru Road Round-about, Nairobi, Kenya
Numéro de téléphone: [+ 254 2] 749606

VISA: Issued by Embassy in Nairobi, Kenya

TANZANIA,
UNITED REPUBLIC OF

High Commission of the United Republic of Tanzania,
9th Floor, Taifa Road, Re-Insurance Plaza
P O Box 47790, Nairobi, Kenya

Telephone N°:	**Telefax N°:**
[+ 254 2] 33 10 56	[+ 254 2] 21 82 69
[+ 254 2] 33 10 57	
[+ 254 2] 33 11 04	
[+ 254 2] 33 10 93	

Telex: 25351 TANREP KE

Office Hours: Monday to Friday
0800 to 1500

High Commissioner
H.E. Major General Mirisho Sam Hagai SARAKIKYA
Muthaiga Road, Nairobi, Kenya

VISA: Issued upon arrival

THAILAND,
KINGDOM OF

Royal Thai Embassy
Rose Avenue, Off Denis Pritt Road
P. O. Box 58349, Nairobi, Kenya

Telephone N°:	**Telefax N°:**
[+ 254 2] 71 52 43	[+ 254 2] 71 58 01
[+ 254 2] 71 57 96	
[+ 254 2] 71 58 00	

E-mail: thainbi@form-net.com

Office Hours:
Monday to Friday
0900 to 1230 1400 to 1700

Ambassador
H.E. Mr. Thanarat THANAPUTTI
Telephone N°: [+ 254 2] 71 57 98

VISA: Issued upon arrival for a stay of up to 15 days

TUNISIE
REPUBLIQUE TUNISIENNE

Ambassade de la République Tunisienne,

BP 100069, Addis Abéba, Ethiopie

Numéro de Téléphone: [+ 251 1] 61 20 63
Numéro de Téléfax: [+ 251 1] 61 45 68

Télex: 21505

E-mail: embassy.tunisia@telecom.net.et

Ambassadeur
vacant

Chargé d'Affaires a.i.:
M. Mourad Ben DHIAB

NO VISA REQUIRED

**TURKEY,
REPUBLIC OF**

**Embassy of the Republic of Turkey
Gigiri Road, Off Limuru Road
P. O. Box 64748, Nairobi, Kenya**

Telephone N°: [+ 254 2] 52 25 62
[+ 254 2] 52 04 04
Telefax N°: [+ 254 2] 52 27 78

E-mail address: embturk.nairobi@unon.org
tcbenair@wanachi.com

Office Hours: Monday to Friday0900 to 1230
1330 to 1700

Ambassador
H.E. Mr. Osman Mengü BÜYÜKDAVRAS

UNITED KINGDOM OF GREAT BRITAIN AND NORTHERN IRELAND

**British High Commission,
P O Box 161, 3rd Floor,
Oliajee Trade Centre, Victoria, Mahé, Seychelles**

Telephone N°: [+ 248] 22 52 25
Telefax N°: [+ 248] 22 51 27

Telex: 2269 UKREP SZ
Website: www.bhcvictoria.sc
E-mail address: bhcsey@seychelles.net

Telegraphic Address: UK REP VICTORIA

Office Hours: Monday to Thursday 0800 to 1600
Friday 0800 to 1500

High Commissioner
H.E. Mr John YAPP (m)
"The Residence", Curio Road, Bel Air, Mahé, Seychelles
Telephone N°: [+ 248] 22 42 84

Deputy Head of Mission:
Mr. David CHAMBERS
769 Machabée, Mahé, Seychelles
Telephone N°: [+ 248] 24 12 21

NO VISA REQUIRED

UNITED STATES OF AMERICA
Embassy of the United States of America,
P O Box 544, 4th Floor, Rogers House,
John Kennedy Street, Port Louis
Republic of Mauritius

Telephone N°:	**Telefax N°:**
[+ 230] 20 82 347	[+ 230] 20 89 534
[+ 230] 20 82 354	
[+ 230] 20 89 763	
[+ 230] 20 89 764	
[+ 230] 20 89 765	
[+ 230] 20 89 757	

E-mail: usembass@intnet.mu
E-mail: usecocom@intnet.mu
Website: http:/www.usembassymauritius.mu

Office Hours: Monday to Friday, 0800 to 1630

Ambassador
H.E. Mr Mark Wylea ERWIN

MaCarty House, Angus Road, Vacoas, Mauritius
Telephone N°: [+ 230] 686 4505

VISA: Issued by Embassy in Port-Louis, Mauritius

VATICAN (LE SAINT-SIEGE)

Nonciature Apostolique du Vatican,
Villa Roma II, Ivandry, B. P. 650,
101 Antananarivo, Madagascar

Numéro de téléphone: Numéro de téléfax:

[+ 261 20] 22 42 376 [+ 261 20] 22 42 384

E-mail: noncapmg@dts.mg

Télex: 22432

Horaires de Travail: Lundi à Vendredi
09h00 à 12h00

Nonce Apostolique
S.E. Monseigneur Bruno MUSARO'
Numéro de téléphone: [261 20] 22 42 376

Secrétaire de la Nonciature:
Rèv. Dr. Mathew AMPONSAH-SAAMOA
Numéro de téléphone: [+ 261 20] 22 42 376

YEMEN, REPUBLIC OF

Embassy of the Republic of Yemen,
P O Box 349, Plot N° 353 United Nations Road, Upanga, Dar Es Salaam, Tanzania

Telephone N°:	Telefax N°:
[+ 255 222] 11 76 50	[+ 255 222] 11 59 24

Telex: 41901 CADFAN TZ

Ambassador
(Vacant)

VISA: Issued by Embassy in Nairobi, Kenya

YUGOSLAVIA, FEDERAL REPUBLIC OF

Embassy of the Federal Republic of Yugoslavia
State House Avenue, P O Box 30504, Nairobi, Kenya

Telephone N°:	Telefax N°:
[+ 254 2] 72 06 70	[+ 254 2] 71 60 54
[+ 254 2] 72 06 71	

E-mail: yuembnbi@wananchi.com

Telegraphic Address: AMBAYUGO, NAIROBI

Working Hours: Monday to Friday
0830 - 1500
Tuesday and Thursday
1100 - 1400

Ambassador
Vacant

Lower Kabet Road
Gen. Mathenge Gardens, Nairobi
Telephone N°: [254 2] 58 30 93

Chargé d'Affaires a.i.: *Mrs Margita LALIC-TERZIC*

NO VISA REQUIRED

ZAMBIA, REPUBLIC OF

High Commission of the Republic of Zambia
Nyerere Road, P O Box 48741, Nairobi, Kenya

Telephone N°:
[+ 254 2] 72 47 96
[+ 254 2] 72 47 99

Telefax N°:
[+ 254 2] 71 84 94

E-mail address: **Zambiacom@swiftkenya.com**

Telex: 22193

Working Hours: Monday to Thursday
0900 - 1230 1400 - 1700
Friday
0900 - 1500

High Commissioner
H.E. Ms. Wendy Wakapembe SINKALA

NO VISA REQUIRED

INTERNATIONAL ORGANIZATIONS

EU
DELEGATION DE L'UNION EUROPEENNE
EUROPEAN UNION

Bureau de la Délégation de L'Union Européenne, B P 1148, 8ème Etage, St James Court Building,
St Denis Street, Port Louis, Ile Maurice

Numéro de téléphone: Numéro de téléfax:

[+ 230] 211 6295 [+ 230] 211 6624
Télex: 4282 DELCECIW
E-mail:: europe@intnet.mu

Délégué
M. Gerd JARCHOW

COI
COMMISSION DE L'OCEAN INDIEN
INDIAN OCEAN COMMISSION

Secrétariat de la Commission de l'Océan Indien,
B.P. 7, Q4, Avenue Sir Guy Forget,
Quatre Bornes, Maurice

Numéro de téléphone: **Numéro de téléfax:**
[+ 230] 425 9564/425 1652 [+ 230] 425 2709

Télex: 5373 IW SECOI

E-mail:: coi@bow.intnet.mu

Secrétaire Général
M. Caabi Elyachroutu MOHAMED

173, Morcellement Bismic, Flic-en-Flac, Maurice
Numéro de téléphone: [+ 230] 453 8467

FAO
ORGANISATION MONDIALE POUR L'ALIMENTATION ET L'AGRICULTURE
FOOD AND AGRICULTURE ORGANISATION

Bureau de l'Organisation Mondiale pour l'Alimentation et l'Agriculture,
135 bis Route Circulaire, Antsakaviro,
BP 3971, Antananarivo 101, Madagascar

Numéro de téléphone: Numéro de téléfax:
[+ 261 20] 2228831/2228312 [+ 261 20] 2234388

Télex: 22516 MG FAO

Représentant
Vacant

Numéro de téléphone: [+ 261 20] 2228337

ILO/BIT
ORGANISATION INTERNATIONALE DU TRAVAIL
INTERNATIONAL LABOUR ORGANISATION

Bureau de l'Organisation Internationale du Travail,

BP 683, Rue Etienne Planton, Villaakila,
Cité Planton, Antananarivo, Madagascar

Numéro de téléphone: [+ 261 20] 2226615

Télex: + 22349

Adresse Télégraphique: INTERLAB ANTANANARIVO

Représentante
Madame Catherine HEIN

UNICEF
UNITED NATIONS CHILDRENS' FUND (UNICEF)
FONDS DES NATIONS UNIES POUR L'ENFANCE

Office of UNICEF, 4th Floor, Ken Lee Building
Edith Cavell Street, Port Louis, Mauritius

Telephone N°:
[+ 230] 211 1725
[+ 230] 212 0257

Telefax N°:
[+ 230] 208 3823

E-mail: mgopaul@unicef.org

Assistant Representative
Mr. Bernard GILBERT

Programme Officer: ***Mrs Mariam GOPAUL***

UNICEF OFFICE IN MADAGASCAR
Rue Robert Ducroq
Behoririka - B.P. 732, Antananarivo, Madagascar

Telephone N°: [+ 261 20] 22 28 083

Telefax N°: [+ 261 20] 22 62 845

E-mail: antananarivo@unicef.org

UNICEF Area Representative
Dr. Sergio SORO

WHO/OMS
WORLD HEALTH ORGANISATION (WHO)
ORGANISATION MONDIALE DE LA SANTE

Liaison Office of the World Health Organisation,
Blue Block, Victoria Hospital, P.O. Box 52,
Mont Fleuri, Mahé, Seychelles

Telephone N°: [+ 248] 22 47 95

Telex: 2403 WHOSEY

Office Hours: Monday to Friday, 0800 to 1600

Liaison Officer
Dr. Stella ANYANGWE

Mount Simpson Estate, Bel Ombre, Mahé, Seychelles
Telephone N°: [248] 24 73 38

UNDP/PNUD
PROGRAMME DES NATIONS UNIES POUR LE DEVELOPPEMENT
UNITED NATIONS DEVELOPMENT PROGRAMME

Bureau du Programme des Nations Unies pour le Développement, BP 253, 6ème Etage, Anglo Mauritius House, Port Louis, Mauritius

Numéro de téléphone:	**Numéro de téléfax:**
[+ 230] 21 23 726	[+ 230] 20 84 871
[+ 230] 21 23 727	

E-mail: undpmar@bow.intnet.mu

Télex: 4259 DEVPRO IW

Horaires de Travail: Lundi à Vendredi, 08h00 à 15h30
Samedi, 09h00 à 12h00

Représentante
Madame Rose GAKUBA

Numéro de téléphone: [+ 230] 68 36 595

UNFPA/FNUAP
UNITED NATIONS POPULATION FUND
FONDS DES NATIONS UNIES POUR LA POPULATION

Office of the United Nations Population Fund,
2nd Floor, Immeuble Merven
2, Victor de la Faye Street,
P.O. Box 253, Port Louis, Mauritius

Telephone N°:	**Telefax N°:**
[+230] 212 3314	[+230] 212 8133

E-mail: unfpa-mar@compuserve.com

Telex: 4259 IW

Programme Officer in Mauritius: ***Mr Kris Valaydon***

Country Director
Dr Bernard COQUELIN
P.O. Box 1348, Antananarivo, Madagascar

Telephone N°: [+261 20] 22 22 657
[+261 20] 22 30 374
[+261 20]22 69 327

Telefax N°: [+261 20] 22 35 742

WMO
WORLD METEOROLOGICAL ORGANISATION

Meteorological Services
P.O. Box 181, Victoria, Mahé, Seychelles

Telephone N°:	**Telefax N°:**
[+248] 37 33 77	[+248] 37 35 94

E-mail: metadmin@seychelles.net

Permanent Representative in Seychelles:
Vacant

Telephone N°: [+248]

UNESCO
UNITED NATIONS EDUCATIONAL, SCIENTIFIC AND CULTURAL ORGANISATION

c/o Ministry of Education
P. O. Box 48, Victoria, Mahé, Seychelles

Telephone N°:	**Telefax N°:**
[+248] 22 40 28	[+248] 22 46 26

President of the Seychelles National Commission for UNESCO
Minister Danny FAURE

Secretary-General of the Seychelles National Commission for UNESCO
Mr. Bernard SHAMLAYE

Telephone N°: [+248] 24 70 51 (home)

E-mail: shambern@seychelles.net

UNEP/PNUE
UNITED NATIONS ENVIRONMENT PROGRAMME (UNEP)
REGIONAL CO-ORDINATING UNIT OF EASTERN AFRICAN REGION (EAF/RCU)

Botanical Gardens, Mont Fleuri
P. O. Box 445, Mahé, Seychelles

Telephone N°: **Telefax N°:**

[+248] 22 46 44 [+248] 32 29 45

E-mail: uneprcu@seychelles.net

***Interim* Co-ordinator**
Mr. Rolph PAYET

Reef Estate, Anse Aux Pins, Mahé, Seychelles
Telephone N°: [+248] 37 64 94
Cellular Tel. N°: [+248] 51 19 15

IOTC/CTOI
INDIAN OCEAN TUNA COMMISSION (IOTC)
COMMISSION THONIERE DE L'OCEAN INDIEN

Headquarters of the Indian Ocean Tuna Commission
P. O. Box 1011, Fishing Port, Victoria,
Mahé, Seychelles

Telephone N°: **Telefax N°:**
[+ 248] 22 54 94 [+ 248] 22 43 64

E-mail: iotcsecr@seychelles.net

Secretary
Mr. David ARDILL

Deputy Secretary: Dr. Alejandro Alberto ANGANUZZI

USEFUL ADDRESSES AND TELEPHONE NUMBERS

TOUR OPERATORS AND TRAVEL AGENCIES

Masons Travel	Victoria, Mahé	(00248) 322642
Creole Holidays	Victoria, Mahé	(00248) 224900
Travel Services Seychelles	Victoria, Mahé	(00248) 322414
7' South	Victoria, Mahé	(00248) 322682
Orchid Travel	Victoria, Mahé	(00248) 224953
Premier Holidays (Pty) Ltd	Victoria, Mahé	(00248) 225777
Sun and Sea Travel	Victoria, Mahé	(00248) 323858
BANKS		
Barclays Bank	Victoria, Mahé	(00248) 224101
Bank Of Baroda	Victoria, Mahé	(00248) 323038
Banque Francaise Commercial	Victoria, Mahé	(00248) 323096
Central Bank	Victoria, Mahé	(00248) 225200
Development Bank Of Seychelles	Victoria, Mahé	(00248) 224471
Habib Bank	Victoria, Mahé	(00248) 224371
Seychelles Savings Bank	Victoria, Mahé	(00248) 225221
Nouvobanq	Victoria, Mahé	(00248) 225011
PLACES OF INTEREST		
Anse Lazio Beach	Anse Lazio, Praslin	
Anse Source d'Argent Beach	Anse Source d'Argent, La Digue	

Aride Bird Reserve	Aride	
Botanical Gardens	Mt. Fleuri, Victoria, Mahé	
Café Des Arts	Anse Volbert, Praslin	(00248) 232131
Codevar	Victoria, Mahé	(00248) 323161
Cousin Bird Reserve	Cousin	
Christy's Art Gallery	Quincy St, Victoria, Mahé	(00248) 321019
Craft Village	Anse Aux Pin, Mahé	(00248) 376100
Curieuse Nature Reserve	Curieuse	
Devoud Art Gallery	Les Mamelles, Mahé	(00248) 344280
Fish Market	Victoria, Mahé	
Kreol Fleurage Parfums	North East Point, Mahé	(00248) 241329
La Marine (authentic craft models)	La Plaine, Mahé	(00248) 371441
Lenstiti Kreol	Anse Aux Pin, Mahé	(00248) 376351
Michael Adams (painter)	Anse Aux Poules Bleuse	(00248) 361006
Mission Lodge	Sans Soucis, Mahé	
National Museum	Independence Ave, Victoria, Mahé	
Sculptor Studio Antonio	Beau Vallon, Mahé	(00248) 247658
Tea Plantation	San Soucis, Mahé	
Tom Bowers (sculptor)	Studio Les Cannelles, Mahé	(00248) 371518
Vallée de Mai National Park	Praslin	
Veuve Reserve	Anse Reunion, La Digue	
Walks and Trails	Tourist Office, Victoria, Mahé	(00248) 225313

EMBASSIES AND CONSULATES

USA	(00248) 225256
USSR	(00248) 221590
Belgium	(00248) 224201
China	(00248) 266808
Cuba	(00248) 224094
Cyprus	(00248) 376215
Denmark	(00248) 224710
France	(00248) 224523
Greece	(00248) 376251
Germany	(00248) 261222
Great Britain	(00248) 225225
India	(00248) 224489
Madagascar	(00248) 344030
Mauritius	(00248) 376441
Monaco	(00248) 233316
Netherlands	(00248) 261200
Sweden	(00248) 224710
Switzerland	(00248) 371050

HOSPITALS, DENTISTS AND POLICE

Victoria Hospital	Mont Fleuri, Victoria, Mahé	(00248) 388000
Hospital	Anse Royal, Mahé	(00248) 371222
Praslin Hospital	Baie St Anne, Praslin	(00248) 233333
La Digue Hospital	La Passe, La Digue	(00248) 234255
Central Police Station	Victoria, Mahé	(00248) 322011
Mont Fleuri Police Station	Mont Fleuri, Victoria, Mahé	(00248) 322011
Beau Vallon Police Station	Beau Vallon, Mahé	(00248) 247242

Anse Royal Police Station	Anse Royal, Mahé	(00248) 371226
Praslin Police Station	Baie St Anne, Praslin	(00248) 233251
La Digue Police Station	La Passe, La Digue	(00248) 234251
FIRE BRIGADE, POLICE AND AMBULANCE EMERGENCIES		DIAL 999
Tourist Dentist and Tourist Doctor can be contacted by the hospital on		(00248) 388000

ENQUIRIES AND TRAVEL

Weather	Met Office	(00248) 373377
Airport - International Flight Enquiries		(00248) 384000
Airport Inter island reservations		(00248) 384405
Helicopter Seychelles	PO Box 595, Mahé	(00248) 375400
La Digue / Mahé Ferry Service	La Belle Edma, La Digue	(00248) 234031
Mahé / Praslin ; Ferry Service	La Belle Praslinoise, Praslin	(00248) 233238
Mahé / Praslin; Fast boat	Cat Cocos	(00248) 324843
Praslin / La Digue Ferry Service	William Rose, Praslin	(00248) 233229

BASIC LAWS AND REGULATIONS AFFECTING BUSINESS[2]

COUTRY	LAW TITLE
Seychelles	Agriculture & Fisheries Incentive Act
Seychelles	Air Navigation (Fees) (Amendment) Regulations, 2004
Seychelles	Airport (regulations) Act (Cap 6)
Seychelles	Anti-money Laundering Act, 1996
Seychelles	Anti-Money Laundering Act, 2006
Seychelles	Beach Control Act (Cap 14)
Seychelles	Birds' Eggs Act
Seychelles	Business Tax Act 2009
Seychelles	Central Bank of Seychelles Act, 2004
Seychelles	Citizenship Act 1994
Seychelles	Civil Aviation Act, 2005
Seychelles	Companies Act 2001
Seychelles	Companies Ordinance, 1972
Seychelles	Constitution of the republic of Seychelles
Seychelles	Credit Union Act 2009
Seychelles	Delegation of Functions (Development Bank of Seychelles Decree) Order 2009
Seychelles	Delegation of Power & Duties (Foreign Exchange Act) Order, 2009
Seychelles	Development Bank of Seychelles Decree
Seychelles	Domestic Banking Regulations
Seychelles	Double Taxation Agreement with Barbados
Seychelles	Double Taxation Agreement with Botswana
Seychelles	Double Taxation Agreement with China
Seychelles	Double Taxation Agreement with Cyprus
Seychelles	Double Taxation Agreement with Indonesia

[2] For ordering texts of specific laws in English, French or other languages, please contact Global Investment Center USA at ibpusa3@gmail.com

Seychelles	Double Taxation Agreement with Malaysia
Seychelles	Double Taxation Agreement with Mauritius
Seychelles	Double Taxation Agreement with Oman
Seychelles	Double Taxation Agreement with South Africa
Seychelles	Double Taxation Agreement with Thailand
Seychelles	Double Taxation Agreement with U.A.E
Seychelles	Double Taxation Agreement with Vietnam
Seychelles	Elections Regulation, 2006
Seychelles	Employment Act 1995
Seychelles	Employment Regulations
Seychelles	Environment Protection Act (Cap 71)
Seychelles	Excise Tax Act 2009
Seychelles	Financial Institutions Act, 2004
Seychelles	Financial Services Development Act 2001
Seychelles	Fire Protection Act (Cap 81)
Seychelles	Fisheries Act 1991
Seychelles	Fisheries Regulations
Seychelles	Foreign Exchange Act, 2009
Seychelles	Forest Reserves Act
Seychelles	Foundations Act, 2009
Seychelles	General Information on Immigration Laws, 2004
Seychelles	Guidance Notes on Anti-Money Laundering
Seychelles	Higher Education Act of Seychelles
Seychelles	Income Tax Act 1995
Seychelles	Insurance Act, 1994
Seychelles	Interactive Gambling Act, 2003
Seychelles	International Business Companies Act 1994
Seychelles	International Corporate Services Providers Act, 2003
Seychelles	International Trade Zone Act, 1995
Seychelles	International Trade Zones
Seychelles	International Trust Act, 1994
Seychelles	Investment Code
Seychelles	Licenses (Public Omnibus) Regulation 2008
Seychelles	Lighting of Fires (Restriction) Act
Seychelles	Limited Partnerships Act, 2003
Seychelles	Maritime Zones Act 1999, Act No. 2 of 1999
Seychelles	Merchant Shipping Act 1994
Seychelles	Misuse of Drugs Act, 1990
Seychelles	Mutual Assistance in Criminal Matters Act, 1995
Seychelles	Mutual Fund & Hedge Fund Act 2008
Seychelles	National Clearance and Settlement Systems Act 2010
Seychelles	National Identity Card Act 1995
Seychelles	National Parks and Nature Conservancy Act 1991
Seychelles	Non Domestic Banking Regulations
Seychelles	Pension Fund Act 2005

Seychelles	Pesticide Control Act
Seychelles	Plant Protection Act 1996
Seychelles	Prevention of Terrorism Act, 2004
Seychelles	Protected Cell Companies Act, 2003
Seychelles	Protected Cell Companies Guidelines
Seychelles	Restricted Goods, 2005
Seychelles	Securities Act, 2007
Seychelles	Seychelles International Business Authority Act, 1994
Seychelles	Seychelles Pesticide Control Act 1996
Seychelles	Seychelles Revenue Commission Act 2009
Seychelles	Social Security (Amendment) Act 2008
Seychelles	Statistics Act 2010
Seychelles	TIA (Amendments of Schedules) Regulations 2008
Seychelles	Tourism (Incentives) (Amendment) Act 2008
Seychelles	Trades Tax Tariff 2006
Seychelles	Trust Act 2001
Seychelles	Wild Animals Protection Act 1991

BASIC TITLES ON SEYCHELLES

BASIC TITLES ON

IMPORTANT!
All publications are updated annually!
Please contact IBP, Inc. at ibpusa3@gmail.com for the latest ISBNs and additional information
Global Business and Investment Info Databank: www.ibpus.com

Title
Seychelles A "Spy" Guide - Strategic Information and Developments
Seychelles A Spy" Guide"
Seychelles Business and Investment Opportunities Yearbook
Seychelles Business and Investment Opportunities Yearbook
Seychelles Business and Investment Opportunities Yearbook Volume 1 Strategic Information and Opportunities
Seychelles Business Intelligence Report - Practical Information, Opportunities, Contacts
Seychelles Business Intelligence Report - Practical Information, Opportunities, Contacts
Seychelles Business Law Handbook - Strategic Information and Basic Laws
Seychelles Business Law Handbook - Strategic Information and Basic Laws
Seychelles Business Law Handbook - Strategic Information and Basic Laws
Seychelles Business Law Handbook - Strategic Information and Basic Laws
Seychelles Constitution and Citizenship Laws Handbook - Strategic Information and Basic Laws
Seychelles Country Study Guide - Strategic Information and Developments
Seychelles Country Study Guide - Strategic Information and Developments
Seychelles Country Study Guide - Strategic Information and Developments Volume 1 Strategic Information and Developments

Title
Seychelles Diplomatic Handbook - Strategic Information and Developments
Seychelles Diplomatic Handbook - Strategic Information and Developments
Seychelles Ecology & Nature Protection Handbook
Seychelles Ecology & Nature Protection Handbook
Seychelles Ecology & Nature Protection Laws and Regulation Handbook
Seychelles Economic & Development Strategy Handbook
Seychelles Economic & Development Strategy Handbook
Seychelles Energy Policy, Laws and Regulation Handbook
Seychelles Foreign Policy and Government Guide
Seychelles Foreign Policy and Government Guide
Seychelles Immigration Laws and Regulations Handbook - Strategic Information and Basic Laws
Seychelles Investment and Business Guide - Strategic and Practical Information
Seychelles Investment and Business Guide - Strategic and Practical Information
Seychelles Investment and Business Guide - Strategic and Practical Information
Seychelles Investment and Business Guide - Strategic and Practical Information
Seychelles Labor Laws and Regulations Handbook - Strategic Information and Basic Laws
Seychelles Land Ownership and Agriculture Laws Handbook
SEYCHELLES Offshore Investment and Business Guide - Strategic and Practical Information
SEYCHELLES Offshore Investment and Business Guide - Strategic and Practical Information
Seychelles Offshore Tax Guide
Seychelles Offshore Tax Guide
Seychelles Recent Economic and Political Developments Yearbook
Seychelles Recent Economic and Political Developments Yearbook
Seychelles Recent Economic and Political Developments Yearbook
Seychelles Taxation Laws and Regulations Handbook
Seychelles: How to Invest, Start and Run Profitable Business in Seychelles Guide - Practical Information, Opportunities, Contacts

38. Cape Verde Country Study Guide Volume 1 Strategic Information and Developments
39. Cayman Islands Country Study Guide Volume 1 Strategic Information and Developments
40. Central African Republic Country Study Guide Volume 1 Strategic Information and Developments
41. Chad Country Study Guide Volume 1 Strategic Information and Developments
42. Chile Country Study Guide Volume 1 Strategic Information and Developments
43. China Country Study Guide Volume 1 Strategic Information and Developments
44. Colombia Country Study Guide Volume 1 Strategic Information and Developments
45. Comoros Country Study Guide Volume 1 Strategic Information and Developments
46. Congo Country Study Guide Volume 1 Strategic Information and Developments
47. Congo, Democratic Republic Country Study Guide Volume 1 Strategic Information and Developments
48. Cook Islands Country Study Guide Volume 1 Strategic Information and Developments
49. Costa Rica Country Study Guide Volume 1 Strategic Information and Developments
50. Cote d'Ivoire Country Study Guide Volume 1 Strategic Information and Developments
51. Croatia Country Study Guide Volume 1 Strategic Information and Developments
52. Cuba Country Study Guide Volume 1 Strategic Information and Developments
53. Cyprus Country Study Guide Volume 1 Strategic Information and Developments
54. Czech Republic Country Study Guide Volume 1 Strategic Information and Developments
55. Denmark Country Study Guide Volume 1 Strategic Information and Developments
56. Djibouti Country Study Guide Volume 1 Strategic Information and Developments
57. Dominica Country Study Guide Volume 1 Strategic Information and Developments
58. Dominican Republic Country Study Guide Volume 1 Strategic Information and Developments
59. Ecuador Country Study Guide Volume 1 Strategic Information and Developments
60. Egypt Country Study Guide Volume 1 Strategic Information and Developments
61. El Salvador Country Study Guide Volume 1 Strategic Information and Developments
62. Equatorial Guinea Country Study Guide Volume 1 Strategic Information and Developments
63. Eritrea Country Study Guide Volume 1 Strategic Information and Developments
64. Estonia Country Study Guide Volume 1 Strategic Information and Developments
65. Ethiopia Country Study Guide Volume 1 Strategic Information and Developments
66. Falkland Islands Country Study Guide Volume 1 Strategic Information and Developments
67. Faroes Islands Country Study Guide Volume 1 Strategic Information and Developments
68. Fiji Country Study Guide Volume 1 Strategic Information and Developments
69. Finland Country Study Guide Volume 1 Strategic Information and Developments
70. France Country Study Guide Volume 1 Strategic Information and Developments
71. Gabon Country Study Guide Volume 1 Strategic Information and Developments
72. Gambia Country Study Guide Volume 1 Strategic Information and Developments
73. Georgia Country Study Guide Volume 1 Strategic Information and Developments
74. Germany Country Study Guide Volume 1 Strategic Information and Developments
75. Ghana Country Study Guide Volume 1 Strategic Information and Developments
76. Gibraltar Country Study Guide Volume 1 Strategic Information and Developments
77. Greece Country Study Guide Volume 1 Strategic Information and Developments
78. Greenland Country Study Guide Volume 1 Strategic Information and Developments
79. Grenada Country Study Guide Volume 1 Strategic Information and Developments
80. Guam Country Study Guide Volume 1 Strategic Information and Developments
81. Guatemala Country Study Guide Volume 1 Strategic Information and Developments
82. Guernsey Country Study Guide Volume 1 Strategic Information and Developments
83. Guinea Country Study Guide Volume 1 Strategic Information and Developments
84. Guinea-Bissau Country Study Guide Volume 1 Strategic Information and Developments
85. Guyana Country Study Guide Volume 1 Strategic Information and Developments
86. Haiti Country Study Guide Volume 1 Strategic Information and Developments
87. Honduras Country Study Guide Volume 1 Strategic Information and Developments
88. Hungary Country Study Guide Volume 1 Strategic Information and Developments
89. Iceland Country Study Guide Volume 1 Strategic Information and Developments
90. India Country Study Guide Volume 1 Strategic Information and Developments

91. Indonesia Country Study Guide Volume 1 Strategic Information and Developments
92. Iran Country Study Guide Volume 1 Strategic Information and Developments
93. Iraq Country Study Guide Volume 1 Strategic Information and Developments
94. Ireland Country Study Guide Volume 1 Strategic Information and Developments
95. Israel Country Study Guide Volume 1 Strategic Information and Developments
96. Italy Country Study Guide Volume 1 Strategic Information and Developments
97. Jamaica Country Study Guide Volume 1 Strategic Information and Developments
98. Japan Country Study Guide Volume 1 Strategic Information and Developments
99. Jersey Country Study Guide Volume 1 Strategic Information and Developments
100. Jordan Country Study Guide Volume 1 Strategic Information and Developments
101. Kazakhstan Country Study Guide Volume 1 Strategic Information and Developments
102. Kenya Country Study Guide Volume 1 Strategic Information and Developments
103. Kiribati Country Study Guide Volume 1 Strategic Information and Developments
104. Korea, North Country Study Guide Volume 1 Strategic Information and Developments
105. Korea, South Country Study Guide Volume 1 Strategic Information and Developments
106. Kosovo Country Study Guide Volume 1 Strategic Information and Developments
107. Kurdistan Country Study Guide Volume 1 Strategic Information and Developments
108. Kuwait Country Study Guide Volume 1 Strategic Information and Developments
109. Kyrgyzstan Country Study Guide Volume 1 Strategic Information and Developments
110. Laos Country Study Guide Volume 1 Strategic Information and Developments
111. Latvia Country Study Guide Volume 1 Strategic Information and Developments
112. Lebanon Country Study Guide Volume 1 Strategic Information and Developments
113. Lesotho Country Study Guide Volume 1 Strategic Information and Developments
114. Liberia Country Study Guide Volume 1 Strategic Information and Developments
115. Libya Country Study Guide Volume 1 Strategic Information and Developments
116. Liechtenstein Country Study Guide Volume 1 Strategic Information and Developments
117. Lithuania Country Study Guide Volume 1 Strategic Information and Developments
118. Luxembourg Country Study Guide Volume 1 Strategic Information and Developments
119. Macao Country Study Guide Volume 1 Strategic Information and Developments
120. Macedonia,Country Study Guide Volume 1 Strategic Information and Developments
121. Madagascar Country Study Guide Volume 1 Strategic Information and Developments
122. MadeiraCountry Study Guide Volume 1 Strategic Information and Developments
123. Malawi Country Study Guide Volume 1 Strategic Information and Developments
124. Malaysia Country Study Guide Volume 1 Strategic Information and Developments
125. Maldives Country Study Guide Volume 1 Strategic Information and Developments
126. Mali Country Study Guide Volume 1 Strategic Information and Developments
127. Malta Country Study Guide Volume 1 Strategic Information and Developments
128. Man Country Study Guide Volume 1 Strategic Information and Developments
129. Marshall Islands Country Study Guide Volume 1 Strategic Information and Developments
130. Mauritania Country Study Guide Volume 1 Strategic Information and Developments
131. Mauritius Country Study Guide Volume 1 Strategic Information and Developments
132. Mayotte Country Study Guide Volume 1 Strategic Information and Developments
133. Mexico Country Study Guide Volume 1 Strategic Information and Developments
134. Micronesia Country Study Guide Volume 1 Strategic Information and Developments
135. Moldova Country Study Guide Volume 1 Strategic Information and Developments
136. Monaco Country Study Guide Volume 1 Strategic Information and Developments
137. Mongolia Country Study Guide Volume 1 Strategic Information and Developments
138. Monserrat Country Study Guide Volume 1 Strategic Information and Developments
139. Montenegro Country Study Guide Volume 1 Strategic Information and Developments
140. Morocco Country Study Guide Volume 1 Strategic Information and Developments
141. Mozambique Country Study Guide Volume 1 Strategic Information and Developments
142. Myanmar Country Study Guide Volume 1 Strategic Information and Developments
143. Nagorno-Karabakh Republic Country Study Guide Volume 1 Strategic Information and Developments

144. Namibia Country Study Guide Volume 1 Strategic Information and Developments
145. Nauru Country Study Guide Volume 1 Strategic Information and Developments
146. Nepal Country Study Guide Volume 1 Strategic Information and Developments
147. Netherlands Country Study Guide Volume 1 Strategic Information and Developments
148. New Caledonia Country Study Guide Volume 1 Strategic Information and Developments
149. New Zealand Country Study Guide Volume 1 Strategic Information and Developments
150. Nicaragua Country Study Guide Volume 1 Strategic Information and Developments
151. Niger Country Study Guide Volume 1 Strategic Information and Developments
152. Nigeria Country Study Guide Volume 1 Strategic Information and Developments
153. Niue Country Study Guide Volume 1 Strategic Information and Developments
154. Northern Cyprus (Turkish Republic of Northern Cyprus)
155. Northern Mariana Islands Country Study Guide Volume 1 Strategic Information and Developments
156. Norway Country Study Guide Volume 1 Strategic Information and Developments
157. Oman Country Study Guide Volume 1 Strategic Information and Developments
158. Pakistan Country Study Guide Volume 1 Strategic Information and Developments
159. Palau Country Study Guide Volume 1 Strategic Information and Developments
160. Palestine (West Bank & Gaza) Country Study Guide Volume 1 Strategic Information and Developments
161. Panama Country Study Guide Volume 1 Strategic Information and Developments
162. Papua New Guinea Country Study Guide Volume 1 Strategic Information and Developments
163. Paraguay Country Study Guide Volume 1 Strategic Information and Developments
164. Peru Country Study Guide Volume 1 Strategic Information and Developments
165. Philippines Country Study Guide Volume 1 Strategic Information and Developments
166. Pitcairn Islands Country Study Guide Volume 1 Strategic Information and Developments
167. Poland Country Study Guide Volume 1 Strategic Information and Developments
168. Polynesia French Country Study Guide Volume 1 Strategic Information and Developments
169. Portugal Country Study Guide Volume 1 Strategic Information and Developments
170. Qatar Country Study Guide Volume 1 Strategic Information and Developments
171. Romania Country Study Guide Volume 1 Strategic Information and Developments
172. Russia Country Study Guide Volume 1 Strategic Information and Developments
173. Rwanda Country Study Guide Volume 1 Strategic Information and Developments
174. Sahrawi Arab Democratic Republic Volume 1 Strategic Information and Developments
175. Saint Kitts and Nevis Country Study Guide Volume 1 Strategic Information and Developments
176. Saint Lucia Country Study Guide Volume 1 Strategic Information and Developments
177. Saint Vincent and The Grenadines Country Study Guide Volume 1 Strategic Information and Developments
178. Samoa (American) A Country Study Guide Volume 1 Strategic Information and Developments
179. Samoa (Western) Country Study Guide Volume 1 Strategic Information and Developments
180. San Marino Country Study Guide Volume 1 Strategic Information and Developments
181. Sao Tome and Principe Country Study Guide Volume 1 Strategic Information and Developments
182. Saudi Arabia Country Study Guide Volume 1 Strategic Information and Developments
183. Scotland Country Study Guide Volume 1 Strategic Information and Developments
184. Senegal Country Study Guide Volume 1 Strategic Information and Developments
185. Serbia Country Study Guide Volume 1 Strategic Information and Developments
186. Seychelles Country Study Guide Volume 1 Strategic Information and Developments
187. Sierra Leone Country Study Guide Volume 1 Strategic Information and Developments
188. Singapore Country Study Guide Volume 1 Strategic Information and Developments
189. Slovakia Country Study Guide Volume 1 Strategic Information and Developments
190. Slovenia Country Study Guide Volume 1 Strategic Information and Developments
191. Solomon Islands Country Study Guide Volume 1 Strategic Information and Developments
192. Somalia Country Study Guide Volume 1 Strategic Information and Developments
193. South Africa Country Study Guide Volume 1 Strategic Information and Developments
194. Spain Country Study Guide Volume 1 Strategic Information and Developments
195. Sri Lanka Country Study Guide Volume 1 Strategic Information and Developments

196. St. Helena Country Study Guide Volume 1 Strategic Information and Developments
197. St. Pierre & Miquelon Country Study Guide Volume 1 Strategic Information and Developments
198. Sudan (Republic of the Sudan) Country Study Guide Volume 1 Strategic Information and Developments
199. Sudan South Country Study Guide Volume 1 Strategic Information and Developments
200. Suriname Country Study Guide Volume 1 Strategic Information and Developments
201. Swaziland Country Study Guide Volume 1 Strategic Information and Developments
202. Sweden Country Study Guide Volume 1 Strategic Information and Developments
203. Switzerland Country Study Guide Volume 1 Strategic Information and Developments
204. Syria Country Study Guide Volume 1 Strategic Information and Developments
205. Taiwan Country Study Guide Volume 1 Strategic Information and Developments
206. Tajikistan Country Study Guide Volume 1 Strategic Information and Developments
207. Tanzania Country Study Guide Volume 1 Strategic Information and Developments
208. Thailand Country Study Guide Volume 1 Strategic Information and Developments
209. Timor Leste (Democratic Republic of Timor-Leste) Country Study Guide Volume 1 Strategic Information and Developments
210. Togo Country Study Guide Volume 1 Strategic Information and Developments
211. Tonga Country Study Guide Volume 1 Strategic Information and Developments
212. Trinidad and Tobago Country Study Guide Volume 1 Strategic Information and Developments
213. Tunisia Country Study Guide Volume 1 Strategic Information and Developments
214. Turkey Country Study Guide Volume 1 Strategic Information and Developments
215. Turkmenistan Country Study Guide Volume 1 Strategic Information and Developments
216. Turks & Caicos Country Study Guide Volume 1 Strategic Information and Developments
217. Tuvalu Country Study Guide Volume 1 Strategic Information and Developments
218. Uganda Country Study Guide Volume 1 Strategic Information and Developments
219. Ukraine Country Study Guide Volume 1 Strategic Information and Developments
220. United Arab Emirates Country Study Guide Volume 1 Strategic Information and Developments
221. United Kingdom Country Study Guide Volume 1 Strategic Information and Developments
222. United States Country Study Guide Volume 1 Strategic Information and Developments
223. Uruguay Country Study Guide Volume 1 Strategic Information and Developments
224. Uzbekistan Country Study Guide Volume 1 Strategic Information and Developments
225. Vanuatu Country Study Guide Volume 1 Strategic Information and Developments
226. Vatican City (Holy See) Country Study Guide Volume 1 Strategic Information and Developments
227. Venezuela Country Study Guide Volume 1 Strategic Information and Developments
228. Vietnam Country Study Guide Volume 1 Strategic Information and Developments
229. Virgin Islands, British Country Study Guide Volume 1 Strategic Information and Developments
230. Wake Atoll Country Study Guide Volume 1 Strategic Information and Developments
231. Wallis & Futuna Country Study Guide Volume 1 Strategic Information and Developments
232. Western Sahara Country Study Guide Volume 1 Strategic Information and Developments
233. Yemen Country Study Guide Volume 1 Strategic Information and Developments
234. Zambia Country Study Guide Volume 1 Strategic Information and Developments
235. Zimbabwe Country Study Guide Volume 1 Strategic Information and Developments

www.ingramcontent.com/pod-product-compliance
Ingram Content Group UK Ltd.
Pitfield, Milton Keynes, MK11 3LW, UK
UKHW051459290926
15471UKWH00008B/1293